"This extraordinary book is the outcome of the experience and thinking of a genuine authority, whose step-by-step program has been validated by scientific studies. Cash is more than a scientist, he is also a creative author. I would like to see this book become part of the standard high school curriculum to help students avoid the harmful consequences of disliking their physical endowments."

—Albert M. Kligman, M.D., Ph.D., Professor of Dermatology at the University of Pennsylvania

THE
Body Image
WORKBOOK

AN 8-STEP PROGRAM FOR LEARNING TO LIKE YOUR LOOKS

THOMAS F. CASH, PH.D.

New Harbinger Publications

As a revised presentation of the author's self-help program, *The Body Image Workbook* is published with the expressed consent of Bantam Books, the original publisher of *What Do You See When You Look in the Mirror?* (© Thomas F. Cash, Ph.D., 1995). Any permission of sublicensing requests for materials originally appearing in *What Do You See When You Look in the Mirror?* should be directed to Bantam Books, 1540 Broadway, New York, NY, 10036.

Copyright © 1997 Thomas F. Cash, Ph.D.
        New Harbinger Publications, Inc.
        5674 Shattuck Avenue
        Oakland, CA 94609

CATHY © Cathy Guisewite. Reprinted with permission of UNIVERSAL PRESS SYNDICATE. All rights reserved.

Cover design by Lightbourne Images.
Text design by Tracy Marie Powell.

Distributed in the U.S.A. by Publishers Group West; in Canada by Raincoast Books; in Great Britain by Airlift Book Company, Ltd.; in South Africa by Real Books, Ltd.; in Australia by Boobook; and in New Zealand by Tandem Press.

New Harbinger Publications Web address: www.newharbinger.com

ISBN 1-57224-062-8 paperback
All rights reserved.
Printed in the United States of America using recycled paper.

10 9 8 7 6 5 4 3 2 1

I am forever indebted to my sons. Ben and T.C., each in his own wonderful way, always enrich the pleasure of my life. Thanks guys!

Contents

List of Helpsheets

Step 5: Critical Thinking—Correcting Your Private Body Talk

Step 6: Hide and Seek—Defeating Your Self-Defeating Behaviors

Step 7: The Good Times—Treating Your Body Right

Step 8: From This Day Forward—Preserving Your Positive Body Image for Life

Preface

We would all agree that the human condition is inherently one of embodiment. The functioning and appearance of the body shapes our lives. This is true both in terms of how others react to our bodies as we interact with our social world as well as in terms of how we perceive and react to our own conditions of embodiment.

The essential purpose of *The Body Image Workbook* is to offer meaningful help to people for whom embodiment is fraught with discontent and discomfort. I firmly believe in the potential and real value of psychological self-help. After all, the ultimate goal of professional help is to provide clients with experiences through which they can learn to solve problems and help themselves. Scientific research has confirmed that "self-help bibliotherapy" can effectively teach people to solve a range of life's problems. For some individuals, however, this goal is more easily attained under the masterful and caring guidance of a therapist or counselor. I did not write this book to replace the professional assistance that any person may need and deserve. In fact, it is my hope that this workbook will help professionals in helping clients improve their experiences of embodiment.

The evolution of *The Body Image Workbook* reflects an integration of psychological theory, research, and clinical practice. It draws substantively from my 1995 book, *What Do You See When You Look in the Mirror? Helping Yourself to a Positive Body Image* (Bantam Books). Unique in its format, this workbook incorporates further innovations and information to promote positive changes in its readers.

From early childhood I recall loving to write. My love of psychology came much later. As a writer, I must find the ideas, the words, the motivation, and the time to communicate—sometimes in the middle of the night. The ultimate product always reflects a lifetime of experiences with many terrific people.

For nearly twenty-five years, I have been a faculty member in the Psychology Department at Old Dominion University. My students contribute greatly to my professional growth. I give special thanks to several generations of my "body image family": Tim Brown, Jon Butters, Sherri Crosson, Jill Grant, Jill Hangen, Andy Labarge, Danielle Lavallee, Jennifer Muth, Pam Novy, Laura Rieves, Melissa Strachan, Marci Szymanski, and Pam Williams.

By sharing their ideas and enthusiasm, psychologists from other universities have enhanced this work. I am especially appreciative of Tom Pruzinsky, James Rosen, and Kevin Thompson.

The Body Image Workbook reflects the valued feedback from the many people who have completed this program to improve the quality of their body images and their lives. Ultimately, it is their collective voice that matters most.

A few years ago, Nellie Sabin became my "word wizard" and facilitated my becoming a better popular writer. I continue to reap the benefits of her wisdom, and I remain sincerely grateful.

I am pleased that New Harbinger is my publisher. Their track record in the production of psychosocial self-help books is reputable. Their excitement and encouragement concerning this project were enormously helpful. I am particularly grateful to Kristin Beck, Farrin Jacobs, and Matt McKay.

The endeavor of writing, hour after hour and day after day, is a challenge that is possible only by having moments to step back, sort out my thoughts, and re-energize. To this end, the beauty, serenity, and vitality of the Chesapeake Bay always gave me clarity of mind and renewal of purpose.

Introduction

Taking Eight Steps to a More Positive Body Image

- ◎ Are you happy with the body that you live in? Or would you rather be living somewhere else?

- ◎ Are there aspects of your physical appearance that you really despise?

- ◎ Do the same old negative thoughts about your looks keep popping into your head?

- ◎ Do you spend too much time worrying about what you look like?

- ◎ Do your feelings about your looks get in the way of enjoying your everyday life?

- ◎ Do these feelings impair your self-esteem?

- ◎ Do you avoid certain activities or situations because you feel self-conscious about how you look?

- ◎ Do you rely to a great extent on clothes or cosmetics to try to cover up the "flaws" in your appearance?

◎ Do you spend a lot of time, effort, and money attempting to "repair" your looks or achieve physical perfection?

◎ Are you often <u>searching for</u> the ultimate diet, the most effective body-shaping exercise, the right clothes, the most flattering cosmetics or hairstyle?

◎ Are you contemplating cosmetic surgery?

All of these questions are about your *body image*. Body image doesn't refer to what you actually look like. It refers to your personal relationship with your body—especially your beliefs, perceptions, thoughts, feelings, and actions that pertain to your physical appearance. What you look like is certainly one aspect of who you are. So is your body image! Having difficulty liking your looks makes it harder to accept yourself.

But here's the good news: A negative, unsatisfying body image can be changed. *The Body Image Workbook* will teach you how to transform your relationship with your body from a self-defeating struggle to an experience of self-acceptance and enjoyment. Before delving into the details of this program, I want to tell you how it came to be and how it can help.

A Scientific Approach to Body Image Improvement

This eight-step program for body image change didn't come to me in a dream or in a rainbow vision on a rainy day. Rooted in scientific psychology, it reflects an active, cognitive-behavioral approach to therapy. Over the past ten years, its effectiveness has been tested in clinical trials at various universities and clinics across the United States.

Without exception, these controlled studies have verified that the program can produce meaningful improvements in how people feel about their bodies. Furthermore, these positive body image changes foster better self-esteem and overall psychological well-being. Researchers have also determined that the program works better than more traditional "talk therapy."

In 1991, I published an audiocassette version of my program, *Body Image Therapy: A Program for Self-Directed Change* (Guilford Publications), to aid professionals in helping clients with body image problems. Despite the value of this version to practitioners, the fact is that most people with a negative body image don't and won't seek professional help for the problem. So, how could I help them?

I was encouraged by a growing collection of scientific evidence that many people can use carefully designed self-help programs to overcome certain psychological or behavioral problems. So, in 1995, psychologist Jill Grant and I sought to find out if my body image therapy program could work in a self-help format. We recruited people who suffered from a negative body image. Half received the program administered by professional therapists. The other half completed the program on their own with minimal professional guidance. We found that participants in both groups became much less unhappy with their looks. They came to feel less socially uncomfortable and less depressed. They developed better self-esteem. Even in a largely self-help format, the program worked!

Our research led to refinements in the program and to my publication of the self-help book, *What Do You See When You Look in the Mirror?* (Bantam Books, 1995). I conducted two scientific tests of this self-help version of the program in collaboration with doctoral student Danielle Lavallee. Both investigations verified the effectiveness of this self-help version of the program for individuals with a negative body image. Take a look at figure 1. It reveals that after a few months of completing the program on their own, people evaluated their looks much more favorably and had fewer distressing experiences related to their appearance. This research further confirmed that the program benefits people in ways that go beyond their body image. It enhances comfort and contentment in interpersonal relations and in feelings of social self-worth. It can reduce the risk of developing an eating disorder.

In addition, our studies informed us of those aspects of the program that our participants said were especially helpful to them. Believing in the value of listening to consumers, I have taken their feedback into account in writing *The Body Image Workbook*.

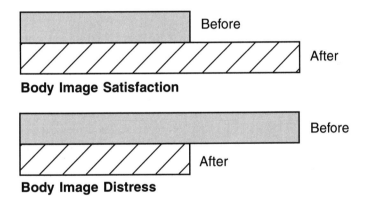

Body Image Satisfaction

Before

After

Body Image Distress

Before

After

Figure 1. Do People Really Change?[*]
Body Image Before and After Self-Help

Help Yourself to What You Need

The Body Image Workbook represents the newest generation of the program. It is updated, reorganized, and presented in a more streamlined, user-friendly manner than previous versions. This workbook is for people who are dissatisfied with their looks and want to do something about it. This workbook is for men as well as women, for teenagers as well

[*]From Cash and Lavallee, 1995; Lavallee and Cash, 1996.

as adults. It is for average-looking folks and for those who "look different"—whether fat or thin, tall or short, disfigured or a "perfect ten." So this workbook is for anyone with a negative body image, right? Actually, it's not. Sometimes a negative body image is part of a more complex problem. The following mental health problems require more than body image self-help:

◎　Anorexia nervosa

◎　Bulimia nervosa

◎　Binge-eating disorder

◎　Body dysmorphic disorder

◎　Major (clinical) depression

Now, let me describe each of these five psychological difficulties. I want you to be sure that *The Body Image Workbook* is appropriate for you.

Do you have an eating disorder that is driven in part by a worrisome body image? The following eating disorders clearly require professional assistance to overcome:

Anorexia nervosa is a potentially lethal disorder of self-starvation in pursuit of thinness. It mostly affects young women, perhaps 1 percent of women in their teens or twenties. Their fear of weight gain and perception of themselves as fat, even when they are emaciated and physically ill, is overwhelmingly intense. Controlling weight seems the only way to control their life.

Bulimia nervosa is an even more prevalent eating disorder, occurring in an estimated 5 percent of young women. This problem entails recurrent binges, the rapid consumption of large quantities of food in a twenty- to thirty-minute period. Usually carried out secretly, these binges feel "out of control." After the binge comes the purge, an attempt to negate the binge and reduce the fear and the likelihood of weight gain. The purge may involve self-induced vomiting, but it may also involve the excessive use of laxatives, diuretics, dietary fasts, or vigorous exercise. People with bulimia nervosa not only hate their body shape and weight, but their eating problem traps them in an unhealthy pattern of self-destruction. Their hatred of their body and feelings of guilt, depression, and self-loathing just keep diminishing their quality of life.

There is a third eating disorder in which binges occur without efforts to purge or to compensate for the excessive food intake. This is *binge-eating disorder*, or compulsive overeating. Understandably, binges often lead to feeling out of control, weight gain, and an even more negative body image. Binge eaters represent about 5 to 8 percent of obese women and men, and about 20 to 30 percent of obese persons who are receiving professional weight-loss treatment.

Persons with eating disorders must gain control over their problematic eating behaviors. But they must also learn to think and feel differently about their looks. Research reveals that without repairing their body image, they risk returning to the same old patterns of self-starvation or binges and purges. While a negative body image is a core aspect of their problems, body image therapy isn't the sole solution for eating disorders.

For some people, obsessive preoccupation with their appearance is an excessive concern known as *body dysmorphic disorder*—the disorder of imagined ugliness. They have a grossly distorted view of what they look like. Others look at them and either think they look fine or have a barely noticeable "defect." Persons with this problem may spend hours every day inspecting the "deformity" in the mirror and attempting to hide it or fix it. Social events are avoided or self-consciously endured. The desire to "fix the flaws" may motivate a relentless search for surgical solutions.

Can the solutions offered in this workbook help those with such an extremely negative body image? Research by Dr. James Rosen and his colleagues at the University of Vermont has verified that this program can help people with body dysmorphic disorder, but the expertise of a professional is needed to provide optimal care for such a life-controlling condition. To learn more about body dysmorphic disorder, read Dr. Katherine Phillips's informative book *The Broken Mirror* (1996).

A final problem that demands more than self-help is *major depression*—an intense and recurring mood disturbance. People who are depressed frequently have a negative body image. In this situation, hating one's looks is symptomatic of the more pervasive problem of self-loathing. With clinical depression, people feel worthless or guilty and are unable to derive much pleasure from daily life. Their minds are filled with negative thoughts about themselves and life events. The future seems so hopeless that sometimes thoughts of suicide make sense.

Combating severe depression requires more than feeling better about your looks. Depression can cause you to believe that you can't do anything to feel better. Does depression about yourself and your life taint your view of your looks, or does your negative body image itself cause despondency? If you're unsure, a professional can help you sort it out.

In recent years, effective treatments have emerged for body dysmorphic disorder, eating disorders, and depression. If you recognize yourself in any of these descriptions, please seek professional help immediately. Because your negative body image is an integral part of your difficulties, together you and your therapist can use this workbook to achieve its maximum benefits.

What If I Want to Transform My Body, Not My Body Image?

If you dislike your looks, you will understandably try to figure out how to change what you look like. Instead of thinking about an attitude adjustment, you contemplate how you can have an appearance adjustment—a slimmer physique, better muscle tone, a more youthful complexion, bigger breasts, thicker hair, or some other item on your body image wish list. Annually, millions of individuals diet to modify their weight, exercise to look fit, purchase cosmetic commodities to conceal flaws, or seek surgery to fix some detested feature. But why? All of these remedies have one basic psychological purpose—to feel better about the body you live in. Consider the provocative possibility that the problem and its solutions have more to do with changing your body image than changing your body.

Because so many of you who are reading these words are either thinking about dieting or about plastic surgery, let me offer you some additional words about each of these two options.

Hey, Weight a Minute!

Weight concerns are the primary complaint of people with a negative body image. Some surveys suggest that, at any given time, about one-half of adult women and one-fourth of adult men are on a weight-loss diet. For many people, dieting is a way of life. Most dieters regain much of their lost weight after a year or two. "Yo-yo dieters" lose weight and regain it in a never-ending cycle that takes its toll on body image. In a 1993 study, for example, I discovered that after taking off an average of fifty pounds, obese dieters' body images did improve. However, after regaining a mere five pounds a few months later, their body image worsened significantly.

Many experts are now questioning the dieting solution. Drs. Janet Polivy and Peter Herman have even published a program, *Breaking the Diet Habit* (1983), to help people stop unhealthy dieting. Chronic dieting can lead to health problems, binges, emotional distress, and a possible metabolic change that increases the likelihood of weight gain.

If you are a compulsive, recurrent dieter, I know I can't readily convince you to take a different path. But I can ask that you ponder what motivates your habitual dieting. Is it a desire for health and physical well-being? Or is it a wish for attractiveness and a "fat phobia"—a fear that if you weigh more than your ideal you'll be a social misfit?

Effective weight management is a good idea. Rather than erratic and drastic dieting, weight control entails a healthy lifestyle that doesn't depend on the number on your bathroom scale. The sensible solution involves good nutrition, spreading out your daily food intake, and regular exercise.

It is a myth that weight loss is the only way you can come to accept your body if it's overweight or just heavier than you would like. University of Vermont researchers provided obese persons with group body image therapy, very similar to the program in this workbook. The program enabled participants to greatly improve how they felt about their bodies, without reductions in their weight.

People who need to lose weight in order to improve their health should separate the goals of weight loss and body acceptance. By first learning to have a positive relationship with your imperfect body instead of a relationship of loathing, desperation, and abuse, the ability to shed excess weight may be strengthened.

Surgical Solutions for Body Dissatisfaction

In growing numbers, men and women are seeking cosmetic surgery to change what they look like. Can surgically changing your body improve your body image? In my 1990 book, *Body Images*, my colleague, Dr. Tom Pruzinsky, and a prominent surgeon, Dr. Milton Edgerton, examined the research on this question. They concluded that for many people plastic surgery can relieve their discontent with some physical characteristic. However, surgery is no magic wand; it is a catalyst for changing one's relationship with one's self. I neither recommend nor reject it. Any surgery carries risks as well as potential benefits, both of which depend upon the physical and psychological makeup of the individual having the surgery, the particular surgical procedure, and the skill of the surgeon.

Certainly, plastic surgery can restore the quality of life for persons whose opportunities for human dignity, productivity, and happiness are diminished by congenital or traumatic disfigurements. But what about surgery for minor, nondisfiguring variations in appearance, such as a few sags or wrinkles or a less-than-perfect nose? Deciding to have surgery should not be like impulsively deciding to get a new hairstyle. It requires thoughtful and knowledgeable deliberation in weighing the pros and cons. So, if you're considering cosmetic surgery, first become an astute consumer by reading Joyce Nash's informative book, *What Your Doctor Can't Tell You About Cosmetic Surgery* (1995). Two eye-opening articles entitled "The Price of Vanity" and "Read This First" from the October 14, 1996, issue of *U.S. News and World Report* are also worth reading.

My advice to you is that before you opt for extensive "exterior remodeling," work on the interior problem—your body image. After you've completed this workbook, you may no longer want to change your looks. And if you do, you'll be more able to reap the emotional benefits you desire.

Building a Better Body Image— One Step at a Time

This workbook offers the science you've waited for—an eight-step program for enduring, gratifying changes in your body image. Figure 2 on page 9 shows the eight building blocks of your program. Let me tell you a little more about each step.

Step 1

First, you'll discover exactly what your body image strengths and weaknesses are. Each of you has your own distinctive appearance and your distinctive experience of your appearance. In this step, you'll take special, scientifically developed self-tests to discover the many facets of your body image. These self-discoveries will allow you to set specific goals for change.

Step 2

Why do you have a negative body image? Through recent research, psychologists have determined that the causes of a negative body image stem from your developmental past as well as from the current forces in your life. I want you to have this latest information so that you can start your program with wisdom. I will also show you how to keep a special journal or diary of your daily body image experiences. In this way you can pinpoint your problems and track your progress.

Step 3

A negative body image is emotionally upsetting and draining. Feeling despondent, ashamed, or self-conscious about your looks impairs your ability to feel in charge of your life. Step 3 teaches you two therapeutic skills so you can feel more at ease with your looks and learn to control your body image emotions.

Step 4

You feel what you think. How you feel about your looks is greatly influenced by your privately held beliefs, interpretations, and thought patterns. Most people have particular assumptions about the importance and influence of looks—unchecked assumptions can lead to trouble. In this step, you'll find out whether you unconsciously harbor ten arguable assumptions and then learn how to "change your mind."

Step 5

This step involves more mind changing. When you think about your own looks, you carry on a type of inner conversation, your *Private Body Talk.* If your Private Body Talk is laden with mental mistakes or distortions, it will devastate your body image. In this step, you'll learn about eight common distortions. You'll listen in on your Private Body Talk, identify your own problematic thought patterns, and create a New Inner Voice to communicate with yourself about your looks.

Step 6

A negative body image leads people to act in ways that protect themselves from self-consciousness and other uncomfortable feelings. Such behaviors range from avoiding certain situations to engaging in frustrating grooming rituals. Many of these self-protective maneuvers can trap you in self-defeating cycles of distress; they make your body image even worse. In this crucial step, you'll learn to understand and eradicate your imprisoning patterns of behavior.

Step 7

Having overcome many negative factors of your body image, it's time to expand the positive ones. Step 7 teaches you how to create a more confident, pleasurable, and affirming relationship with your body.

Step 8

You'll begin this step by taking stock of your successful changes. But will they last? By being attuned to the Achilles heels of your body image and planning ahead for possible adversities, you can strengthen your new body image and ward off tough times. This final step of preventative maintenance is your insurance policy.

Good Summary!

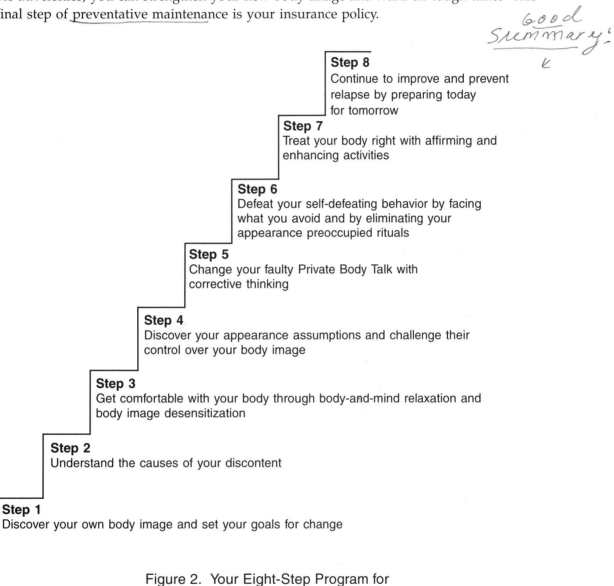

Step 8
Continue to improve and prevent relapse by preparing today for tomorrow

Step 7
Treat your body right with affirming and enhancing activities

Step 6
Defeat your self-defeating behavior by facing what you avoid and by eliminating your appearance preoccupied rituals

Step 5
Change your faulty Private Body Talk with corrective thinking

Step 4
Discover your appearance assumptions and challenge their control over your body image

Step 3
Get comfortable with your body through body-and-mind relaxation and body image desensitization

Step 2
Understand the causes of your discontent

Step 1
Discover your own body image and set your goals for change

Figure 2. Your Eight-Step Program for
Building a Better Body Image

How to Maximize Your Body Image Benefits

The Body Image Workbook is not just for reading—it's for *doing*. You won't achieve the desired results from this program by being a "bedtime reader," sleepily scanning a chapter or two each night until you reach the end. Each program step has the necessary self-tests to diagnose your personal body image difficulties and shows you how to bring about the experiences necessary for change. These experiences require that you think, plan, and act in new ways.

Each step in this program builds on the ones before it. If you're like most people, you probably want your body image problem fixed today. Unfortunately, that's impossible. But, since each step only takes about a week or two to carry out completely, you'll be on your way in no time. If you'd like, first spend about an hour skimming through the entire workbook to appreciate the overall structure of the program. Then, having reviewed the roadmap for your journey, venture forth—one destination at a time.

Throughout this workbook are special "Helpsheets" you will use in learning to like your looks. Concluding each step is a section called "Your Path for Progress" that summarizes what you should be doing to help yourself at that point.

If you were my client and we were meeting face-to-face, together we would tailor this program to your unique individual needs. Carrying it out on your own means that you determine how best to fit the many elements of the program to suit your specific personal needs. The various self-tests and self-discovery assignments in the workbook will enable you to adapt the program in ways that are just right for you.

Another great idea for maximum benefits is to have one or more "Body Image Buddies." Rather than going it alone, get an interested friend or relative to complete the program with you. Get together regularly to talk about what you're doing, to solve difficulties, and to encourage one another. If you don't have a buddy who wants to carry out the program, there may be someone close to you, like a spouse, parent, or roommate, who is willing to be your cheerleader. Enlist his or her support.

Perhaps you've heard the riddle that asks, "How many psychologists does it take to change a light bulb?" The answer is "Only one—but the light bulb must *really* want to change." Bad jokes aside, my program is based on the premises that you really want to have a better body image and that you are willing to do something to change.

So, I turn this opportunity for change over to you. And with your turn of the pages, you can begin learning how to like your looks.

Words of Advice for Therapists

This program has been used successfully by professional therapists in helping their clients overcome distressing body image experiences. If you are a therapist and plan to use this program with your clients, I offer these recommendations:

◎ *The Body Image Workbook* can make your provision of body image therapy more systematic and efficient. workbook assignments and helpsheets offer clear guidance to promote change. In face-to-face sessions, you review the client's workbook entries and provide the support, feedback, and problem-solving that the client needs.

◎ The program is structured as eight discrete steps, in a manner that cumulatively builds the client's skills and integrates therapeutic techniques. However, professional judgment should dictate your priorities in introducing and pacing the components of the program to fit the individual client.

◎ In clinical practice, clients with a negative body image may exhibit a range of other psychological disorders or difficulties. Thus, your thorough assessment of the client's functioning and primary complaints is essential. You must have an accurate understanding of the functional significance of the client's body image in relation to other aspects of his or her psychosocial problems. The program should never, of course, be the sole treatment for clients who, for example, are clinically depressed or anxious, exhibit eating disorders, or have sexual dysfunctions. However, you can effectively integrate the program with the proper treatments of these problems.

◎ *Body Image Workbook* can be used in either individual or group formats by therapists with knowledge and skill in the cognitive-behavioral therapies.

◎ I recommend that you read at least one of the following published articles that provide a detailed, practitioner-oriented overview of cognitive-behavioral body image therapy:

Cash, T, F. 1996. The treatment of body image disturbances. In J. K. Thompson (ed.), *Body Image, Eating Disorders, and Obesity: An Integrative Guide for Assessment and Treatment* (83–107). Washington, D.C.: American Psychological Association.

Cash, T. F., and J. R. Grant. 1996. The cognitive-behavioral treatment of body-image disturbances. In V. Vat Hasselt and M. Hersen (eds.), *Sourcebook of Psychological Treatment Manuals for Adult Disorders* (567–614). New York: Plenum.

Finally, I suggest that you read the following article on the use of bibliotherapy in clinical practice:

Pantalon, M. V., B. S. Lubetkin, and S. T. Fishman. 1995. Use and effectiveness of self-help books in the practice of cognitive and behavioral therapy. *Cognitive and Behavioral Practice*, 2:213–228.

Step 1: Know Thyself

Discovering Your
Personal
Body Image

Let me introduce Darlene to you. She is a twenty-eight-year-old woman—bright, professional, interesting—whom most people would describe as nice looking. She is average in her weight and height, with pretty hazel eyes and a contagious smile. But that's not the way Darlene sees herself. "My huge rear and thunder thighs totally destroy everything," she complains. She admits liking the color and style of her strawberry blonde hair, and she feels her upper body shape is "nice enough." But she's neutral about most other areas of her body.

Whenever Darlene meets someone new at work or at a social event, she's struck by a wave of self-consciousness and feels as if her appearance is under a microscope. Another upsetting situation occurs whenever she weighs herself and sees that she's a few pounds heavier than she'd like. She gets especially bothered about her body whenever she wears any snug clothing—for example, a bathing suit at the pool, or a leotard in aerobics class. A familiar pattern of thoughts runs through Darlene's mind in these situations: "I'm the fattest person here. I hate having a pear-shaped body. I look like a blimp. I wish I could be invisible." Rarely does she have pleasant thoughts about her looks, unless a friend compliments an outfit she's wearing. But these thoughts readily give rise to self-critical ones, like "The outfit would look a lot better if my butt didn't stick out so much."

Darlene's distress about her looks takes its toll on her. To avoid uncomfortable encounters, she sometimes stays away from parties, especially if she has to meet new people. She also avoids going to the beach or pool. When attending her aerobics class, Darlene sneaks into the back of the room after the class has begun. She weighs herself only if she's confident that her latest diet has slimmed her by several pounds. Her husband, Kevin, thinks Darlene looks terrific. Her "insane obsession with her looks" makes no sense to him, and he gets exasperated with her.

Now I'd like you to meet Arnie. He is a forty-five-year-old, divorced computer programmer. Arnie absolutely hates his receding hairline and thinning scalp. He's also dissatisfied with his stature of five feet, four inches. He feels "cheated in the looks department." Once his thoughts zoom in on his appearance, as they so often do, Arnie is irritable for the rest of the day. He's convinced that no woman will ever find him attractive enough to date. Sometimes, if someone does seem interested he wonders what's wrong with her.

Several situations predictably trigger Arnie's body image distress. When he's with people he thinks are good-looking or those taller than he is, Arnie is filled with bitterness. Mirrors are also maddening to him. Before going to work, he stares at himself in the mirror, inspects his balding head, and tries to comb his remaining locks to conceal the thinning spots. Arnie's thoughts about his looks are sadly disparaging. "I look like a damned midget. It's totally unfair." And he thinks, "I look worse every day. The more hair I lose, the dumber I look. I can't win."

So how does Arnie cope? To escape feeling too short, he avoids being with taller people as much as he can. He rarely stands around chatting with people who "make me look like a shrimp," especially taller women. Arnie wears baseball caps, even indoors, to hide his hair loss. He's tried Rogaine but it didn't work for him. Rather than asking any woman for a date and risking rejection, he goes to movies and parties alone, if at all. He nervously belittles himself to others with half-hearted jokes about looking like "E.T., the little space alien," with the exit punch line that he has to go "phone home." People laugh. Arnie doesn't.

Self-Discovery with the Body Image Self-Tests

Body image is like a fingerprint. Both Darlene and Arnie have a negative body image, but if you look more closely you see the experience is unique to each individual: They dislike different physical features, are distressed by different triggering events, have different thoughts and emotions, and handle their problems differently. What these two people do have in common is that, like you, they are tired of struggling with a negative body image.

Now it's time to discover more about your own unique body image—both your body image strengths and vulnerabilities.

✳   On the following pages, you'll complete a series of self-tests that probe your individual body image experiences in detail. Each scientifically developed test provides a fine-tuned, informative summary of certain facets of your body image.

❖ After you've taken each test, I'll show you exactly how to score it. It's best to use a calculator to recheck the accuracy of your math.

❖ Once you've computed a test score, enter it on your Personal Body Image Profile, located on pages 31 and 32. Then compare your scores with the test's norms. Because the norms sometimes differ for men and women, there is a different Personal Body Image Profile form for each gender.

❖ The Profile has five categories to depict how your scores compare with the results for people of your gender: A *very low* score means that at least 80 percent of your peers scored higher than you did. A *very high* score means that at least 80 percent scored lower than you. A *low* score is one exceeded by 55 percent to 80 percent of your peers. A *high* score means you exceeded 55 percent to 80 percent of them. An *average* score indicates that your answers were typical of your gender. Depending on the test, higher scores may mean good news or bad news about your body image.

❖ Immediately after you chart each score in your Profile, I'll guide you in its interpretation. Ultimately though, the most important insights must come from you. Take some time to think about what I suggest. Does it fit? In discussing your test results, I will ask you as much as I tell you.

1. The Body Areas Satisfaction Test

On this first body image self-test, you evaluate how satisfied (or dissatisfied) you are with various aspects of your body. If there are features you don't like that aren't listed (for example, your teeth, your knees, a scar, or a birthmark), simply write them in on lines 9 and 10 and rate your level of discontent.

❖ ❖ ❖ ❖ ❖

The Body Areas Satisfaction Test

*low score –
dissatisfied*

How satisfied are you with each aspect of your body?

1	2	3	4	5
Very Dissatisfied	*Mostly Dissatisfied*	*Neither Satisfied Nor Dissatisfied*	*Mostly Satisfied*	*Very Satisfied*

_____ 1. Face (facial features, complexion)

_____ 2. Hair (color, thickness, texture)

_____ 3. Lower torso (buttocks, hips, thighs, legs)

_____ 4. Mid torso (waist, stomach)

_____ 5. Upper torso (chest or breasts, shoulders, arms)

_____ 6. Muscle tone

_____ 7. Weight

_____ 8. Height

_____ 9. Any other area/aspect you dislike: _____

_____ 10. Any other area/aspect you dislike: _____

❖ ❖ ❖ ❖ ❖

Scoring Your Body Areas Satisfaction Test

To obtain your Body Areas Satisfaction score,

◎ Add your ratings for items 1 through 8. (For now, ignore items 9 and 10).

◎ Make sure your score is between 8 and 40.

◎ Enter your score in the space provided on your Personal Body Image Profile on page 31 or 32. Then circle the appropriate numbers on the Profile grid.

Self-Discovery: "Where Does It Hurt?"

People with low or very low scores on the Body Areas Satisfaction Test usually find a lot to complain about and are less satisfied than the majority of persons of their gender. Because most of you are reading this book to overcome a negative body image, don't be surprised if you have a low score. There are three possible reasons for this:

❖ Low scores could reflect several distinct sources of displeasure. Being overly critical of your looks, you find a number of different physical attributes that you cannot accept as they are. Your body is a moving target for your discontent.

❖ Then, there's the spillover factor. Not liking your weight, for example, may spill over to any body area that you think betrays your weight. You actually have only one complaint, but it affects your evaluation of several features.

❖ Finally, you may be body neutral and have no strong feelings, good or bad, about any facet of your looks. Men especially tend to evaluate their looks this way. Being neutral about your body may prevent the pain of discontent, but it also precludes chances to appreciate and enjoy your best features.

Those of you with average or higher scores may feel pleased with much of your appearance, but there's still something about your looks that troubles you. Your body image discontent is focused. For you, maybe it's a scar, or some facial feature, or your chest size that's tough to accept.

Whatever your score and whatever imperfections you focus on, eliminating any dissatisfaction is worth the effort.

2. The Wishing Well Test

This second self-test examines your views of your body as it is and your body as you wish it could be. Each test item describes a physical characteristic. For each, think about how you see yourself as you actually look. Then think about how you wish you looked. In some instances, your looks may closely match your ideal. For other attributes, they may differ greatly.

Some of your physical ideals may be very important to you. You strongly desire that you look a certain way, whether you do or not. In other areas, your ideals may be less important to you. For each item, rate not only how closely you resemble your personal ideal (Part A), but also how important your ideal is to you (Part B).

✻ ✻ ✻ ✻ ✻

low score – happy c self

The Wishing Well Test

For each item, <u>first rate how much you look like your ideal.</u> <u>Then rate how important this ideal is to you.</u> Enter your ratings in the blank to the left of each scale.

_____ 1. A. My ideal height is

0	*1*	*2*	*3*
Exactly	*Almost*	*Fairly*	*Very*
As I Am	*As I Am*	*Unlike Me*	*Unlike Me*

_____ B. How important to you is your ideal height?

0	*1*	*2*	*3*
Not	*Somewhat*	*Moderately*	*Very*
Important	*Important*	*Important*	*Important*

_____ 2. A. My ideal skin complexion is

0	*1*	*2*	*3*
Exactly	*Almost*	*Fairly*	*Very*
As I Am	*As I Am*	*Unlike Me*	*Unlike Me*

_____ B. How important to you is your ideal skin complexion?

0	*1*	*2*	*3*
Not	*Somewhat*	*Moderately*	*Very*
Important	*Important*	*Important*	*Important*

_____ 3. A. My ideal hair color is

0	*1*	*2*	*3*
Exactly	*Almost*	*Fairly*	*Very*
As I Am	*As I Am*	*Unlike Me*	*Unlike Me*

_____ B. How important to you is your ideal hair color?

0	*1*	*2*	*3*
Not	*Somewhat*	*Moderately*	*Very*
Important	*Important*	*Important*	*Important*

_____ 4. A. My ideal hair texture and length are

0	1	2	3
Exactly	Almost	Fairly	Very
As I Am	As I Am	Unlike Me	Unlike Me

_____ B. How important to you are your ideal hair texture and length?

0	1	2	3
Not	Somewhat	Moderately	Very
Important	Important	Important	Important

_____ 5. A. My ideal facial features (eyes, nose, ears, facial shape) are

0	1	2	3
Exactly	Almost	Fairly	Very
As I Am	As I Am	Unlike Me	Unlike Me

_____ B. How important to you are your ideal facial features?

0	1	2	3
Not	Somewhat	Moderately	Very
Important	Important	Important	Important

_____ 6. A. My ideal muscle tone or definition is

0	1	2	3
Exactly	Almost	Fairly	Very
As I Am	As I Am	Unlike Me	Unlike Me

_____ B. How important to you is your ideal muscle tone or definition?

0	1	2	3
Not	Somewhat	Moderately	Very
Important	Important	Important	Important

_____ 7. A. My ideal body proportions are

0	1	2	3
Exactly	Almost	Fairly	Very
As I Am	As I Am	Unlike Me	Unlike Me

_____ B. How important to you are your ideal body proportions?

0	1	2	3
Not	Somewhat	Moderately	Very
Important	Important	Important	Important

_____ 8. A. My ideal weight is

0	1	2	3
Exactly	Almost	Fairly	Very
As I Am	As I Am	Unlike Me	Unlike Me

_____ B. How important to you is your ideal weight?

0	1	2	3
Not	Somewhat	Moderately	Very
Important	Important	Important	Important

_____ 9. A. My ideal physical strength is

0	1	2	3
Exactly	Almost	Fairly	Very
As I Am	As I Am	Unlike Me	Unlike Me

_____ B. How important to you is your ideal physical strength?

0	1	2	3
Not	Somewhat	Moderately	Very
Important	Important	Important	Important

_____ 10. A. My ideal physical coordination is

0	1	2	3
Exactly	Almost	Fairly	Very
As I Am	As I Am	Unlike Me	Unlike Me

_____ B. How important to you is your ideal physical coordination?

0	1	2	3
Not	Somewhat	Moderately	Very
Important	Important	Important	Important

❋ ❋ ❋ ❋ ❋

Scoring Your Wishing Well Test

You've rated how much you differ from your personal ideal and how important your ideal is to you for ten physical characteristics. Here's the way to calculate your test score:

◉ For each characteristic, multiply your rating from Part A (how much you differ from your ideal) by your rating from Part B (the importance of your ideal). Their product can range anywhere from 0 to 9. For example, if your ideal weight is fairly unlike you (2) and being your ideal weight is very important to you (3), your score on this item is 2 x 3 = 6.

◉ Now add your scores for all ten items. Your Wishing Well total score can range from 0 to 90.

◉ Enter your score on your Body Image Profile and mark the appropriate box.

Self-Discovery: "How Do I Measure Up?"

The results of the Wishing Well Test can tell you what physical characteristics you want but don't think you have. Wishing for physical ideals that you believe you lack will diminish your body image. The more you value a particular ideal, the more it will bother you if you feel you don't measure up to it. Your Wishing Well score takes into account both of these elements—whether you believe you measure up and how much this matters to you.

❧ If your score is very high or high, your body image may be ruled by *shoulds* that you feel you don't measure up to—"I should be taller" or "I should have perfect skin." Your perfectionistic standards for your appearance are a demanding force behind your negative body image.

❧ If your Wishing Well score is average or lower, you aren't necessarily saved from *shoulds*. There are probably some physical ideals that you still expect of yourself. There are times you are critical of yourself for not living up to these standards.

Future steps in this workbook will enable you to understand how your physical ideals are interfering with your self-acceptance. Wishing for perfection is not wishing well!

3. The Distressing Situations Test

Negative body image emotions, such as anxiety, disgust, despondency, anger, envy, shame, or embarrassment, crop up in different situations for different people. In the next self-test, you'll think about occasions when you have been in each of fifty situations. Using a 0 to 4 scale, convey how often you have had negative feelings about your appearance in each situation. Of course, there may be some listed situations that you haven't encountered or some that you avoid. If so, merely indicate how often you probably would have negative body image emotions if you were in such situations.

❋ ❋ ❋ ❋ ❋

The Distressing Situations Test

How often do (would) you have negative feelings about your appearance in each of the following situations? Enter your rating in the blank to the left of each situation.

0	1	2	3	4
Never	Sometimes	Moderately Often	Often	Always or Almost Always

_____ 1. At social gatherings where I know few people

_____ 2. When I'm the focus of social attention

_____ 3. When people see me before I've "fixed myself up"

_____ 4. When I'm with attractive people of my sex

_____ 5. When I'm with attractive people of the other sex

_____ 6. When someone looks at parts of my appearance that I dislike

_____ 7. When people can see me from certain angles

_____ 8. When someone compliments me on my appearance

_____ 9. When I think someone has ignored or rejected me

_____ 10. When the topic of conversation pertains to appearance

_____ 11. When someone comments unfavorably on my appearance

_____ 12. When somebody else's appearance gets complimented and nothing is said about my appearance

_____ 13. When I hear someone criticize another person's looks

_____ 14. When I recall any kidding or unkind things people have said about my appearance

_____ 15. When I'm with people who are talking about weight or dieting

_____ 16. When I see attractive people on television or in magazines

_____ 17. When I'm trying on new clothes at a store

_____ 18. When I'm wearing certain "revealing" clothes

_____ 19. If I'm dressed differently than others at a social event

_____ 20. When my clothes don't fit just right

_____ 21. After I get a new haircut or hairstyle

_____ 22. When I am not wearing any makeup (for women)

_____ 23. If my hair isn't fixed just right

_____ 24. If my friend or partner doesn't notice when I'm "fixed up"

_____ 25. When I look at myself in the mirror

_____ 26. When I look at my nude body in the mirror

_____ 27. When I see myself in a photograph or on a videotape

_____ 28. When I have my photograph taken

_____ 29. When I haven't exercised as much as usual

_____ 30. When I'm exercising

_____ 31. After I've eaten a full meal

_____ 32. When I get on the scale to weigh myself

_____ 33. When I think I have gained some weight

_____ 34. When I think I've lost some weight

_____ 35. When I'm already in a bad mood about something else

_____ 36. When I think about how I looked earlier in my life

_____ 37. When I think about what I wish I looked like

_____ 38. When I think about how I may look in the future

_____   39. When anticipating or having sexual relations

_____   40. When my partner sees me undressed

_____   41. If my partner touches me in body areas that I dislike

_____   42. If my partner doesn't show sexual interest

_____   43. When I am with a certain person (Specify whom: _____)

_____   44. At particular times of the day or evening (Specify when: _____)

_____   45. During particular times of the month (Specify when: _____)

_____   46. During particular seasons of the year (Specify when: _____)

_____   47. During certain recreational activities (Specify which: _____)

_____   48. When I eat certain foods (Specify which: _____)

_____   49. Any other difficult situation? _____

_____   50. Any other difficult situation? _____

❆   ❆   ❆   ❆   ❆

Scoring Your Distressing Situations Test

Here's how you compute a Distressing Situations score:

◉   Add your ratings for the first forty-eight items. Ignore the last two.

◉   Be sure your score falls between 0 and 192.

◉   Enter your score on your Body Image Profile and then circle the appropriate numbers.

Self-Discovery: "What Situations Provoke Distress?"

The first two self-tests have revealed what you dislike about your looks and what idealized images lead to your dissatisfaction. Now let's learn more about the situations and events that trigger your troubles.

❋   If your score is high or very high, there are a lot of situations in which you become bothered or upset about your looks. Daily life is like crossing a minefield, with the potential for eruptions of negative emotions and experiences almost everywhere. In this workbook, you'll focus on your most provocative situations—the ones in which you're conditioned to react emotionally—and learn to handle these situations differently.

❋   Scores that are average or low on this self-test indicate that you have some times and places that intensify your body image displeasure. Even if your distress is triggered by limited circumstances, you don't need the grief and can learn to eliminate it.

4. The Body Image Thoughts Test

In the course of day-to-day life, thoughts about your physical appearance run through your mind. The following self-test samples some of these thoughts.

  ❊ The first portion of the self-test lists negative thoughts. The second part consists of positive thoughts.

  ❊ Simply read each thought and decide how often, if at all, it has occurred to you in your daily life during the past week. Use the 0 to 4 scale to rate the frequency of each thought.

  ❊ In making this decision, don't take any listed thought too literally. Your own thoughts might be similar in content, but consist of different words. For example, you may not have the identical thought "I am unattractive," rather you may have equivalent thoughts like "I'm ugly," or "I look awful."

❊ ❊ ❊ ❊ ❊

The Body Image Thoughts Test

In the last week, how often have you had each of these thoughts?

0	1	2	3	4
Never	*Sometimes*	*Moderately Often*	*Often*	*Always or Almost Always*

A. Negative Thoughts

_____ 1. My life is lousy because of how I look.

_____ 2. My looks make me a nobody.

_____ 3. I don't look good enough to be here (i.e., in some specific situation).

_____ 4. Why can't I ever look good?

_____ 5. It's just not fair that I look the way I do.

_____ 6. With my looks, nobody is ever going to love me.

_____ 7. I wish I were better looking.

_____ 8. I must lose weight.

_____ 9. They think I look fat.

_____ 10. They're laughing about my looks.

_____ 11. I'm not attractive.

_____ 12. I wish I looked like someone else.

_____ 13. Others won't like me because of how I look.

_____ 14. I'll never be attractive.

_____ 15. I hate my body.

_____ 16. Something about my looks has to change.

_____ 17. How I look ruins everything for me.

_____ 18. I never look the way I want to.

_____ 19. I'm so disappointed in my appearance.

_____ 20. I feel unattractive, so there must be something wrong with my looks.

_____ 21. I wish I didn't care about how I look.

_____ 22. Other people notice right off the bat what's wrong with my body.

_____ 23. People are thinking I'm unattractive.

_____ 24. They look better than I do.

_____ 25. I especially think that I'm unattractive when I'm with attractive people.

_____ 26. I can't wear stylish clothes.

_____ 27. My body needs more definition.

_____ 28. My clothes just don't fit right.

_____ 29. I wish others wouldn't look at me.

_____ 30. I can't stand my appearance anymore.

_____ 31. Any other frequent negative thought? Specify: _____

_____ 32. Any other frequent negative thought? Specify: _____

B. Positive Thoughts

_____ 1. Other people think I'm good looking.

_____ 2. My appearance helps me to be more confident.

_____ 3. I'm proud of my body.

_____ 4. My body has good proportions.

_____ 5. My looks seem to help me socially.

_____ 6. I like the way I look.

_____ 7. I still think I'm attractive even when I'm with people more attractive than I am.

_____ 8. I'm at least as attractive as most people.

_____ 9. I don't mind people looking at me.

_____ 10. I'm comfortable with my appearance.

_____ 11. I look healthy.

_____ 12. I like the way I look in my bathing suit.

_____ 13. These clothes look good on me.

_____ 14. My body isn't perfect, but I think it's attractive.

_____ 15. I don't need to change the way I look.

_____ 16. Any other frequent positive thought? Specify: _____

_____ 17. Any other frequent positive thought? Specify: _____

❀ ❀ ❀ ❀ ❀

Scoring Your Body Image Thoughts Test

For this self-test, you calculate two scores—a Negative Thoughts score and Positive Thoughts score.

◎ Add your ratings for the first thirty items in Part A, the Negative Thoughts section. Ignore the last two items.

◎ Enter your score, which can range from 0 to 120, on your Body Image Profile.

◎ Now, add your answers for the first fifteen items of Part B, the Positive Thoughts section. Omit the last two items.

◎ Enter the Positive Thoughts score on your Body Image Profile. It can range from 0 to 60.

◎ As usual, for each score, mark the appropriate box.

Self-Discovery: "How Thought Provoking is My Body Image?"

It's important to find out how often certain thoughts, both positive and negative, run through your head. With the Body Image Thoughts Test, you're beginning to read your own mind.

❀ A high or very high Negative Thoughts score means you tend to think the worst about your looks and you think it often. You've probably convinced yourself that these mental self-criticisms are really true. As you mull over aspects of your appearance, you focus on your "flaws." You ruminate over what other people think about your looks and probably assume they judge you as disapprovingly as you do. Once caught up in the stream of these thoughts, it's hard for you to ignore them.

❀ If your score is average, you may either be milder in your self-critical thoughts, or you may berate your body in a more focused fashion, picking on some single feature. Either way, you are needling yourself—needlessly.

Now let's look at the other side of the coin. How open is your mind to pleasant, approving thoughts about your body?

❋   If your Positive Thoughts score is low or very low, your mind is closed and won't admit nice things about your appearance. Why would you do this? Perhaps you don't believe there's anything good to think about. You're oblivious to your physical assets. Or maybe you shove aside any complimentary thoughts with a "Yes but . . . ," followed by some self-criticism. For example, "I look pretty nice with this hairstyle, but I'm still fat."

❋   Another reason for a deficit of self-affirming thoughts could be that you've come to believe that only vain, egotistical people think favorably of their looks. If so, then any mental compliment about your appearance may lead to a brief guilt trip. So you dismiss the positive thought with "I shouldn't be thinking that." Later in this workbook, you'll learn to give yourself permission to acknowledge and enjoy your best features—without the guilt. Some self-approving thoughts will help you withstand the onslaught of belittling thoughts. Now that's food for thought!

5. The Body/Self Relationship Test

Do you ever stop to consider that you have a relationship with your body, just like you have relationships with friends, family, and other folks? This final self-test lists some ways you might think, feel, or behave in relation to your body. Some of the items on this test pertain to your physical appearance, while others deal with your physical activities and health. To begin to understand your relationship with your body, rate (from 1 to 5) how descriptive each statement is of you.

❋ ❋ ❋ ❋ ❋

The Body/Self Relationship Test

How well does each statement describe you?

1	2	3	4	5
Definitely Disagree	Mostly Disagree	Neither Agree Nor Disagree	Mostly Agree	Definitely Agree

_____   1. My body is sexually appealing.

_____   2. I like my looks just the way they are.

_____   3. Most people would consider me good-looking.

_____   4. I like the way I look without my clothes.

_____   5. I like the way my clothes fit me.

_____   6. I dislike my physique.

_____   7. I'm physically unattractive.

_____   8. Before going out in public, I always notice how I look.

_____   9. I am careful to buy clothes that will make me look my best.

_____   10. I check my appearance in a mirror whenever I can.

_____   11. Before going out, I usually spend a lot of time getting ready.

_____   12. It is important that I always look good.

_____   13. I'm self-conscious if my grooming isn't right.

_____   14. I take special care with my hair grooming.

_____   15. I'm always trying to improve my physical appearance.

_____   16. I usually wear whatever is handy without caring how it looks.

_____   17. I don't care what people think about my appearance.

_____   18. I never think about my appearance.

_____   19. I use very few grooming products.

_____   20. I easily learn physical skills.

_____   21. I'm very coordinated.

_____   22. I'm in control of my health.

_____   23. I'm seldom physically ill.

_____   24. From day to day, I never know how my body will feel.

_____   25. I'm a physically healthy person.

_____   26. I would pass most physical-fitness tests.

_____   27. My physical endurance is good.

_____   28. My health is a matter of unexpected ups and downs.

_____   29. I do poorly in physical sports or games.

_____   30. I often feel vulnerable to sickness.

_____   31. I know a lot about things that affect my physical health.

_____   32. I have deliberately developed a healthy lifestyle.

_____   33. Good health is one of the most important things in my life.

_____   34. I don't do anything that I know might threaten my health.

_____   35. I do things to increase my physical strength.

_____   36. I often read books and magazines that pertain to health.

_____   37. I work to improve my physical stamina.

_____   38. I try to be physically active.

_____   39. I know a lot about physical fitness.

_____   40. Being physically fit is not a strong priority in my life.

_____   41. I am not involved in a regular exercise program.

_____   42. I take my health for granted.

_____   43. I make no special effort to eat a balanced and nutritious diet.

_____   44. I don't care to improve my abilities in physical activities.

❖ ❖ ❖ ❖ ❖

Scoring Your Body/Self Relationship Test

This self-test is really four tests in one, therefore you'll have to compute four scores. You'll use specific formulas to adjust for the fact that some items are worded positively while others are stated negatively. In each formula, first you add ratings on certain items, next you subtract the sum of ratings on other items, and finally you add a specific number of points to adjust the score.

A. To determine your Appearance Evaluation score

◎   Step 1. Add your ratings on items 1–5   _____

◎   Step 2. Add your ratings on items 6–7   _____

◎   Step 3. Subtract the amount in step 2 from the amount in step 1   _____

◎   Step 4. Add 12 points to the step 3 amount   __+12__

◎   Enter the final amount on your Body Image Profile. Make sure it falls somewhere between 7 and 35. Mark the appropriate box.   _____

B. To determine your Appearance Orientation score

◎   Step 1. Add your ratings on items 8–15   _____

◎   Step 2. Add your ratings on items 16–19   _____

◎   Step 3. Subtract the amount in step 2 from the amount in step 1   _____

◎   Step 4. Add 24 points to the step 3 amount   __+24__

◎   Enter the final amount on your Body Image Profile. It should fall somewhere between 12 and 60. Mark the appropriate box.   _____

C. To determine your Fitness/Health Evaluation score

◎ Step 1. Add your ratings on items 20–27 _____

◎ Step 2. Add your ratings on items 28–30 _____

◎ Step 3. Subtract the amount in step 2 from the amount in step 1 _____

◎ Step 4. Add 18 points to the step 3 amount ___+18___

◎ Enter the final amount on your Body Image Profile. Is it a number between 11 and 55? Mark the appropriate box. _____

D. To determine your Fitness/Health Orientation score

◎ Step 1. Add your ratings on items 31–39 _____

◎ Step 2. Add your ratings on items 40–44 _____

◎ Step 3. Subtract the amount in step 2 from the amount in step 1 _____

◎ Step 4. Add 30 points to the step 3 amount ___+30___

◎ Enter the final amount on your Body Image Profile. Your score should fall between 14 and 70. Mark the appropriate box. _____

A.

Self-Discovery: "What's the Sum of My Discontent?"

Disliking some aspect of your body doesn't guarantee that you cannot accept your overall looks. However, it will if you hate one physical characteristic, such as your body shape or some facial feature, and are convinced that this one aspect ruins everything. Your Appearance Evaluation score (Part A) captures this "big picture," your overall perception or judgment of your looks.

❋ Is your Appearance Evaluation score low or very low? If so, you probably have a nearsighted vision of your body. Your view of your looks as a whole is clouded by how you see some part of your appearance. You may perceive yourself as homely and doubt that anyone could see you differently. This program will enable you to become more clear-sighted and acquire a more accurate view of your appearance—its parts and its totality.

❋ It is possible that even though your Body Areas Satisfaction score is low or very low, you scored in the average or higher categories on Appearance Evaluation. This means that, to some extent, you're able to keep your particular dissatisfactions from influencing how you feel about your looks overall. And that's good.

B.

Self-Discovery: "How Much Do I Bank on My Looks?"

Part B of this self-test gives your Appearance Orientation score. This facet of your body image refers to how psychologically invested you are in your appearance, how much you emphasize your looks over other qualities you possess.

❄ If your Appearance Orientation score is in the high to very high range, your appearance is exceedingly important to you. You probably devote considerable time, effort, and mental energy to your appearance and the pursuit of attractiveness. Your looks may define how you see yourself as a person.

❄ Consider this: If you have a negative body image, then you've invested heavily in something that's not paying many dividends. Like a smart investor who diversifies to minimize losses, you need to invest your sense of self-worth in areas other than your appearance. For fashion models, whose livelihood depends on their looks, a blemish, wrinkle, or ten-pound weight gain can cost thousands of dollars. For you, the price is an emotional expense.

❄ Scoring average or lower on Appearance Orientation doesn't mean you consider your looks to be irrelevant in your life. Because society works overtime teaching people to invest in their appearance, few fail to learn the lesson. Most people, male or female, are quite appearance oriented, so that even an average level of investment in your appearance relative to your peers still may be too much. It's still a big gamble.

❄ Some individuals scoring low in Appearance Orientation may actually care about their appearance, but they feel that any attempts to improve it would be hopeless. Because they feel that even their best is woefully inadequate. So why try? If your score is low or very low, ask yourself this: Have I abandoned my looks because I believe that any improvements are doomed to fail?

Self-Discovery: "Is There More to Me than the Eye Can See?"

Your Fitness/Health Orientation score (Part C) reveals how much you're invested in something about your body besides its looks—what your body can *do*. Fitness-and health-oriented people are active and exercise regularly. They make intentional, healthy choices about what they eat and how they eat. They create a lifestyle that can prevent sickness and promote health.

❄ I hope your Fitness/Health Orientation score places you in the high or very high category. If not, you're neglecting a tremendous source of body satisfaction. A later step of this program will help you discover this facet of your experiences of embodiment.

❄ How does your Fitness/Health Orientation level compare with your Appearance Orientation level? If you emphasize your appearance more than your fitness and health, you'll need to shift the balance and devote more energy to your physical well-being. Contrary to the quip by one of comedian Billy Crystal's characters, it is *not* "better to look good than to feel good."

❄ If you are strongly invested in fitness and health, ask yourself *why*. If you regularly exercise and carefully select your diet, is health really your goal? Or is your aim to *look* thin, *look* muscular, or *look* healthy? Fitness/Health Orientation is sometimes Appearance Orientation in disguise. Is it for you?

Self-Discovery: "Do I Feel Fit and Healthy?"

Your Fitness/Health Evaluation score (Part D) is an index of the returns on investment in health and fitness. Higher scores represent positive payoffs. Lower sco. reveal displeasure with how well your body functions. You feel out of shape or un. healthy. Later in this workbook, you'll find ways to enhance and enjoy your physical well-being.

Translating Self-Discoveries into Goals for Change

Having taken and interpreted all the self-tests, your body image is coming into sharper focus. You should now see patterns, both strengths and vulnerabilities, that were not apparent to you before. You may be tempted to chastise yourself—"I can't believe my body image is so bad. I'm such a total mess!"—but I urge you to take a different, certainly more helpful perspective. Your self-discoveries give you insight into exactly what you need to change. And this insightful knowledge is power! You could not change without it.

The Personal Body Image Profile for Women

Score the tests as explained in the text. Enter each test score in the blank provided below. Then, to classify your score, from "very low" to "very high," circle the appropriate numbers.

Body Image Self-Test	Score	Very Low	Low	Average	High	Very High
1. Body Areas Satisfaction Test	___	8–22	23–25	26–27	28–32	33–402
Wishing Well Test	___	0–8	9–17	18–26	27–50	51–90
3. Distressing Situations Test	___	0–50	51–72	73–80	81–110	111–192
4. Body Image Thoughts Test						
A. Negative Thoughts	___	0–8	9–17	18–21	22–39	40–120
B. Positive Thoughts	___	0–16	17–26	27–32	33–39	40–60
5. Body/Self Relationship Test						
A. Appearance Evaluation	___	7–17	18–23	24–25	26–29	30–35
B. Appearance Orientation	___	12–40	41–46	47–48	49–53	54–60
C. Fitness/Health Evaluation	___	11–33	34–40	41–42	43–47	48–55
D. Fitness/Health Orientation	___	14–41	42–49	50–52	53–59	60–70

The Personal Body Image Profile for Men

Score the tests as explained in the text. Enter each test score in the blank provided below. Then, to classify your score from "very low" to "very high," circle the appropriate numbers.

Body Image Self-Test	Score	Very Low	Low	Average	High	Very High
1. Body Areas Satisfaction Test	____	8–25	26–28	29–30	31–33	34–40
2. Wishing Well Test	____	0–8	9–17	18–26	27–50	51–90
3. Distressing Situations Test	____	0–24	25–43	44–49	50–65	66–192
4. Body Image Thoughts Test						
A. Negative Thoughts	____	0–7	8–15	16–17	18–32	33–120
B. Positive Thoughts	____	0–13	14–21	22–25	26–34	35–60
5. Body/Self Relationship Test						
A. Appearance Evaluation	____	7–19	20–24	25–26	27–29	30–35
B. Appearance Orientation	____	12–36	37–42	43–44	45–50	51–60
C. Fitness/Health Evaluation	____	11–36	37–42	43–44	51–55	45–50
D. Fitness/Health Orientation	____	14–41	42–49	50–52	53–59	60–70

What Do You Need?

So let's translate your self-discoveries into specific directions for improvement. Take a look at the Needs for Change Helpsheet on page 34. Identify and write down two or three important needs for change based on your results of each body image self-test. The Helpsheet is neatly organized into specific topics so that you can easily translate your self-discoveries into an individualized plan for change.

Do you remember Darlene, whom you met at the beginning of this chapter? Here are examples from her Needs for Change Helpsheet:

"I need to stop loathing my lower body."

"I need fewer self-critical thoughts about my weight."

"I need to get more comfortable with my looks at social events (especially at the pool)."

"I need to be able to look in the mirror and not get upset."

"I need to spend less time trying to decide what to wear before going out."

"I need to emphasize my looks less and start paying more attention to my physical fitness."

"I need to quit comparing myself to every good-looking person I see (especially in the beauty mags)."

Here are some excerpts from Arnie's needs list:

"I need to stop making fun of myself for having some hair loss."

"I need to accept the fact that I'm not a tall guy and the reality that I never will be."

"I need to spend less time criticizing myself when I'm looking in my mirror."

"I need to give myself more credit for the fact that I work out regularly and I'm in good shape."

"I need to stop thinking that women consider me to be boring because of my looks."

"I need to appreciate the fact that I have nice skin and an attractive beard."

"I need to be friendlier to tall guys. It's not their fault they're taller than I am."

Final Words of Encouragement

Each subsequent chapter of your *Body Image Workbook* contains opportunities to discover additional assets and liabilities affecting your body image. And always, after learning what's wrong, you'll then learn how to make it better.

Such a detailed discovery of what's wrong with their body image can leave some folks feeling as though they're at the bottom of a mountain that they'll never be able to climb. I understand. A journey is often hardest at its start. Realize that the climb isn't really as steep or as treacherous as it may seem at the moment. Others have taken the same path you will take, and they have succeeded. You have translated your difficulties into positive directions for change and can accomplish your goals one step at a time. I commend you for completing this first important step. Onward!

Step 1
Your Path for Progress

★ You've taken, scored, and interpreted the body image self-tests. You're gaining valuable insights into the strengths and vulnerabilities of your body image.

★ Having translated your test results into what you need to change, you're setting your goals. You're committed to work toward improving your body image.

Helpsheet for Change: My Needs for Change

Physical characteristics I need to feel better about:

I need to _____ .

I need to _____ .

I need to _____ .

Body image emotions I need to control or eliminate:

I need to _____ .

I need to _____ .

I need to _____ .

Physical ideals (*shoulds*) I need to emphasize less:

I need to _____ .

I need to _____ .

I need to _____ .

Negative thoughts I need to get rid of:

I need to _____ .

I need to _____ .

I need to _____ .

Positive thoughts I need to have more of:

I need to _____ .

I need to _____ .

I need to _____ .

Situations I need to learn to handle better:

I need to _____ .

I need to _____ .

I need to _____ .

Appearance-invested behaviors I need to change:

I need to _____ .

I need to _____ .

I need to _____ .

Fitness/health-oriented behaviors I need to change:

I need to _____ .

I need to _____ .

I need to _____ .

Step 2: The Psychology of Physical Appearance

Harnessing Knowledge for Change

A few years ago, I surveyed over a hundred people and asked them: "What do you see when you look in the mirror?" I was so struck by the poignancy of their written responses, I reprinted some of them in my previous book, for which this question was the title. Here are a sample of these and further "reflections":

What I see is a body I regret to call my own. I wasn't fond of it as a child. I really disliked it as a teenager. My twenty-five adult years have been constant contempt of my ugly fat body. I would trade it in for almost anything.

(White man, age forty-five)

What I see I really hate. I hate my thighs. I hate my butt. My mouth is too big. My eyes are too big. My hair is too straight. I wish I didn't have to spend so much time on my looks. Tomorrow I'll start working out.

(White woman, age twenty-five)

I see a slim, healthy looking woman, until I look into her eyes. What am I going to do about these growing bags under my eyes? I look pretty good for thirty-two. But what will I see when I'm fifty or sixty? Perish the thought!

(White woman, age thirty-two)

I see a person who's not short and not tall. She's not thin and not fat. She's not pretty yet not ugly. Everything I see is average—boringly average.

(White woman, age twenty-one)

I see a woman whose face I've grown to love and accept. I look at the nose I hated when I was a teenager. It's the exact same nose but I don't see it the same way. My past worries about the size of my nose were really misguided worries about my worth as a Black person.

(African-American woman,
age twenty-one)

What I try to see (but can't) is what I dream about being: Rich! Rich enough to afford to have plastic surgery on my nose and to have my teeth fixed plus a chin implant. Rich enough to have my makeup and hair done professionally. Then, there are the fashionable clothes. Dream on! I'm always going to be a plain Jane.

(White woman, age thirty-three)

I see an average-looking dude. I wish I was bigger. I wish my hair was fuller. I wish I was a couple of inches taller. Why am I kidding myself? I'm less than an average-looking dude. I'd settle for average.

(African-American man, age twenty-six)

I see an old fart. When did this happen?

(White man, age sixty-three)

I see a tall, well-built young man, who has a crippling injury of his right hand. If it weren't for my deformity, I'd be the happiest person in the world.

(White man, age nineteen)

I see a nice-looking guy with a warm smile and friendly eyes. I like his haircut too. He looks healthy and happy. Not bad. I'm glad he's me!

(Hispanic man, age thirty-four)

I see a woman who looks like a girl. If it weren't for my big nipples I'd have no breasts at all.

(White woman, age thirty-one)

What do I see? Are those spots in front of my eyes? Nope, just freckles everywhere. So get out your pencil and let's play connect the dots—on my body.

(White woman, age twenty-seven)

What I see has looked worse. And it'll probably look worse again.

(Asian-American woman, age thirty-nine)

I see a fairly attractive young lady who can't stop thinking about the things that keep her from being a very attractive young lady.

(White woman, age twenty-eight)

I see a tall, skinny guy. I see a receding hairline. I see acne scars. I see a loser!

(Hispanic man, age thirty-one)

I see a short girl with an hourglass figure, but the sand stays settled in the bottom.

(White woman, age nineteen)

I see a gal who looks pretty good. Just don't ask her to take her clothes off. Then you'll get another story. But I'll spare you the ugly details.

(Hispanic woman, age forty-one)

I see a girl who needs to lose weight. My arms are covered with dark hair that I'm always hiding or bleaching. Why can't I look as pretty as the other girls?

(White woman, age twenty-two)

I see a guy who looks like Ross Perot with a goatee. If only I could flap these ears I could fly.

(White man, age forty-six)

When I look in the mirror, I see nothing. That's because I'm too scared to open my eyes. Sorry.

(Pacific Islander woman, age nineteen)

All I see is a guy in a wheelchair with skinny legs. Unfortunately, I know that's all everybody else sees too.

(Asian-American man, age forty-eight)

I see my father's great big nose. Damn him!

(White woman, age eighteen)

I see zits and fat cheeks. Yuck!

(White woman, age nineteen)

Mirror, mirror on the wall, who's the fairest of them all? It ain't me, babe!

(Hispanic woman, age thirty-eight)

Discovering the Physical and Mental Reflections in Your Mirror

Unfortunately, most of these comments don't reveal a very favorable body image. What about your own reflections? Using the Helpsheet on page 39, carry out a self-discovery exercise in your mirror. Take a little time to see what this experience is like.

Looking at Looks: The Inside View

Being objectively good-looking does not guarantee a positive body image, just as homeliness does not dictate a lifetime of self-loathing. In 1986, I appeared on ABC-TV's *20/20* news program to discuss my research on the psychology of physical appearance. Reporter John Stossel also interviewed professional models, both men and women, about how they felt about their beautiful bodies. Here were people who are prototypes of what many of us wish to look like, yet most of them were self-critical. They zeroed in on specific physical features that really bugged them. Their candid comments and complaints conveyed a fundamental truth that research has also confirmed: Your body image has little to do with your outward appearance. Body image is really a state of mind.

What Are We Complaining About?

How common is a negative body image? Among people who are unhappy with their appearance, what physical characteristics are the sources of their discontent? In 1985, my colleagues and I conducted a national survey on body image in *Psychology Today* magazine. With over thirty thousand replies to our questionnaire, we found that nearly two out of every five women and about one in three men said they disliked their overall appearance. *Psychology Today* conducted a similar body image survey in 1996. Results revealed dissatisfaction with overall appearance among 56 percent of women and 43 percent of men.

Thus, while women are more prone to having a negative body image, men are clearly not immune to body image problems. People mistakenly believe that only women focus on hating their bodies, in part because women more readily verbalize their body image concerns. In doing so, they "normalize" their dissatisfaction and their misery finds company. Men suffer silently, feeling that "real men" are not supposed to be bothered about their looks. Having body image difficulties threatens their sense of masculinity.

So why are women more dissatisfied than men? One key reason is that women in general are more psychologically invested in their physical appearance. It's more central to their sense of who they are. As I'll discuss later on, girls and women are more intensely programmed by society to regard their own personal worth as dependent on their physical attractiveness. Scientific studies reveal that the more people invest in their looks, the more vulnerable they become to a negative body image and to day-to-day distress about it.

What do people with a negative body image complain about? Take a look at the results from the 1972, 1985, and 1996 *Psychology Today* surveys, summarized in table 2.1. Weight and the weight-sensitive lower and middle torso areas are the most disliked attributes. For example, 66 percent of women and 52 percent of men are currently dissatisfied with their weight. Women mostly despair about being too fat. Men are as worried about being skinny as they are about being fat. The old adage that "You can never be too rich or too thin" isn't entirely true of how men feel. Attesting to the notion that body image is more a state of mind than body, we discovered in 1985 that among those at a healthy weight, about one-half of the women and one-fourth of the men actually believed they were overweight. Overall body image and self-esteem are more closely related to what people believe about their weight than to what their scale says.

Self-Discovery Helpsheet:
Reflections in My Mirror

Alone, in the privacy of your room, stand in front of a full-length mirror.
Describe what you see when you look in the mirror.

_____

_____

_____

_____

_____

What thoughts run through your mind as you look at your reflection?

_____

_____

_____

_____

_____

How do you feel as you look at your reflection?

_____

_____

_____

About one-third of both sexes aren't content with their upper torso or chest area. The attributes of least concern are face and height, with less than 20 percent of women and men reporting dissatisfaction. Muscle tone is a fairly typical focus of body image displeasure—for 57 percent of women and 45 percent of men surveyed in 1996.

Most people dislike something about their looks. In our 1985 survey, only 28 percent of men and 15 percent of women were accepting of all seven body areas listed. Thus, complete contentment is the exception and not the rule. Furthermore, what is important is whether some specific discontent erodes overall satisfaction with one's looks. In Step 1, you discovered the extent to which this is true of you.

Table 2.1
Sources of Discontent:
The Results of Three U.S. Surveys on Body Image

Disliked Physical Attributes	1972 Survey		1985 Survey		1996 Survey	
	Men	Women	Men	Women	Men	Women
Mid Torso	36%	50%	50%	57%	63%	71%
Lower Torso	12%	49%	21%	50%	29%	61%
Upper Torso	18%	27%	28%	32%	38%	34%
Weight	35%	48%	41%	55%	52%	66%
Muscle Tone	25%	30%	32%	45%	45%	57%
Height	13%	13%	20%	17%	16%	16%
Face	8%	11%	20%	20%	n.a.	n.a.
Overall Appearance	15%	23%	34%	38%	43%	56%

Adapted from Berscheid, Walster, and Bohrnstedt (1973), Cash, Winstead, and Janda (1986), and Garner (1997); n.a. designates data not available.

As you perused the percentages from three decades of body image surveys in Table 2.1, did you start comparing numbers to answer the important question "Are people's body images getting better or worse?" Let me help you with this answer. The news is bad. For most physical attributes and for overall appearance, body images have progressively worsened. Furhtermore, this seems to be as true for men as it is for women.

Is there any good news? Yes, the good news is that you personally have decided to do something about your negative body image. If enough people make the choice that you have made, I'm hopeful that the tide of body image discontent in our society will turn before the next decade—in the twenty-first century.

Does Your Body Image Really Matter?

Body image problems spawn other problems in living. The following are some of the most frequent troubles. How much do they apply to you?

✻ A poor body image often lowers *self-esteem*. Poor self-esteem means feeling inadequate as a person; it means you have low self-worth. Studies confirm that as much as one-fourth to one-third of your self-esteem is related to how positive or negative your body image is. If you don't like your body, it's difficult to like the person who lives there—you!

❊ Body image is integral to *gender identity*—your feelings of manliness or masculinity, or your feelings of womanliness or femininity. Some people believe that they don't have the physical qualities necessary to experience themselves as particularly masculine or feminine. This can diminish their sense of acceptability as a person.

❊ A negative body image can cause *interpersonal anxiety*. If you can't accept your looks, you most likely assume others don't like your looks either. As a result, you feel self-conscious and inadequate in some of your social interactions. Perhaps these are interactions with members of your gender. Perhaps they involve relating to individuals of the other gender. Fearful of social inspection and social rejection, you may even shy away from situations in which you feel that your appearance is on trial. And of course, if nothing is ventured nothing is gained—like fun and friendships.

❊ If your physical self-consciousness spills into your sexually intimate relationships, it can jeopardize your *sexual fulfillment*. If you believe your naked body is ugly or unacceptable, sex becomes anxiety producing. Sex researchers and therapists know that one cause of sexual difficulties is *spectatoring*—a self-conscious scrutiny of one's own body during sex instead of immersion in the sensate experience itself. By dwelling on worries about your attractiveness or on maneuvers to hide your body from your partner's view or touch, sex becomes an act of apprehension and avoidance. If you switch off the lights to cloak your body in darkness, you may be switching off your pleasure as well! For example, Dr. Jill Hangen and I conducted a study of body image and sexuality. We compared fifty women who were highly self-conscious about their body's appearance during sex and fifty women who weren't. Body-conscious women reported that they had orgasms in an average of only 42 percent of their lovemaking occasions—versus an average of 73 percent of the time for less physically self-conscious women. A negative body image can make it hard to give and receive sexual intimacy.

❊ As mentioned in the workbook's introduction, *depression* and a negative body image are often intertwined. Depression can lead people to detest their looks and vice versa. Self-disparagement and thoughts of hopelessness and helplessness about what you look like are depressing. In turn, this despondency, like quicksand, can further trap you in self-criticisms of your body. It's a vicious cycle of despair.

❊ Also indicated earlier, a negative body image can bring about *eating disturbances*, such as anorexia nervosa or bulimia nervosa. These are problems that gradually build over time. If you worry that you look fat, you may diet and exercise to excess. Scientific studies reveal that chronic dieting may lead to binge eating, which can precipitate purging. Not only does having a negative, "fat phobic" body image predispose disturbed patterns of eating, but having an eating disorder undermines body image. Changing a negative body image is as important to preventing eating disorders as it is to conquering them.

Now, having seen the troubles that a negative body image can bring, answer the questions on the following Self-Discovery Helpsheet to find out how much your body image influences various aspects of your life.

Self-Discovery Helpsheet:
How a Negative Body Image Affects My Life

Fill in the value on the 0 to 4 rating scale that best describes the extent to which your body image negatively affects each of these areas.

0	1	2	3	4
No Negative Effect	*Slight Negative Effect*	*Moderate Negative Effect*	*Considerable Negative Effect*	*Extreme Negative Effect*

_____ My self-esteem—feelings of personal adequacy and self-worth

_____ My gender identity—feelings of masculinity or femininity

_____ My feelings of comfort and confidence in my social interactions in general

_____ My feelings of comfort and confidence interacting with people of my own gender

_____ My feelings of comfort and confidence interacting with people of the other gender

_____ My feelings of comfort and confidence during sexual relations

_____ My responsiveness as a sexual partner

_____ My enjoyment of sex

_____ My desires and efforts to modify my weight by dieting

_____ My desires and efforts to modify my weight by exercising

_____ My feelings of being in control of my eating behavior

_____ My feelings of dejection, despondency, or depression

_____ My overall quality of life

The Development of a Negative Body Image: Voices from the Past

People don't just wake up one day to the conviction that they cannot stand their looks. They've usually felt this way for quite some time. Body image forms gradually, beginning in childhood. Many factors lead some people to relate to their bodies in a positive and satisfying way, while others travel down a less enjoyable path. We can divide these influential factors into two basic categories:

 ❖ The *historical influences* are the forces from your past that shaped how you came to view your appearance in the ways that you do.

 ❖ The *current influences* are the experiences of everyday life that determine how you think, feel, and react to your looks.

You must explore each of these two influences in greater detail so that you can begin to understand your personal body image development.

Your basic sense of identity is rooted in your experience of being embodied. The body is a boundary between you and everything that is not you. By the age of two years, most children have self-awareness and can recognize their physical self as a reflection in the mirror. More and more, their bodily being comes to represent who they are in their own eyes. And they begin to reflect upon how other people view their appearance.

Preschool children have already started to learn how society views various physical characteristics. Little kids know that lovely Cinderella wins the handsome prince; her ugly and mean step-sisters lose out. They know that Barbie and Ken have the good life, with bodies to match. Body image takes shape as children absorb conceptions of what is valued as attractive—how they *should* look. Kids also form images of what is not attractive—how they should *not* look. Most importantly, they judge their own bodily appearance—how well does it live up to the *shoulds*? The answer affects feelings of self-worth.

Cultural Reflections

From the word *go*, society dictates social values and the meanings of physical appearance. For example, it teaches that well-toned thinness for women and tallness and muscularity for men are desirable. Let's briefly take a closer look at the lessons we are taught by our culture.

My Fair Lady

The worship of thinness hasn't occurred in some cultures to the extent that it has in Western society. Societies in which food is scarce, for example, view a heavier body as evidence of successful survival. In earlier times, a full-figured physique was the epitome of feminine beauty. Rounded hips and thighs of prehistoric goddesses symbolized feminine fertility. In the art of the fifteenth to eighteenth centuries, full-bodied women were the standard of beauty. In the ancient Orient, a fat wife was such a symbol of honor for her husband that some men force-fed their wives to enhance their own social standing.

In the twentieth century, however, a thinner and less curvaceous body type has increasingly been promoted as the standard of feminine attractiveness. Fashion models, film stars, and beauty pageant contestants have become thinner, even as the female population has gotten heavier. As rates of anorexia nervosa and bulimia nervosa have steadily increased, emaciated "waif models" appear on magazine covers and in television ads. The broadcasted messages are not only "thin is in and feminine," but also that today's woman needs to look fit and strong as well. And as reflected in the prevalence of breast augmentation surgery and the record sales of the Wonder Bra, shapely breasts have become more important to the cultural ideal.

For the sake of beauty, women in our society are told to shave or wax their legs and armpits, pluck their eyebrows, dye and either curl or straighten their hair, pierce their ears, paint their faces and all twenty nails, and walk around in uncomfortable high heels. Women are also told that they should worry about unsightly age spots, split ends, the sprouting of a single gray hair, a chipped nail, and a visible panty line. Who can wonder why so many girls and women find so many things faulty about their looks!

The Handsome Prince

Though less demanding than women's appearance standards, societal norms and expectations definitely exist for men. Guys are supposed to be tall, have broad shoulders, a muscular chest and biceps, a small rear, strong facial features, and a full head of hair. Most "manly heroes" and "leading men" are handsome hunks—Arnold Schwarzenegger, Denzel Washington, Tom Cruise, Kevin Costner, Richard Gere, Brad Pitt, Michael Jordan, Sylvester Stallone, Superman. John "Duke" Wayne protected his masculine, "stand tall" image by refusing to appear "topless" in public—that is, without his hairpiece.

These masculine body image prescriptions lead some boys and men to jeopardize their health with steroid abuse and excessive exercise. Now more than ever before, men seek cosmetic surgery, including hair transplants, pectoral implants, face lifts, and liposuction. Men, too, feel growing pressures to be physically attractive, believing that good looks are a prerequisite for succeeding in relationships and life in general.

From Cultural Images to Body Images

In various cultures at various times, attractiveness has required decorative scars on the face, a shaved head, tattoos fully covering the body, jewels placed in holes drilled in the teeth, large disks inserted in the lips, stacked rings to elongate the neck, and the maiming of women's feet to make them petite. All these things have been done, and most still are, in service of societal standards of attractiveness.

Just as you may dismiss foreign appearance standards as "really crazy," I urge you to begin to question the mandates of our own culture. Who are the appearance masters that you feel obliged to serve? Throughout this program, I'll help you defend yourself against these unhealthy messages. Right now, I want you to think about these two crucial facts:

❋ *Societal standards can't harm you unless you buy into them.* You don't have to adopt these ideals and pressure yourself to live up to them. You don't have to allow your sense of self-worth to be determined by voices not of your choosing. Plenty of research shows that if you think you should possess some trait that you believe you lack, you'll experience distress in situations that remind you of this "inadequacy." People with extreme standards for how they should look are vulnerable to shame, anxiety, and depression. These worrisome emotions lead to self-defeating behaviors such as avoiding certain situations, dieting excessively, or spending considerable time and money trying to look "right." Events that remind you of your physical ideals and your "shortcomings" trigger self-conscious thoughts, feelings of inadequacy, and attempts to defend yourself against distress. On the other hand, if you hold ideals that are more moderate and realistic, and stop beating yourself over the head with unreasonable yardsticks, your more favorable body image will promote self-acceptance.

✣ *Other people don't judge you as harshly as you judge yourself.* Let me tell you what several scientific investigations have found. Researchers asked men and women to specify their physical ideals for themselves and for the other sex. They were also asked what they believed the other sex is most attracted to. The findings indicate that many people demand more physical "perfection" of themselves than they *think* others expect of them, even more than others *truly* expect. People are often out of touch with reality. Men are often more appreciative of a heavier female body type than women believe men are. Guys don't idealize blonde beauty to the degree women assume. Likewise, lots of women don't worship the same narrow images of "macho" male attractiveness that men assume women do.

Whatever your gender, *The Body Image Workbook* will help you adjust your ideals so that you can stop making inaccurate and unfair evaluations of your worth.

Remembrance of Things Past: "Hey Fatso . . . Hey Crater Face"

In the development of an unhappy body image, the media aren't the only messengers. Socialization about the meaning of the body goes beyond the television commercials and magazine ads that convey that you must look a certain way to succeed and be happy, or that you should desperately fear being fat, or that you should do all you can to disguise the natural wrinkles of aging. There are other voices as well—those of peers, parents, and other loved ones.

Your family has most likely taught you about your own body. How many times have you heard this: "You're not really going to leave the house looking like that, are you?" Parents remind you to brush your hair, put on clean clothes with patterns and colors that don't clash, and stay trim. Families also communicate expectations by what psychologists call *modeling*. For example, if you grow up with a parent or sibling who constantly complains about his or her appearance, you learn that looks can be something to worry about. If you have a brother or sister doted on for being attractive, you may come to feel shortchanged by your looks. You may feel resentful and envious that you aren't as nice-looking.

Being repeatedly criticized, taunted, or teased about your appearance during the childhood or teen years can leave a lasting effect on body image development. Many adults who dislike their appearance can recall experiences of being teased or criticized as children because of their looks. Deeply etched in their memories are episodes of rebuke or ridicule for being too chubby or too skinny, too tall or too short, for having a large nose or big ears, or for how they dressed or wore their hair.

In one study that graduate student Laura Rieves and I recently conducted, 72 percent of college students revealed that, while growing up, they had been repeatedly teased or criticized for an average of over six years, usually about their facial features or weight. Many reported having had an unwelcome nickname—Bubble Butt, Pinocchio, Freckles, Pizza Face, Four Eyes, Carrot Top, Beanpole. Of those who had been teased, 71 percent said it had been moderately to very upsetting. Table 2.2 summarizes some of the interesting findings of our study, including information on what physical characteristics people were teased about and who the perpetrators were. We found in an earlier study that 65 percent said that appearance teasing had marred their body image. Both studies revealed that a history of such treatment was linked to a more negative adult body image.

As the Years Go By

The human body changes dramatically at puberty. This time can also bring intense preoccupation with these changes and with physical appearance in general. Having the "right" body type, clothes, or hairstyle becomes far more important than algebra or geography. The relative timing of physical maturation can be pivotal in body image development. Girls whose hips and breasts develop earlier than those of their classmates may feel self-conscious. They don't appreciate their new shape as a sign of approaching womanhood. Many girls can only see it as grotesque fat. Boys whose spurt in height and muscularity is slower than that of their peers may privately worry that their body will never catch up.

The teen years are a tough time for body image. Teenagers' feelings of social adequacy depend in part on how they think their appearance is perceived by peers and how that will affect their chances in the dating game. One common occurrence during adolescence is facial acne. Acne can have a profound effect on body image and social adjustment. In a series of extensive studies in 1996, I found that 74 percent of teenagers with moderate to severe facial acne reported that it had a damaging effect on their body image, and 43 percent indicated it had negatively affected their social lives. Their blemishes were more than skin deep.

As you can see, body image is very much the consequence of cultural and interpersonal conditioning. Sometimes the physical focus of your discontent—the chubby body, the zits, the knobby knees, or whatever—improves with time, but an emotional "afterimage" still burns in your private perceptions of yourself. Your body image remembers.

Let me give you some examples of this phenomenon. In a 1990 study, I compared the current body images of three groups: average-weight women who had never been overweight, average-weight women who had been overweight, and women now overweight. I discovered something quite interesting—something I call *phantom fat*. In many respects, currently and formerly overweight groups had a comparable body image. Despite the fact they had eventually lost their excess weight, the previously overweight women hadn't lost the nagging feeling that their body is unacceptable. Somehow it still *felt* fat, even though it wasn't anymore. At one time, their body had been their enemy; it's hard to forget your enemies.

This phenomenon goes beyond matters of body weight. Evidence from my teen acne studies also confirmed that "adult survivors of adolescent acne" had a more nega-

---

Table 2.2. Appearance Teasing/Criticism during Childhood and Adolescence

This table summarizes the experiences of persons who reported having been recurrently teased or criticized about appearance in childhood or adolescence. It shows what physical attributes were the targets of such maltreatment and indicates who had teased them and who the "worst teasers" were.

What Was Teased?[a]		*Who Were the Teasers?*	*Ever*	*Worst*
Face and head	45%	Brother(s)[b]	79%	33%
Weight	36%	Peers in general	62%	28%
Upper torso	19%	Friends	47%	16%
Height	17%	A specific peer	31%	13%
Clothes/attire	13%	Mother	30%	11%
Hair	12%	Sister(s)[b]	36%	8%
Lower torso	11%	Father	24%	6%
General appearance	10%	Other relatives	23%	4%
Hands/feet	3%	Other adults	20%	1%
Mid torso	2%	Teachers	6%	0%
Muscle tone	1%			
Miscellaneous	6%			

Information adapted from Rieves and Cash (1996)

[a] Percentages sum to over 100% because respondents may have been teased or criticized about more than one physical characteristic.
[b] These percentages are based on only those respondents who had brothers or sisters.

tive body image years later, as compared to their peers who had had minimal or no acne. Physical scars faded, yet some emotional scars remained. Again, the body image remembers!

Bodies don't stand still. They change naturally over time. You are able to control some aspects of your appearance—for example, you can get a new hairstyle or choose what clothes to wear. But other changes are beyond your complete control. For better or worse, heredity and life events influence your looks. Take hereditary pattern hair loss for instance. My own scientific research indicates that some folks—men and women—feel helplessly unhappy about their progressively thinning locks, while others just take it in stride—"hair today gone tomorrow."

People also struggle to cope with their altered appearance following traumas, such as a mastectomy or severe facial burns. These unwanted changes certainly challenge one's body image. But the inspiring fact is that many of these people come to accept such drastic changes, incorporate them in a healthy body image, and move forward in their lives.

I want you to appreciate the important point I'm conveying here: *How your body appears on the outside does not have to determine how you feel on the inside.* Among people born with a disfiguring condition, some agonize that they don't look "normal," yet many others have little difficulty "looking different." Some folks whose appearance you envy are more unhappy with their looks than you would assume. Your appearance doesn't mandate how you must feel. If you're faced with unwelcome changes in your appearance, understand that it is possible to accept and accommodate the changes. This program will teach you how to accept your body—no matter what.

Different People, Different Paths

The arrows of adversity aimed at us by our culture, family, or peers do not affect everyone's body image identically. Some of us have been able to transcend ill effects of our culture's prescriptions, our peers' teasing, our pimples on prom night, and even disfiguring conditions. Who are these resilient people?

They are people with solid self-esteem—they believe in themselves. Self-esteem is a powerful ally in facing and defeating life's challenges. The child, adolescent, or adult who has a secure sense of self—as being competent, lovable, and invested in hope and in living—doesn't so easily fall prey to societal *shoulds* or assaults on his or her physical worth. Self-fulfillment doesn't rely on aspirations for a perfect appearance.

On the other hand, people whose nature and nurture have handed them a basic sense of inadequacy are all too eager to find fault with themselves. Their infection of inner insecurity easily spreads to their "outer" self.

Although poor self-esteem can pave the way for developing a negative body image, it's only a predisposition—it's *not* a predestination. Learning to improve body image is possible for everyone. If your self-esteem is as negative as your body image, working on improving your self-esteem can benefit your body image as well. In fact, a colleague and I recently tested this proposition by studying the body image changes among people who completed a self-help program for enhancing self-esteem, without ever focusing on body image per se. Guess what? Their body images got better! In the final chapter of this workbook, I'll say more about working on your self-esteem.

Understanding Your Body Image: From Then to Now

I'm about to shift from the historical influences to the current causes of your dissatisfaction with your body. But first, based on what you've learned so far in Step 2, I want you to get in touch with your own personal body image history. On the following page is a Self-Discovery Helpsheet, called "My Body and My Body Experiences from Then to Now." Write down your descriptions of your body and your body image for specific periods in your life. What events and experiences shaped your body image during each period?

The Pivotal Power of Now: The Eyes of the Beholder Belong to You

Past experiences and social conditioning can certainly program you to develop a negative body image. But history isn't everything. Even more important are the current causes— the here-and-now factors that affect your body image experiences in everyday life. These influences can propagate and reinforce your personal body image distress, or they can extricate you from your past programming. If past conditioning was omnipotent, a positive body image would be practically impossible. Yet, as you've learned, most people find ways to transcend the lessons of the past and accept their overall appearance, despite physical imperfections.

Inherently, human beings are "explainers." Moving beyond the past, however, requires that you relinquish explaining your complaining. Perhaps nothing is more upsetting than to be upset and not understand why. So, you search for the reasons you do what you do and feel what you feel. You explain your misery to yourself. You point the finger of blame at your dysfunctional family, tactless friends, lousy genes, hormonal fluctuations, bad luck, or astrological sign. Blaming your past or forces outside of your control may help you justify having a problem, but it doesn't help you solve it. Instead you conclude you are a helpless victim and you try to change nothing.

Change can only occur if you take responsibility for the choices you make today. After all, today is tomorrow's history, and that's history you can do something about. Taking responsibility for change starts with a simple realization: You feel what you think. Your *judgments* and *interpretations* of events, not the events themselves, govern your emotional reactions. Consider the following two examples:

Every Wednesday just before noon as I entered the elevator to go to my private-practice office on the third floor, I encountered a woman in the lobby. Each time, I held the elevator door open for her; each time, she nervously declined to get on. Finally, after several weeks, she informed me that she was phobic of riding elevators and that someone always came down and unlocked the stairwell door so that she could walk up to the third floor. I replied by mentioning that I was a psychologist and understood her fear. "You're a psychologist?" she exclaimed. "Well, in that case, I'll ride the elevator with you." And she did, with no visible signs of anxiety. Apparently, in her mind, she was safe with me.

Self-Discovery Helpsheet:
My Body and My Body Experiences from Then to Now

At each period of your life listed below, what did you look like? What were the key influences on how you felt about your looks? Be sure to mention important cultural and interpersonal influences.

Early Childhood (up to age 8)

My Body:

Influential Events and Experiences:

Later Childhood (age 8 to puberty)

My Body:

Influential Events and Experiences:

Early Adolescence (during the physical changes of puberty)

My Body:

Influential Events and Experiences:

Later Adolescence (up to age 21)

My Body:

Influential Events and Experiences:

Adulthood (age 21 to last year)

My Body:

Influential Events and Experiences:

The Past Year of My Life

My Body:

Influential Events and Experiences:

Now, imagine that an acquaintance promises to call you to invite you to his party. You're excited, but as the day of the party comes and goes without a call, you're disappointed. You wonder why he never called. When you think that he forgot, you feel really annoyed that he could be so thoughtless. Then you think that maybe he didn't forget; maybe he didn't want you to come. Why not? Maybe he thinks you're boring. Maybe he doesn't like you. Now you begin to feel hurt, to feel insecure. For a few days, when you think about it, you feel dejected. You wonder whether other people really don't like you. A week later you run into a friend who mentions that the party was canceled because the host had the flu. Now how do you feel?

You do feel what you think! Your body image emotions also are driven by your thoughts. The often subtle and unspoken messages you give yourself—your assumptions, perceptions, and interpretations—decisively dictate your feelings about your looks. Your patterns of relating and interacting with yourself produce a negative body image. You create your own conditioning. While the seeds of body image distress may have been planted in your cultural and interpersonal history, a negative body image exists and grows in "your presence of mind."

Right now I want you to do the following:

◎ Think about the aspect of your appearance you like least.

◎ Picture it clearly in your mind's eye.

◎ Now think these thoughts about this attribute: "It looks awful. Ugly. It's really ugly. I hate it. I really hate it. Everybody hates looking at it. People think I'm ugly. I'm really, really ugly."

◎ After saying these things to yourself, over and over, for one entire minute, check your feelings.

For many people, this little exercise gives rise to unhappy body image feelings. With only a few moments of immersing your mind in self-critical thinking, you may start to feel homely and hopeless. Did this exercise have a familiar ring to it? This pattern of thought may resemble what happened earlier in the "Reflections in My Mirror" exercise, when you recorded your thoughts and perceptions while gazing at your body in the mirror.

About ten years ago, psychologists at Dartmouth University conducted an eye-opening experiment. The investigators used theatrical makeup to create a facial scar on their research subjects before they were to interact face-to-face with a stranger. The stranger worked with the researchers and was trained to act in a standard neutral way with each subject. Unbeknownst to the subjects, however, the hideous scar had actually been removed before their conversation with the stranger. After the conversation, subjects were asked questions about how the stranger had related to them. Compared to a control group who hadn't been given a "scar," participants who believed they had the facial scar "witnessed" more discomfort in the stranger's behavior—like staring or avoiding looking at them. They reported experiencing the self-conscious and adverse effects of their facial "flaw," even though no flaw existed. Obviously, since there was no actual scar, these people created their own reality. Their experiences reflected what they believed about their looks, not the objective facts of the situation.

This fascinating experiment demonstrates a profoundly important truth: the most influential dictators of negative body image emotions are your own ways of judging and thinking about your looks. Many of your thought patterns may have become so automatic and habitual that you're not conscious of them as they occur. Particular events might trigger these thoughts, but once they begin, the emotional damage ensues, which breeds more self-critical ruminations and, in turn, even more despair.

To cope with your self-inflicted distress, you may avoid those people or situations that activate your negative thoughts and feelings. Or, you may carry out time-consuming rituals in which you try to fix or hide the "flaws" in your appearance. These self-protective efforts obviously don't fix your longstanding body image problems. They provide only temporary relief and actually perpetuate your problems.

Figure 2.1 is an informative diagram of the causes of a negative body image. It shows the historical factors that can predispose negative body image development. The diagram also shows the current influences—a vicious cycle of self-defeating thoughts, emotions, and behaviors. Overcoming a negative body image is accomplished by taking control and breaking the cycle. It's too late to alter the events of your past; the history is written! If you single-handedly changed society and halted its unhelpful messages, you would surely receive lots of thank-you notes. But we both know that's a bigger job than any one person can undertake. So what can you do? You can learn to change yourself—how you think, act, and feel—now and in the future.

The Body Image Workbook will help you unlearn the self-defeating patterns of a negative body image. In this program, you'll discover new, satisfying ways to experience your body and yourself.

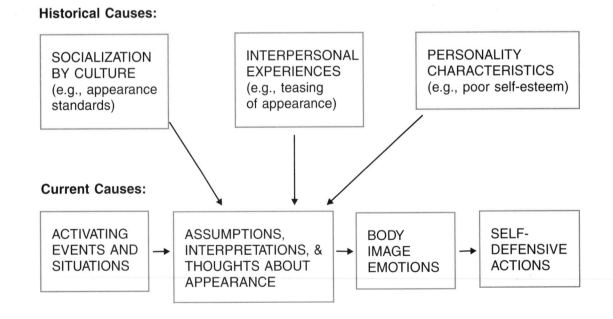

Figure 2.1. The Development of a Negative Body Image

In her book *Revolution from Within: A Book of Self-Esteem*, feminist Gloria Steinem reveals her own attempts to reconcile past, present, and future body image experiences (1992, 248):

> Looking in the mirror, I see the lines between nose and mouth that now remain, even without a smile, and I am reminded of a chipmunk storing nuts for the winter. This is the updated version of my plump-faced child. When I ask what they have to say for themselves, nothing comes back. They know I don't like them, so until I stop with the chipmunk imagery and learn to value them as the result of many smiles, they're not communicating. I'll have to work on this—and many other adjustments of aging yet to come.

Understanding Your Body Image in Everyday Life

In Step 1, you summarized your self-discoveries in your Personal Body Image Profile. It highlights how you generally think, feel, act, and so forth. However, each occurrence, or "episode," of body image distress has its own unique elements—specific thoughts, emotions, and behaviors—that unfold in reaction to particular situations and events. Changing your body image requires that you examine and understand the specifics of each distressing episode as it takes place. This is possible by keeping a special journal or diary that will work almost like a videotape recording the moment-to-moment expression of your body image. I'm going to teach you how to successfully monitor your experiences and capture them in your Body Image Diary.

The Mastery of Self-Monitoring

A basic tenet of most therapies is that people can solve their personal problems if they can learn to examine their own minds and actions with objectivity and accuracy. If you no longer want to be controlled by negative emotions, you must be able to step back from your subjective experience and ask the following questions:

- ◎ What am I feeling?

- ◎ What just happened to cause me to feel this way?

- ◎ What am I saying to myself about this situation?

- ◎ How am I reacting behaviorally to this experience?

Asking and answering these questions reflects a powerful process called *self-monitoring*. Self-monitoring is analogous to eavesdropping on yourself. You become consciously attuned to your own ongoing experience. You observe precisely what's going on. When body image feelings occur, you identify what emotions you're having. You pinpoint what's happened in the situation that has triggered these emotions. You listen objectively to the thoughts and perceptions that are running through your mind. You also monitor how you behave in reaction to these thoughts and emotions.

Self-monitoring isn't as easy as it may sound. It is a skill, and skills can only develop through practice. Most people with a negative body image focus only on being upset and on blaming their appearance for their unhappiness. They just feel what they feel and do what they do. They reflexively react and never step back to calmly dissect their experience.

Because your negative body image emotions may interfere with learning to self-monitor, start off by monitoring experiences from your recent past. Soon you'll be able to use your new ability in the midst of upsetting body image episodes.

Plenty of people respond to the notion of self-monitoring by claiming they already do it and it doesn't help. They say, "I'm always analyzing my looks. I'm always focusing on how crummy I feel about my body." Being intensely aware of your appearance or deeply immersed in emotion is *not* self-monitoring—it's actually part of the problem you need to change. And to change, you must develop a more objective view of your experiences. If you've loathed your looks for many years, it's difficult to separate the hatred from whatever it is that you hate. Besides, if you've persuaded yourself that your body is the problem, then your body image miseries will seem justified. "My awful looks make me feel awful," you argue. In time, you'll see that you're wrong, so bear with me. You can become open, observant, and objective enough to monitor reality and change your body image experiences.

Some of my clients initially insist that they don't have individual episodes of body image distress. All they see is that "life is one big, nonstop episode." Let me explain what I mean by an episode. While you may "always" dislike your nose, your weight, or some other attribute, you aren't constantly thinking about it, nor are you continually upset about it. Like a sleeping dragon, your discontent is sometimes dormant, and other times it breathes fire. Something happens to rouse your dissatisfaction. Then, as you dwell on it, your emotions are aroused and become especially negative and intense. These particularly troublesome times are what I mean by body image episodes.

Learning Your Body Image ABCs

You probably have some episodes that repeat themselves like a broken record. Take some time now to recollect several recent episodes of body image distress, ones that you expect to recur. You will identify the following three elements of each episode and record them in your Body Image Diary. These three elements make up the *ABC Sequence*, as depicted in the diagram on the next page.

* *A* stands for the *Activators*. What events activated or triggered your negative feelings about your looks? In your diary, you'll write down a brief description of the particular situation and occurrences that immediately preceded your distress. Be specific.

* *B* stands for your *Beliefs*—your perceptions and interpretations of the activating event. What thoughts were running through your mind at the time? Try to replay the tape—the mental conversation you were having with yourself. How were you viewing the situation? What were you saying to yourself about the events? Recalling your thoughts out of their actual context can be difficult. Re-

mind yourself by filling in the blank: "I was thinking _____," or "I was probably thinking _____."

 ✻ C stands for the *Consequences* of your thoughts and perceptions. How did you react emotionally? How did you react behaviorally?

In your diary, you will describe the Consequences in terms of the *TIDE* of the episode. I use TIDE as an acronym that will help you analyze the four essential aspects of consequences that occur.

 ✻ T stands for the *Types* of emotions you felt in the situation. Anxiety? Anger? Depression? Shame? Disgust? Envy? Embarrassment? Identify the feeling or feelings that you had.

 ✻ I stands for the *Intensity* of your emotions. Rate their strength at their peak, from 0 for "not at all intense" to 10 for "extremely intense."

 ✻ D stands for the episode's *Duration*. How long did your distress last? About how many minutes or hours did it take before you felt noticeably better?

 ✻ Finally, the E stands for the *Effects* of the episode on your behavior. Your actions at this point are often reflexive efforts to cope with or defend yourself against your unwanted emotions. Did you try to get out of the situation? Did you become sullen and withdraw? Did you attempt to fix or conceal the part of your body that you were bothered about? Did you take your feelings out on others? Did you take them out on yourself?

The more types of emotions you feel with greater intensity for a longer duration and with more behavioral effects, the more powerful the episode—like being caught up in a turbulent TIDE.

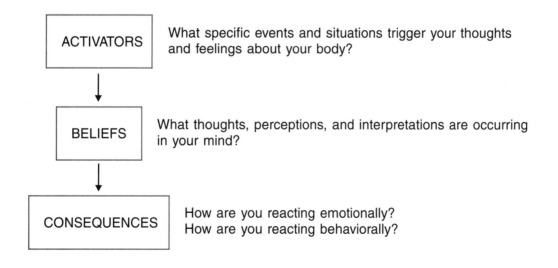

Figure 2.2. The ABC Sequence of Your Body Image Experiences

How to Keep Your Body Image Diary

A personal Body Image Diary is an essential tool for learning to like your looks. The Helpsheet on page 57 shows the format for monitoring, dissecting, and recording the ABC Sequences of your negative body image episodes. Just write out the format of the diary in a personal notebook. (This is more convenient than photocopying the Helpsheet and having lots of unbound sheets of paper to keep up with.)

Before beginning your Body Image Diary, here are three things to do:

◎ First, to see how to complete the diary for an episode, examine the three sample diary entries on pages 58 to 60.

◎ Then, go back to Step 1 and review your answers to the Situational Distress Test and the Body Image Thoughts Test. This will remind you of the Activators and the Beliefs that produce your own troublesome Consequences.

◎ Next, complete your Body Image Diary for as many different recent episodes of distress as possible. To become more skilled in identifying your body image ABCs, over the next several days, analyze and enter ten or more recent episodes. For each, mentally recreate the experience. Close your eyes and picture the situation. Replay your "tape" of the episode—the triggering events, your thoughts, your emotions, and your actions.

After analyzing the ABC Sequence and Emotional TIDE of past episodes, you'll be ready for current self-monitoring. This is what you'll do:

◎ For four or five days, monitor any episode as it occurs. Don't try to change the episode; just mentally monitor its ABCs as they unfold.

◎ Afterward, as soon as possible, make a diary entry.

◎ Monitoring and recording these experiences may lead you to recognize items to add to your Needs for Change Helpsheet from Step 1. Having specific goals for change and then fine-tuning them are important ingredients of success.

Final Words of Encouragement

It is of paramount importance that you self-monitor and keep your diary *throughout the entire program*. Any thoughts you may have about bypassing the diary keeping are bad ideas! Later, you'll rely on valuable self-discoveries from your diary to promote positive changes in your body image. If you were my client, we would review your diary in every session. We'd learn from it each time. I encourage you to start on your diary today.

Now that you're armed with a better understanding of the ways that you currently create your own body image despair, change is just around the corner. In the next important phase of your program, I'll be teaching you how to take control of your negative feelings about your looks. After you've worked on your diary for about a week, I'll meet you in Step 3.

Helpsheet for Change:
The Body Image Diary for _____

Date: _____

ABC Sequence

ACTIVATORS (Triggering events and situations):

_____

_____

_____

_____

BELIEFS (Thoughts and interpretations of the situation):

_____

_____

_____

_____

CONSEQUENCES (Emotional **TIDE**):

Types of emotions: _____

_____

Intensity of emotions (0 to 10): _____

Duration of the episode: _____

Effects of the episode on your behavior: _____

_____

_____

_____

Helpsheet for Change:
The Body Image Diary for <u>Shiana</u>

Date: <u>3-14</u>

ABC Sequence

ACTIVATORS (Triggering events and situations):

<u>Watching the Miss America Beauty Pageant on TV</u>

BELIEFS (Thoughts and interpretations of the situation):

<u>I was thinking how pretty all the contestants are and how I wish I could be</u>

<u>that beautiful. I hate being short and chunky.</u>

CONSEQUENCES (Emotional **TIDE**):

Types of emotions: <u>Envious of them. Sad and disgusted with myself.</u>

Intensity of emotions (0 to 10): <u>5</u>

Duration of the episode: <u>about 3 hours</u>

Effects of the episode on your behavior: <u>Looked at my body in the mirror with</u>

<u>disgust. Went to bed to try to stop thinking about it.</u>

Helpsheet for Change:
The Body Image Diary for <u>Matt</u>

Date: <u>8-29</u>

ABC Sequence

ACTIVATORS (Triggering events and situations):

<u>Making out with Bev, my girlfriend,</u>

BELIEFS (Thoughts and interpretations of the situation):

<u>Thinking how unmuscular my body is and wondering if she's thinking I'm bony</u>

<u>and unappealing.</u>

<u>Preoccupied with what she thinks when she touches me.</u>

CONSEQUENCES (Emotional **TIDE**):

Types of emotions: <u>Anxiety and self-consciousness.</u>

<u>Shame.</u>

Intensity of emotions (0 to 10): <u>8</u>

Duration of the episode: <u>30 minutes</u>

Effects of the episode on your behavior: <u>Couldn't get into sex because of being</u>

<u>self-conscious, so I made up an excuse about being hungry. Stopped making</u>

<u>out and left the room.</u>

Helpsheet for Change:
The Body Image Diary for *Fran*

Date: __10-10__

ABC Sequence

ACTIVATORS (Triggering events and situations):

Trying on tops at Dillard's dept. store.

BELIEFS (Thoughts and interpretations of the situation):

I think nothing looks good on me. I think my little breasts and big hips make it impossible to find peace with myself. I start thinking about getting breast implants.

CONSEQUENCES (Emotional **TIDE**):

Types of emotions: Frustration; disgust

Intensity of emotions (0 to 10): 9

Duration of the episode: an hour

Effects of the episode on your behavior: Left the store without buying a top. Headed to Ben and Jerry's to soothe my soul with ice cream.

Step 2
Your Path for Progress

★ With the "Reflections in My Mirror" exercise, you've discovered what you see and how you think and feel when you look at your body in the mirror.

★ You've learned how a negative body image can impair various aspects of life. You've identified the unwanted effects of your own body image.

★ You've acquired knowledge from the psychology of physical appearance to understand the forces behind the development of a negative body image. You can take solace in knowing that you are not alone in your discontent and your desire to change.

★ Aided by the Helpsheet "My Body and My Body Experiences from Then to Now," you're beginning to understand how cultural conditioning and your past social and physical experiences have left their mark, as demanding and critical "voices from your past."

★ You are recognizing the power of the present in creating your negative body image. Using your Body Image Diary to monitor the ABC Sequence—Activators, Beliefs, and Consequences (including the emotional TIDE)—you can see your body image experiences as they unfold. Having spent a few days to record your most common, distressing episodes from the recent past, you graduate to monitoring your ongoing episodes. You enter them in your diary.

★ As other revelations turn up in your Body Image Diary, you are adding to your Needs for Change Helpsheet, setting and fine-tuning your goals for a better body image.

Step 3: Destroying Distress

Creating Comfortable Reflections

Whenever Joyce thinks about her figure she gets a sinking, hopeless feeling deep down inside. She is repulsed by the size of her thighs and hips. When her fiancé, Jeff, catches a glimpse of her as she emerges naked from the shower, Joyce at first feels intensely self-conscious. Then, as she quickly cloaks her body in a towel, she is filled with embarrassment and Joyce makes up some excuse to banish him from the bathroom. Her embarrassment gives way to anger. She is irritated that he saw her body so closely, and angry with her body for the betrayal. She retreats to the guest bedroom to get dressed without Jeff being able to see her. Joyce becomes terribly frustrated as she tries to find the "right outfit" to conceal the curves of her lower torso. This emotional roller coaster is one that Joyce rides daily, without amusement.

David has always been a thin guy throughout his childhood, his teen years, and now at the age of thirty-four. You'd think he would accept his slender body by now, but he doesn't. In reality, he's far from a "ninety-eight-pound weakling." Yet David worries that other people see him as "skinny," "bony," or "scrawny." Sometimes when he looks at his body in the mirror, he feels disgust. He works out regularly at the gym but gets discouraged when he sees other guys there with bulging biceps. At his apartment complex, David must confront his ever-familiar anxiety in order to go to the swimming pool. Once there, the feeling of shame about his body overshadows any fun he might have.

Discovering Your Body Image Emotions

Obviously, a negative body image causes emotional distress. Different emotions, however, may dominate in different people. When you think about your looks, how often do you feel the negative emotions listed on the following Self-Discovery Helpsheet? Use the 0 to 4 rating scale to convey how often you feel each specific emotion in your day-to-day life because of some aspect of your appearance.

Self-Discovery Helpsheet: My Body Image Emotions

0	1	2	3	4
Never or Rarely	*Sometimes*	*Moderately Often*	*Often*	*Very Often*

_____ agitated   _____ gloomy

_____ angry   _____ happy

_____ annoyed   _____ hopeless

_____ anxious   _____ impatient

_____ ashamed   _____ irritated

_____ contented   _____ joyful

_____ dejected   _____ nervous

_____ disappointed   _____ proud

_____ discontented   _____ sad

_____ discouraged   _____ satisfied

_____ disgusted   _____ self-conscious

_____ elated   _____ sullen

_____ embarrassed   _____ tense

_____ forlorn   _____ unhappy

_____ frustrated   _____ worried

Having inventoried your body image emotions, now go back and circle any emotions that you rated as a 1 or 2. Double circle those you rated as a 3 or 4. How many negative emotions were in each of these two categories? How many positive emotions did you circle? Take a few minutes to really think about your answers. What particular emotions typify your feelings about your body?

The Importance of Taking Control

Behavioral scientists have amassed plenty of studies confirming that a sense of control is crucial to psychological well-being. When you think you aren't in control over important events events at school or at work or in relationships guess what happens? You become stressed and upset. Anxiety occurs if you are uncertain of your ability to manage these hassles. Depression strikes if you are certain that you have no control. Your anger begins to boil if people or events unfairly impede your efforts to take control and reach a goal.

You don't have to be a victim of your negative body image emotions. Step 3 will help you to start taking emotional control and to realize that body image distress doesn't have to be inevitable. This type of control is quite different from all the other things you probably do to feel less bothered by your body image—things like hiding your flaws, primping, preening, and avoiding whatever makes you self-conscious. You're probably better at managing your physical appearance than you are at managing your body image emotions.

As you discovered in the last chapter, you have a history that has most likely conditioned you to have negative feelings about the image of your body, whether in the reflections of your mirror or the reflections in your mind. You need to develop new skills with which you can undo your previous conditioning and become more comfortable with your body—weight, warts, and all!

If you think back to times when you learned a new skill—whether it was learning to make super Caesar salad, mastering a new dance, or figuring out how to use a computer—the challenge was best accomplished if broken down into easy-to-do steps and practiced. That's what you're going to do to develop the skills in this workbook.

Body-and-Mind Relaxation

The first step in taking command of your body image discomfort is *Body-and-Mind Relaxation*. An indisputable fact is that relaxation is the physiological and psychological opposite of distress. You can't be uptight or upset *and* be "cool, calm, and collected" at the same time. Body-and-Mind Relaxation will enable you to become more comfortable with your looks and bring to a halt any "runaway train" of negative body image thoughts and emotions. Body-and-Mind Relaxation consists of the following four simple components:

- ✽ *Muscle relaxation.* When you're troubled or distressed, your brain sends messages that signal your muscles to contract. Because these messages get stored, your muscular tension can linger and you stay vulnerable to emotional irritation—about your body image or even something unrelated. So managing physical tension is crucial for emotional control.

- ✽ *Diaphragmatic breathing.* When you're under stress, your breathing becomes irregular and produces physical sensations that further undermine your feelings of control. With deep, rhythmic diaphragmatic breathing, however, you can re-establish control and amplify relaxation.

❋ *Mental imagery*. When fretting about your appearance, you probably replay frustrating or frightful situations in your mind. These images evoke adverse emotions. Being able to turn off upsetting images and to turn on pleasant ones cultivates inner serenity.

❋ *Self-instructions*. Words are as influential in arousing emotions as mental pictures are. How do words like "unattractive," "homely," "ugly," "fat," or "gross" make you feel? How about the words "relaxed," "peaceful," "content," "confident"? People who meditate use special words, or "mantras," to enhance experiences of focused contentment. Body-and-Mind Relaxation also involves using soothing self-instructions to control mental mood states.

The Right Time and Place

Sounds great, right? To learn these Body-and-Mind Relaxation skills, follow these simple suggestions:

◎ Set aside a thirty-minute tranquil period in your day. Pick a time when you're alert, not when you're tired or tense.

◎ For this brief time, you'll want to be somewhere that is quiet and free of distractions. Tell family members or friends that you do not wish to be interrupted. Unplug the phone.

◎ You should have a comfortable chair or recliner. Your bed is okay, but prop pillows behind you so that you can comfortably sit up with your legs outstretched.

◎ Dress comfortably.

People with busy lives (that's pretty much everyone) can't fathom the idea of taking time to "do nothing." Frankly, letting your body image discontent control your life is worse than doing nothing. But learning and practicing Body-and-Mind Relaxation is really doing something. Acquiring emotional control is a productive use of your time and energy. It will be an experience that you deserve and will look forward to. And there's another reason to learn this skill: its ultimate benefits will extend beyond body image into all facets of your emotional life.

Your Script to Relax and Take Control

When teaching my clients Body-and-Mind Relaxation, I give them an audiotape that I made in a recording studio. I'm giving you the transcript of this tape. Because trying to read the script and relax at the same time doesn't work very well, you too will eventually want a Body-and Mind-Relaxation tape. I'll teach you how to make your own tape in the next section. At this point, I want you to just read through the following script to get a feeling for its flow. Check out each of its four components—the tension-relieving muscle relaxation, the tranquilizing deep breathing, the calming mental imagery, and the soothing self-instructions.

Settle into the chair. . . . Get really comfortable. . . . Gently close your eyes. . . . Take five slow, deep breaths. Breathe evenly from your diaphragm [the lowest part of your chest at your abdomen]. *Breathe so that your stomach slowly rises and falls. . . . Notice the soothing flow of air in and out of your lungs. . . .* [Continue this deep, regular breathing throughout the exercise.]

To begin, make a tight fist with both of your hands. [If your nails are long, just turn your fingers under, put them on the outside of your palm, and press.] *Pay close attention to the tightness in those muscles of your hands. Notice the tension. Study it. . . . Now, let go of the tension and just relax those muscles. Notice the tension flowing out. . . . Notice the difference between the relaxation that you feel now in those muscles and the tension that you felt only a moment ago. . . .*

Okay, do this again. Make sure when you tense your muscles that you tense only those muscles and not other muscles in your body. You're making a tight fist now with both hands. Study the tension in those muscles. . . . Now let go and relax. Notice the sensations of relaxation. . . . Let your hands be completely loose and limp. . . .

Next, tense your biceps and only your biceps. As if you're showing off your muscles, bring your arms up and flex your biceps. Study the tension that you feel in each of your upper arms . . . your left arm . . . your right arm. . . . Notice these sensations. Notice the difference as you relax. Just let go of the tension . . . let your arms drop. . . . Notice the pleasant difference. . . .

Now, tense your triceps [the muscles just under your biceps]. *Turn your arms so that your palms are facing up and extend your arms in front of you and tense them. Notice the tension there in your triceps—a tight, uncomfortable feeling. Study this tension . . . concentrate on it. . . . Now, let go and relax these muscles, noticing the difference as the tension leaves and the relaxation and comfort take its place. . . . Focus on this pleasant difference between the earlier tension and the current relaxation. . . .*

The next muscles are in your shoulders and the upper part of your back. Simply extend your arms in front of you and pull your shoulders forward, stretching forward. Notice the tension in your shoulders and the upper part of your back. Study the sensations. . . . Now be very aware of the difference as you let go completely and relax these muscles. . . . Just settle back, noticing the heavier, warmer feeling in these muscles. . . .

Now push your shoulders back. Do this by leaning forward slightly and moving your arms back so as to push your chest out. Notice the tension in your shoulders. . . . Now feel the difference as you relax those muscles. . . . Let go completely and relax. . . .

The next series of muscles are in the neck. [These muscles are a bit easier to strain than most, so I want you to tense them only enough to feel the muscles tighten but not hard enough to hurt yourself.] *First, simply push your head down so that your chin almost touches your chest. Notice the unpleasant tightness in your neck. Study this sensation. . . . Now, slowly lift your head and completely let go of the tension. Notice the relaxation flowing into those muscles. . . . Be aware of the contrast between the tension that you felt a moment ago and the pleasant relaxation you feel right now. . . .*

Sit forward slightly and lean your head back. Push your head back with your face upward, noticing the tension underneath your chin and in your neck. Focus on the sensations there. . . . Now face forward again and relax those muscles. Notice any sensations that you associate with relaxation. . . . Just let the relaxation soothe you. . . .

Tilt your head to the left, until you feel a tightness in the muscles on the right side of your neck. . . . Notice how it feels as you bring your head back up, as you let go of that tension and just relax. . . . Now tilt your head to the right. Focus on the tightness in the muscles on the left side of your neck. . . . Now bring your head back up, release the tension, and relax. . . . Just enjoy the sensations. . . .

Next, we'll move to the muscles of your face. Let's begin with the muscles around your mouth. Open your mouth as wide as you can as if you were yawning. Feel the tension around your mouth and in your jaw. . . . Now, let go and enjoy. . . . Simply enjoy your sensations of relaxation. . . .

And now push your lips together as hard as you can. Again, notice the uncomfortable tightness in the muscles around your mouth. . . . Okay, let go totally and relax these muscles. . . . Just feel the relaxation there. . . .

Press your tongue against the roof of your mouth, noticing the tight sensations in your mouth, your tongue, your jaw . . . and now, completely relax. . . . Just let that tension flow out and be gone. . . .

Now, scrunch up your nose so that all the muscles around your nose become tense. Notice the tight, tense sensations in those muscles. . . . Feel the pleasant difference as you relax those muscles. . . . Notice the sensations of relaxation. . . .

Close your eyes tightly to tense the muscles there. Concentrate on the tension. . . . Feel the difference as you relax the muscles around your eyes. . . . Just release all of the tension. . . .

Next, tense the muscles of your forehead by frowning. Notice the tightness there. . . . And now relax. . . . Just enjoy the sensations of warmth beginning to flow through your face. . . .

You are continuing to breathe from your diaphragm. Your slow, even breathing makes your stomach go up . . . and down . . . up . . . and down. . . . Simply think the word "peaceful" as you inhale. Think the word "calm" as you exhale. Ready now, "peaceful" . . . and "calm" . . . "peaceful" . . . and "calm" . . . "peaceful" . . . "calm." . . . "peaceful" . . . "calm." . . . As you breathe smoothly and deeply, you become more and more relaxed. . . .

The next muscles to tense are the muscles in your stomach. Without changing your slow, even pattern of breathing, just pull your stomach in and notice the uncomfortable tightness of these muscles. . . . Now, as you exhale, let go of that tension and relax. . . .

As you continue breathing smoothly and deeply, tense your stomach muscles again—this time by pushing your stomach out. Really notice the tension there. . . .

Now, while exhaling, totally relax those muscles. . . . Notice the sensations of warmth, heaviness, and relaxation throughout your midsection. . . .

Next, as you inhale, tighten the muscles in your buttocks. Study the tension. . . . And while exhaling, let go and relax these muscles. . . . Simply enjoy any sensations of relaxation in these muscles. . . .

Now, focus your attention on your legs. Extend your legs in front of you and raise them just slightly, tensing the muscles of your thighs. Feel the uncomfortable strain in your thighs. . . . Notice the difference as you exhale and let go of that tension. Lower your legs and completely relax. . . . Feel the warm flow of relaxation moving through your thighs. . . .

Now, flex your toes back toward your head so that the muscles around your ankles and your calves become tense. Just tip your feet back slightly. Notice the hard tightness in your calves. . . . And while exhaling, release that tension and simply relax. . . . Now point your toes away from you, and again sense the tension in your feet and your lower legs. . . . And while exhaling, simply let go and relax. . . . Just let all the tension flow out of your legs. . . .

Now, deepen the relaxation that you feel throughout your entire body by taking three or four smooth breaths from the diaphragm. . . . Just breathe evenly . . . comfortably. . . . Feel the relaxation flow through your body from your hands . . . up through your arms . . . to your shoulders . . . up through your head and neck . . . and down your chest . . . through your midsection . . . all the way down your legs . . . into your feet. Each complete inhalation and exhalation of air increases the depth of relaxation. . . .

As you breathe smoothly, allow yourself to become aware of any slight tension that you feel in any muscle in your body. . . . Simply tense that muscle and release the tension as you've done before.

[Pause for thirty seconds]

Let yourself enjoy the wonderful inner sensations of relaxation as they flow through your body. In your enjoyment, you are becoming more and more relaxed . . . sinking into the chair . . . feeling peaceful and calm, contented, very pleasant feelings. . . . Use your breathing to enhance your relaxation even more, sinking more comfortably and deeply into relaxation. Each time you exhale, feel more tension flowing out of your body and more calm, peaceful feelings flowing into your body.

[Pause for thirty seconds]

And now, allow your imagination to paint a pleasurable picture in your mind to help you feel even more calm and content and relaxed. Simply place yourself, in your mind, in a springtime scene, on the beach or in the mountains or in the countryside—whichever pleases you most.

Begin to paint your mental picture vividly and experience your pleasant scene as if you are really there. . . . You hear the melody of birds, singing so sweetly. . . . You see the colors of nature around you. . . . You feel the soothing, gentle warmth of the sun. . . . Against your skin you feel a soft breeze that caresses your body. . . .

[Pause for thirty seconds]

Simply enjoy your pleasant scene. . . . You haven't a worry in the world, absolutely nothing to do but simply relax . . . feeling so relaxed and peaceful. . . . You are giving way totally to the experience.

[Pause for thirty seconds]

Now, in your mind's eye, picture a small circle of your favorite color located in the center of your body. . . . This circle contains feelings of well-being, of contentment, of confidence, of being in control. . . . Using your deep, slow breathing, make the circle grow, ever so gradually. . . . The expanding circle fills you more and more. . . . It fills you more and more with your very real experience of contentment and confidence and control. . . . As you inhale, let the circle expand . . . and as you exhale let the experience of contentment and confidence and control spread and radiate throughout your body. . . . Allow the feeling to grow, to spread, to fill you up completely . . . more and more as you breathe in . . . and out. . . . So peaceful and calm . . . very content, very confident, very much in control.

[Pause for sixty seconds]

Gradually, counting backward from ten to one, feel yourself—refreshed and alert—slowly reactivating your body . . . ten, nine, eight . . . moving your hands a little bit whenever you're ready . . . seven, six, five . . . moving your feet . . . four, three . . . and moving your legs . . . and two, one . . . slowly moving your head. . . . And now, whenever you're ready, open your eyes.

[Script from *What Do You See When You Look in the Mirror?* (Cash 1995) and based on *Body Image Therapy* (Cash 1991)]

How to Record Your Own Body-and-Mind Relaxation Tape

A lot of people become more relaxed just by reading over the script. Imagine how terrific it will be having an audiotape that guides you through the steps. A tape with your own voice can be especially helpful. After all, once you've eventually mastered Body-and-Mind Relaxation, you will be the one guiding yourself in your own mind. If dissatisfaction with your voice is one of your sore spots, it's okay to ask a friend or loved one to record the tape for you. Here's what you do:

◎ Use a portable cassette recorder and a ninety-minute tape. You'll need about thirty to thirty-five minutes of one side.

◎ Find a very quiet place to make your recording, so that it contains only the voice speaking the words. Ultimately, sneezes and sniffles, your phone ringing, a neighbor's dog barking, or your toilet flushing won't be particularly relaxing to hear!

◎ Before turning the recorder on, read through the script at least once to get the hang of it. Read it softly, in an even, slightly monotonous tone of voice.

◎ Notice the special punctuation in the script. *Italicized words* are those ones you read aloud. Words enclosed in brackets [like this] are instructions and should not be read aloud on your tape. Ellipses (*that look like this . . . or this. . . .*) tell you to insert a five-second pause. Just let the tape continue while you silently count out five seconds. Some instructions in the script call for longer pauses.

◎ Ideally, you should record the script in one continuous reading, because stopping or pausing and then restarting the recorder may create distracting clicks on your tape. Feel free to play some soft background music or natural sounds, like rainfall or sea sounds. Use mellow classical or New Age instrumental music. Jimi Hendrix, Beastie Boys, Kiss, or John Philip Sousa are not exactly the mood setters you'll want.

◎ Making your own tape is both easy and enjoyable. Nevertheless, if you'd rather use one that's professionally produced, my Body-and-Mind Relaxation tape can be ordered from Guilford Publications for $12.95. Phone them at 1-800-365-7006 and request item #9652.

◎ Here's a suggestion to try before you use a recorded script: If you are completing this program with someone else, your "Body Image Buddy," take turns relaxing each other. Even a spouse or friend who isn't carrying out the body image program might love learning Body-and-Mind Relaxation. Just ask!

How to Learn Body-and-Mind Relaxation

Once a day, for the next week, give yourself the full Body-and-Mind Relaxation experience. Follow this regimen:

◎ For the first four days, use your tape to guide your experience.

◎ On the fifth and sixth days, guide yourself through the experience without the tape. Following is an outline of the steps of Body-and-Mind Relaxation for your handy reference.

◎ On the seventh day, omit the muscle-tensing procedures. Just take a few initial minutes to tell your body to let go of muscle tension, before moving on to your slow breathing, pleasant imagery, and mental phrases like, "peaceful and calm," "pleasant and content," and "relaxed and comfortable."

Your Body-and-Mind Relaxation Helpsheet

You'll be pleasantly surprised how repeated practice will deepen your relaxation and your experiences of emotional control. Use the Body-and-Mind Relaxation Helpsheet on page 73 for tracking these experiences and monitoring your progress. The Helpsheet has spaces for one week of daily practice. But because you'll continue relaxation over the course of the program, you may want to photocopy the Helpsheet or copy its format into

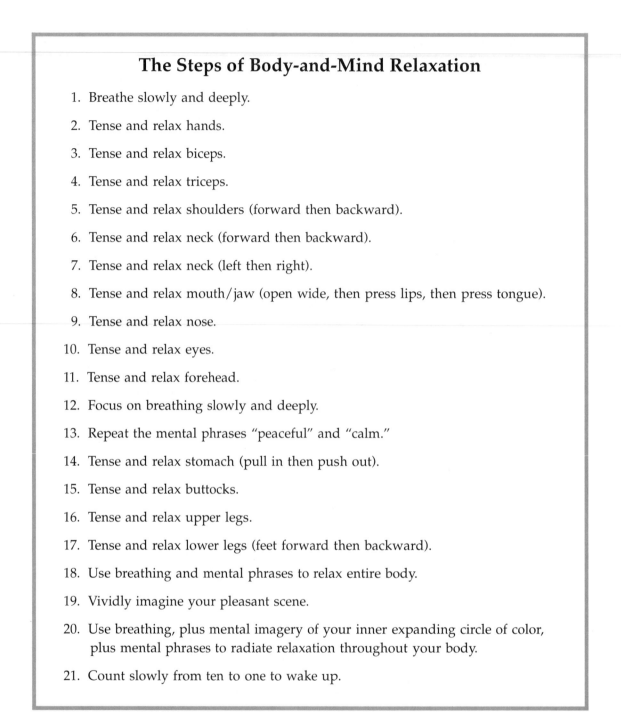

The Steps of Body-and-Mind Relaxation

1. Breathe slowly and deeply.

2. Tense and relax hands.

3. Tense and relax biceps.

4. Tense and relax triceps.

5. Tense and relax shoulders (forward then backward).

6. Tense and relax neck (forward then backward).

7. Tense and relax neck (left then right).

8. Tense and relax mouth/jaw (open wide, then press lips, then press tongue).

9. Tense and relax nose.

10. Tense and relax eyes.

11. Tense and relax forehead.

12. Focus on breathing slowly and deeply.

13. Repeat the mental phrases "peaceful" and "calm."

14. Tense and relax stomach (pull in then push out).

15. Tense and relax buttocks.

16. Tense and relax upper legs.

17. Tense and relax lower legs (feet forward then backward).

18. Use breathing and mental phrases to relax entire body.

19. Vividly imagine your pleasant scene.

20. Use breathing, plus mental imagery of your inner expanding circle of color, plus mental phrases to radiate relaxation throughout your body.

21. Count slowly from ten to one to wake up.

the notebook that serves as your Body Image Diary. Before and after each session, ask yourself these two basic questions:

◎ *How physically relaxed do I feel?* Rate your physical relaxation anywhere from 0, for extremely tense and uptight, to 10, for totally relaxed.

◎ *How contented, confident, and in control do I feel?* Similarly, rate your degree of mental relaxation from 0 to 10.

In addition, jot down noteworthy insights—for instance, that certain tension-prone muscles require repeating the exercise to relax them more fully. Or you may realize that particular mental imagery really facilitates your sense of control.

After a week of practice, you should have sufficient skill to apply Body-and-Mind Relaxation in a special way, that is, to control negative body image emotions. Until then, just relax!

Mellowing Out the Misery of Your Body Image

Now, after a week of practice, you should be ready to apply Body-and-Mind Relaxation directly to your body image problems. The procedure that you'll use to achieve this is called *Systematic Desensitization*. This is a scientifically proven therapy that can help peo-

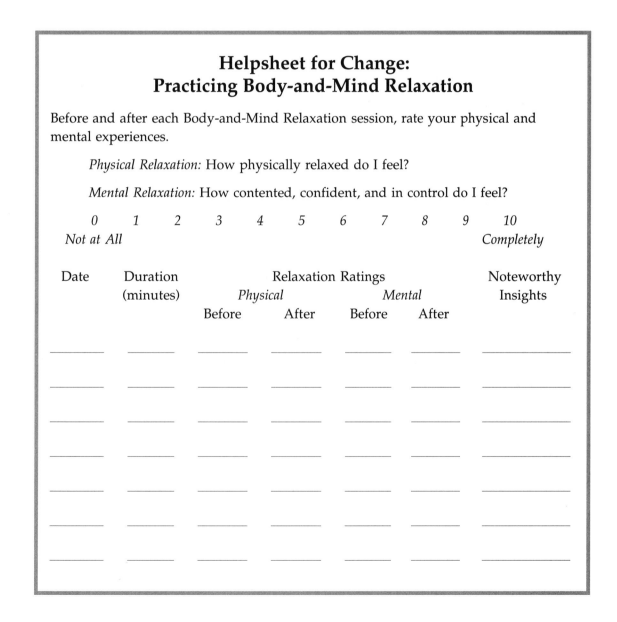

Helpsheet for Change: Practicing Body-and-Mind Relaxation

Before and after each Body-and-Mind Relaxation session, rate your physical and mental experiences.

Physical Relaxation: How physically relaxed do I feel?

Mental Relaxation: How contented, confident, and in control do I feel?

0	*1*	*2*	*3*	*4*	*5*	*6*	*7*	*8*	*9*	*10*
Not at All										*Completely*

Date	Duration (minutes)	Relaxation Ratings				Noteworthy Insights
		Physical		*Mental*		
		Before	After	Before	After	
___	___	___	___	___	___	___
___	___	___	___	___	___	___
___	___	___	___	___	___	___
___	___	___	___	___	___	___
___	___	___	___	___	___	___
___	___	___	___	___	___	___
___	___	___	___	___	___	___

ple become less distressed by things that agitate them. It helps them feel in control of their lives. Originally the technique was developed as a treatment for anxieties and phobias, but subsequently it has been used to aid people in taking control of a variety of distressing difficulties.

As a therapist for twenty-five years, I've witnessed many clients benefit greatly from systematic desensitization. I recall one woman whom desensitization enabled to surmount a longstanding fear of air travel. For others, it was valuable in overcoming their anxiety about taking tests, giving speeches, or asking people out on dates.

My earliest use of desensitization for a body image problem was nearly two decades ago. It helped a young man whose port-wine birthmark on the side of his neck made him terribly self-conscious. He usually wore turtleneck shirts, or would try to position himself to keep the birthmark away from the view of other people. Desensitization greatly enhanced his confidence and comfort in social situations.

Destroying Distress with Desensitization

Desensitization involves facing your discomfort, so it's a good place to start in taking control over how you feel about your appearance. It's an exercise by which you say to yourself, "I want to begin to be more comfortable with my body, even though there are aspects of my looks that I don't like."

Systematic desensitization essentially reprograms your reactions to disturbing situations. As a result of past experiences, you are conditioned to feel anxiety, disgust, shame, or other negative emotions when focusing on certain aspects of your appearance. This is called *classical conditioning*; it's been going on for so long that your reactions have become automatic. All you have to do is see or think about those disliked physical characteristics (the ones you pinpointed in Step 1) and you feel lousy.

Desensitization enables you to take conscious control over your past conditioning and weaken the subliminal emotional reactions. Through *counter-conditioning*, you replace the troublesome conditioning with a new and favorable experience. You train yourself to control your reactions, which clears the path for a more satisfying body image.

How does this work? It's simple. You "turn on" your Body-and-Mind Relaxation while you simultaneously view various aspects of your appearance. Gradually, you'll progress from experiencing images with which you feel fairly at ease to those that now churn up discomfort; you'll climb a ladder of your discomforts to achieve success.

Building Your Body Image Ladder

First, develop a list, called a *hierarchy*, or *ladder*, using the My Ladder of Body Areas Helpsheet that follows.

◎   On this Ladder of Body Areas, there are six spaces for listing specific body areas. Review your Body Areas Satisfaction Test from Step 1 and choose one physical characteristic with which you feel mostly *satisfied*. Write down this physical attribute at the bottom of the ladder.

◎   Now, identify at least five aspects of your appearance with which you are *dissatisfied*. Use a scale from 0 to 10 to specify how much discontent or distress you associate with each area. (Note here that higher numbers mean more discomfort, whereas the opposite was the case for your Body-and-Mind Relaxation sessions).

◎ On the top rung of the ladder, fill in the body area or feature that disturbs you the most. Rung 4 will be somewhat less distressing, Rung 3 slightly less, and so forth. Try to have each step up the ladder involve about the same increase in distress points. You may insert more than six areas if needed.

◎ To understand how to develop your ladder, consider the one constructed by Joyce, whom you met at the beginning of the chapter. She likes her eyes, so they are at the base of her hierarchy, with a discomfort rating of 0. Then, her ladder's steps include her hands (rated 1), her upper arms (rated 3), her calves (rated 5), her thighs (rated 7), and her hips (rated 9).

◎ Once you've constructed your own Ladder of Body Areas, I'll show you how to climb it to success.

Helpsheet for Change:
My Ladder of Body Areas

Body Area or Aspect

Rating of Discontent or Distress (0—10)

(the most distressing body area)

Rung 5 _____

Rung 4 _____

Rung 3 _____

Rung 2 _____

Rung 1 _____

Rung 0 _____

(a satisfying area)

Desensitization: Reflections in Your Mirror

Step by step, guided by your Ladder of Body Areas, you're about to do some *Mirror Desensitization*. First, you'll look at yourself in a mirror. Then, you'll actively use your Body-and-Mind Relaxation skills to dissolve any feelings of tension, distress, or discomfort while viewing your appearance.

For Mirror Desensitization, you obviously will need a full-length mirror, like those on a closet or bathroom door. Don't use a handheld mirror or the one on your medicine cabinet—they're too little to give you "the full picture." If you don't own a full-body mirror (maybe because mirrors trigger your body image jitters), buy one or borrow one from a friend. The purpose of Mirror Desensitization is to help you to re-establish feelings of control, so don't use a cheap, distorted mirror that makes you feel like you're in a Salvador Dali painting or a carnival funhouse.

Many people are reluctant to carry out desensitization because they might feel silly or self-conscious looking at themselves in the mirror. This is understandable. After all, if you don't like your appearance, viewing your reflection will generate discomfort, just as someone who dislikes snakes will feel uneasy looking at a snake. The fact here is that being uptight beholding your own body, even in the privacy of your own home, is symptomatic of your body image problem. The more you want to avoid Mirror Desensitization, the more you probably need it. It teaches you to confront and control rather than avoid body image distress. Both you and your mirror will survive!

You'll carry out Mirror Desensitization under two different conditions. First, you'll climb your Ladder of Body Areas while dressed in comfortable indoor clothing, preferably in shorts and a T-shirt—overcoats aren't permitted! Having mastered this experience, you will re-ascend your ladder while unclothed and without any make-up—viewing your natural, unadorned body. I recommend that you do this right after a relaxing bath or shower.

Here are the straightforward steps of the procedure:

◎ Put your mirror in a place, like your bathroom or bedroom, where you'll have privacy during your sessions. For Mirror Desensitization, you won't be seated in your normal relaxation spot; however, you may want to start out there while you get highly relaxed, and then go stand in front of the mirror, at a distance of about three or four feet.

◎ Begin with the physical attribute listed at the bottom of your ladder. First carry out a preparation experience by standing in front of the mirror with your eyes closed and visualizing this body area in your mind's eye for about fifteen seconds.

◎ Then, shift back to your relaxed mental state and let it deepen for a few moments.

◎ Next, directly look at this body area in the mirror for about fifteen seconds, then close your eyes and deepen your relaxation for a while.

◎ Open your eyes and view this area for a little longer—about thirty seconds. Again, shut your eyes and continue to relax.

◎ Then, look at the body area in the mirror for a full minute and relax afterward.

◎ After mastering this, move up one rung.

◎ Again, prepare by mentally visualizing this body area for fifteen seconds, followed by a brief period of relaxing.

◎ Open your eyes and view this body area in the mirror for fifteen seconds, then relax.

◎ Next, look at it for thirty seconds before relaxing.

◎ Then view it for a full minute, followed by relaxation.

◎ In this systematic way, move up one rung at a time—successfully climbing your "ladder of distress" until you've reached the top.

◎ Use the following Helpsheet to record your experiences after each session. Always conclude each session with calming imagery and diaphragmatic breathing—never end on a negative note.

◎ Don't try to progress too quickly up the ladder. Climb only one or two rungs each time. Take three or four separate sessions to make it all the way to the top. Begin each session on the rung you successfully reached in the session before.

◎ After mastering Mirror Desensitization, carry out a final victory session in which you view each area for a full minute while actively maintaining a mellow, pleasant state of body and mind.

Final Words of Encouragement

If you're reading this chapter for the first time and have not yet learned Body-and-Mind Relaxation or carried out Mirror Desensitization, you may be somewhat skeptical about their value. That's okay, just don't let doubts hinder your potential for success. Initially, many people are resistant, thinking they already know how to relax. But after several Body-and-Mind sessions they appreciate what true relaxation feels like. In fact, my research reveals that program participants deem this as one of the most enjoyable and useful aspects of the program.

Mirror Desensitization is definitely difficult for most people with a negative body image. They have to confront how uptight they get while looking at their body, especially their naked body. Even supermodel Cindy Crawford was quoted as saying in a Princeton University speech, "Believe me, I don't want to look at my naked body in a three-way mirror any more than you do." So face the fear and persevere!

Body-and-Mind Relaxation can help control tension and distress arising from other hassles of daily life as well. When your negative, stressed feelings start to get the better of you, you can use this skill to "back off" and reestablish control. You can even construct ladders and desensitize yourself to other unsettling situations and experiences. Whether

Helpsheet for Change:
Mirror Desensitization

Using your Ladder of Body Areas, record each successful desensitization step. Note any important feelings, thoughts, or difficulties. Remember, start at the bottom and work up.

Body Area	Mirror Viewing Duration	DATES COMPLETED	
		Dressed	Undressed
5. _____	1 min.	_____	_____
	30 secs.	_____	_____
	15 secs.	_____	_____
4. _____	1 min.	_____	_____
	30 secs.	_____	_____
	15 secs.	_____	_____
3. _____	1 min.	_____	_____
	30 secs.	_____	_____
	15 secs.	_____	_____
2. _____	1 min.	_____	_____
	30 secs.	_____	_____
	15 secs.	_____	_____
1. _____	1 min.	_____	_____
	30 secs.	_____	_____
	15 secs.	_____	_____
0. _____	1 min.	_____	_____
	30 secs.	_____	_____
	15 secs.	_____	_____

START

Observations and Experiences:

_____

_____

_____

you fear public speaking, going to the physician for a physical exam, dancing at a party, or asking somebody for a date, desensitization can really destroy distress. So keep on rehearsing and applying your new skills. Take control of your body image and your emotional life.

Step 3
Your Path for Progress

★ You've learned Body-and-Mind Relaxation and, if possible, you practice it each day. With your Body-and-Mind Relaxation Helpsheet, you track your progress.

★ Having constructed your Ladder of Body Areas, you have systematically applied your relaxation skills with Mirror Desensitization. You've carried out desensitization for body areas that you dislike—both dressed and undressed in front of your mirror. You've recorded your progress.

★ You are continuing to monitor your negative body image episodes as they occur in your life. In your Body Image Diary, you are regularly recording the Activators, your Beliefs, and the Consequences of these events.

★ You're applying your new skills in everyday life. You're learning to exert control over your disturbing body image emotions as they arise in particular situations.

Step 4:
Arguable Assumptions

Establishing
Reasonable Doubts

Are you talking to yourself again? Of course you are! Everyone talks to themselves in the privacy of their own minds. This is called an *internal dialogue,* or mental conversation. Your silent dialogues consist of thoughts that reflect your perceptions and interpretations of actual or potential events in your life. These inner conversations also entail *self-statements*—thoughts and inferences or conclusions about yourself. Your emotions emanate from how you talk *to* yourself *about* yourself.

Your internal discourse often happens without you realizing that you're talking to yourself. These mental processes are so ingrained that they occur automatically. They require no deliberate, conscious thought. This habitual, automatic-pilot mode of thought just flows and, in a sense, is mindless—because you aren't thinking about your thinking.

Among the obvious liabilities of mindlessness is that you don't know your own mind. You don't see the crucial connections between your silent assumptions, thoughts, and interpretations, and how you feel. You only notice the emotions that these dialogues deliver. So, you end up having to deal with these feelings, especially if they are negative and intense. Seldom do you reverse the mental tape and listen carefully to the inner conversations that led you astray. But that's exactly what must be done.

The Voices Within: Your Private Body Talk

To overcome your body image difficulties, you must first become aware of your inner conversations, especially those that deal with your physical appearance. I call this your *Private Body Talk*. Fortunately, you're already in training. For a while now, since Step 2, you've been monitoring and keeping a diary of the ABC Sequence of your body image experiences—the Activators, the Beliefs, and the Consequences. What happens during the B stage will influence your emotional responses to the activating events. It will also influence how you try to defend yourself against your negative emotions. Of course, B is where your Private Body Talk takes place—where irrational, self-defeating conversations occur.

The following illustrates how pivotal different styles of Private Body Talk can be:

Kerri and Sherri are identical twins. One day, they're together in the dressing room at a health club. After working out, both are in a pretty good mood. Before leaving, each looks at herself in the mirror for a few moments. Afterward, Kerri leaves feeling "bummed out" and down on herself. Sherri, on the other hand, walks away feeling particularly confident and positive about herself. Given that these two women look exactly alike, we must wonder what happened here.

What happened was the Private Body Talk that each had while looking in the mirror. Kerri's Private Body Talk said: "Oh God, I look so ugly. I absolutely hate the way I look. I'm too fat. Nobody will ever like me if I don't lose ten pounds. I hate my face. Look at my stupid fleshy cheeks. Everybody who knows me thinks I'm repulsive." No wonder Kerri walked away from the mirror feeling miserable and wishing she could crawl in a hole and hide.

Sherri's Private Body Talk was hardly identical: "Gee, I look kind of nice today. I really like this new lip gloss. It makes me want to smile, which shows my nice teeth. This blue blouse accentuates my blue eyes. I love blue. I'd like to lose a few pounds, but the world won't end if I don't. Besides, my body really feels energized from the workout today."

Whose Private Body Talk sounds more like yours? Like Kerri, do you torture yourself with a continuing chain of nasty remarks and dire predictions? How derogatory are the dialogues that you've recorded in your diary? To change your self-demeaning inner conversations you must ask another important question: "Why do I do this to myself? Why do I carry on such self-disparaging dialogues in the first place?"

I'll tell you why. Let's go back to the twins and ask this question. Why did Sherri have an inner conversation that gave her contentment and confidence, while Kerri's Private Body Talk had nothing nice to say? You might guess that their parents or peers may have interacted more favorably with Sherri than with her sister. Maybe people somehow preferred her and praised her looks more. Maybe it stemmed from when she was six and her Uncle Fred nicknamed her "my little chipmunk." Maybe she had a more bothersome bout with teen acne than Sherri did. Maybe it was because Kerri used to have a boyfriend who badgered her to lose weight because he "liked the cheerleader look."

Maybe, maybe, maybe . . . you could go on forever guessing about the differences in the twins' personal histories that forged different Private Body Talk. You'd probably be accurate in some of your speculations. It's true that disturbing events can have a lasting effect on your body image and how you think about yourself. Such unfortunate events may have taught you something—something that fed upon itself and remains with you still. This "something" drives your negative Private Body Talk and causes you body image distress. Now I'll explain to you exactly what this "something" is and what you can do about it.

Silent Assumptions About Your Appearance

Whether due to traumatic insults ("Hey, Butt Face!"), family messages ("Look how pretty your sister is" or "Your complexion looks terrible"), or cultural socialization ("Thin is in" and "Blondes have more fun"), you've learned certain basic beliefs or *assumptions* about the meaning of your looks in your life. These core assumptions, which psychologists call *schemas*, determine how you interpret reality. They operate like templates or guides that influence what you pay attention to, how you think about life events, and how you think about yourself. Your schemas are so much a part of you that you cease to be aware of them; they are "self-evident truths" that you take for granted.

You have various schemas that guide your thoughts about all kinds of things—such as love and relationships, success and failure, and the meaning of gender or race. You also have assumptions that direct how you think about your own physical characteristics. I call these self-schemas *Appearance Assumptions*. Appearance Assumptions are your core beliefs about the relevance and influences of your looks in your life. You probably never stop to question their accuracy. Most likely, you ignore or reject any evidence that your Appearance Assumptions might be off base. Appearance Assumptions are your body image "rulers"—in both senses of this word. They are the dictators of your Private Body Talk, and they are the yardsticks by which you measure your physical acceptability.

Take a look at the following diagram. It shows how Appearance Assumptions eventually lead to the emotions you feel that relate to your appearance.

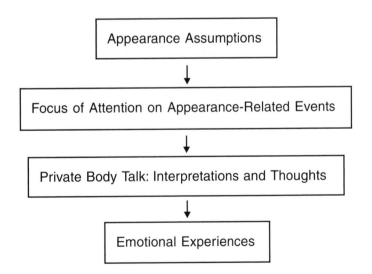

Figure 4.1. From Assumptions to Distress

Core Appearance Assumptions:
The Dictators of Discontent

From my research and clinical work, I've identified ten common Appearance Assumptions that are real troublemakers for body image. They are listed in the following Helpsheet. First, fill out this Helpsheet and indicate how much you believe each statement listed. Afterward, we'll see what your answers mean.

Self-Discovery Helpsheet:
Ten Appearance Assumptions

Read each statement below and decide how much you agree with it. Then, use the 1 to 5 rating scale to express how closely the statement matches your own personal belief. Be completely honest with yourself.

1	2	3	4	5
Strongly Disagree	Mostly Disagree	Neither Disagree nor Agree	Mostly Agree	Strongly Agree

_____ 1   Physically attractive people have it all.

_____ 2. The first thing that people will notice about me is what's wrong with my appearance.

_____ 3. One's outward physical appearance is a sign of the inner person.

_____ 4. If I could look just as I wish, my life would be much happier.

_____ 5. If people knew how I *really* look, they would like me less.

_____ 6. By controlling my appearance, I can control my social and emotional life.

_____ 7. My appearance is responsible for much of what has happened to me in my life.

_____ 8. I should always do whatever I can to look my best.

_____ 9. The media's messages make it impossible for me to be satisfied with my appearance.

_____ 10. The only way I could ever like my looks would be to change them.

How Appearance Assumptions Dictate Your Discontent

To how many of the Appearance Assumptions did you assign a rating of 4 or 5? Although I suspect they seem like obvious "truths," each of these silent assumptions acts as a faulty premise with disastrous consequences for your Private Body Talk.

Let me provide you with proof. My computer stores data from several hundred people who answered the Appearance Assumptions questionnaire and the same body image self-tests that you took in Step 1. I divided these people into two groups. The first group are "Assumers"—those who agreed with most of the Appearance Assumptions. The second group, "Doubters," disagreed with most assumptions. Then, I compared Assumers and Doubters to find out what percentage of each group had a negative body image on each of three self-tests. The results, depicted in Figure 4.2, are quite striking. Here's what they reveal:

On each of the self-tests, about three-fourths of Assumers had a problematic body image. Their evaluations of their overall looks were quite negative. They were dissatisfied with most areas or aspects of their appearance. They more often felt body image distress in a range of situations. Unlike these Assumers, the Appearance Assumption Doubters seldom had a negative body image. The majority of Doubters, about 85 percent to 90 percent, had a positive view of their appearance, liked most of their body areas, and had fewer episodes of body image distress.

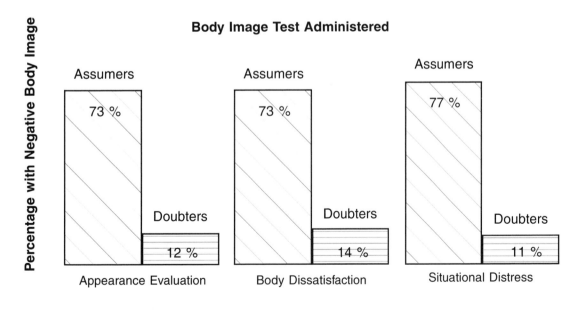

Figure 4.2.
How Do Appearance Assumptions Affect Your Body Image?

Assumers' Private Body Talk always seems to disrupt their peace of mind, while Doubters are clearheaded about their looks. Step 4 will help you become a Doubter instead of an Assumer.

The Helpsheet on page 88, "My Appearance Assumptions in Action," will help you discover exactly how your own assumptions foster disturbing Private Body Talk. To illustrate how to complete this Helpsheet, I've given you a sample Helpsheet. This individual, Louise, indicates how five of her Appearance Assumptions set in motion lots of problems. Look at her experiences and then record your own:

◎   First, list those assumptions you rated as 4 or 5. Write these down on the lines that begin, "When I assume."

◎   Then, write down what each assumption leads you to focus your attention or dwell on.

◎   Next, what thoughts run through your Private Body Talk? Review your Body Image Diary for instances of how your assumptions come into play.

◎   Finally, for each of your assumptions, write down the emotions you subsequently experience. As you'll see, there's a connection between your Appearance Assumptions and your body image distress.

Arguing with Your Assumptions: Your New Inner Voice

Self-esteem comes from the ability to experience yourself honestly and accurately. There are two psychological forces that may lead you to play mind games, in which you hold a distorted view of yourself and your body image. These forces prevent you from making worthwhile changes. The first is *self-deception*. Because honest self-awareness can make you uncomfortable with your shortcomings, you may deceive yourself to achieve a false sense of self-acceptance. For example, you gloss over or deny how demeaning your Private Body Talk is because you'd prefer not to think of yourself as so viciously self-critical. A second force that may lead you to play mind games is based on a need for *self-consistency*. You've decided that your view of yourself is the absolute truth, so you can only see things that consistently confirm these self-perceptions, however unflattering. For example, you convince yourself that your nasty inner conversations about your looks are the only valid view that could exist. You insist that you "should" have a negative body image. Obviously, self-deception and self-consistency will interfere with your being able to change what you need to change in order to be happier with your appearance and yourself.

Cognitive therapy can help you develop honest and accepting self-awareness. This approach teaches you how to find, listen to, and nurture something I call your *New Inner Voice*. This voice speaks in ways that are understanding, tolerant, fair, realistic, logical, and assured. This New Inner Voice doesn't care where you are on anybody's scale of physical attractiveness. It cares about you! It doesn't sound like the old critical voice of your upsetting Private Body Talk.

Self-Discovery Helpsheet:
Louise's Appearance Assumptions in Action

When I assume: *attractive people have it all (#1)*

Then I focus on: *my flaws*

And I think: *I'll never have it all*

And I feel: *depressed*

When I assume: *people notice my flaws first (#2)*

Then I focus on: *my fat tummy*

And I think: *I need to diet; I need to hide*

And I feel: *disgusted and self-conscious*

When I assume: *people won't like what I really look like (#5)*

Then I focus on: *everything gross about my body*

And I think: *I'm fat and ugly underneath my clothes and makeup*

And I feel: *depressed*

When I assume: *my looks are responsible for what's happened in my life (#7)*

Then I focus on: *my shape and all the past disappointments*

And I think: *I've been ripped off*

And I feel: *very irritated*

When I assume: *I have to change my looks to like them (#10)*

Then I focus on: *all the things I wish I could change*

And I think: *I'm never going to be satisfied*

And I feel: *sad, hopeless*

Self-Discovery Helpsheet:
My Appearance Assumptions in Action

When I assume: _____

Then I focus on: _____

And I think: _____

And I feel: _____

When I assume: _____

Then I focus on: _____

And I think: _____

And I feel: _____

When I assume: _____

Then I focus on: _____

And I think: _____

And I feel: _____

When I assume: _____

Then I focus on: _____

And I think: _____

And I feel: _____

When I assume: _____

Then I focus on: _____

And I think: _____

And I feel: _____

When I assume: _____

Then I focus on: _____

And I think: _____

And I feel: _____

When I assume: _____

Then I focus on: _____

And I think: _____

And I feel: _____

When I assume: _____

Then I focus on: _____

And I think: _____

And I feel: _____

When I assume: _____

Then I focus on: _____

And I think: _____

And I feel: _____

When I assume: _____

Then I focus on: _____

And I think: _____

And I feel: _____

When I assume: _____

Then I focus on: _____

And I think: _____

And I feel: _____

Impeaching your longstanding Appearance Assumptions isn't easy. The first words of your New Inner Voice will simply question the validity and value of your assumptions, purposefully challenging their authority over your thoughts and emotions. Each assumption paints a picture, and your New Inner Voice will ask, "What's wrong with this picture?" Each is an arguable assumption, containing a bit of truth and a lot of falsehood. Taking on the ten Appearance Assumptions, one at a time, will make you more aware of the falsehoods and leave you with a more reasonable mind-set.

Assumption 1: Physically Attractive People Have It All.

Society's preoccupation with and marketing of physical attractiveness reinforces the assumption that being good-looking pays bigger benefits than it actually does. The undeniable truth is that being good-looking is helpful sometimes. However, as the French author Stendhal observed in 1822, "Beauty is only the promise of happiness." For numerous reasons, attractiveness doesn't keep most of its promises. There are also plenty of reasons why being average looking or less doesn't close off opportunities for happiness. To help you challenge Appearance Assumption 1, I want to take a few pages here to explain to you why looks aren't everything. These aren't reasons that I made up; these are facts established by scientific research on the psychology of physical appearance.

◎ *Fact 1: "Beauty is as beauty does."* It's true. Actions speak more loudly than looks. Friendliness, intelligence, honesty, a sense of humor, and social sensitivity are highly valued human traits, regardless of what you look like. Think about people who have impressed you or are important in your life. Are they all "10"s on the appearance scale? I'll bet their looks aren't crucial to how you feel about them.

◎ *Fact 2: First impressions don't always last.* Our initial reactions to someone's appearance are not frozen forever in our minds. We come to see good people as increasingly good-looking. Have you ever met a person whose appearance wasn't so appealing, but as your relationship evolved, the person's looks seemed more and more interesting and attractive? On the other hand, have you ever noticed how the halo of physical attractiveness can fade over time? Playwright George Bernard Shaw aptly asserted, "Beauty is all very well at first sight, but who ever looks at it when it has been in the house three days?" (1903).

◎ *Fact 3: Birds of a feather do flock together.* We are attracted to people who are similar to us in certain ways. For example, we seek out those with shared interests, ethnic heritage, religious or philosophical values, and educational background. This is true of physical appearance as well. Many times, best friends, dates, and mates are comparable in their physical attractiveness. This pairing off based on similarity of attractiveness has the fortunate result that nobody gets left out.

◎ *Fact 4: Beauty can backfire by implying egotism.* Appearance Assumption 1 ignores the "ugly faces of beauty." Paradoxically, the assumed advantages of physical attractiveness cause disadvantages. If we believe that good-looking people are desirable and have social benefits, we may also figure that they are well aware of their good looks and their privileged status. So we infer that they must be sold on themselves and opportunistic. Then, we may assume they are less responsible or trustworthy as friends, romantic partners, or parents. This negative stereotype of attractive people cancels out some of the benefits of their looks.

◎ *Fact 5: Beauty can backfire because of sexism.* Another factor that undermines the power of attractiveness is the sex-typing stereotype of appearance. Pretty women are sometimes presumed to possess "feminine" personality traits like passivity and emotionality. Handsome men are sometimes presumed to have "masculine" characteristics such as dominance and unemotionality. Although these stereotypes are untrue, research reveals that such sexist biases about physical attractiveness erode some of its positive power.

◎ *Fact 6: Beauty breeds envy and jealousy.* The eighteenth century historian Edward Gibbon once said that "Beauty is an outward gift which is seldom despised, except by those to whom it has been refused." Have you ever heard anyone exclaim, "They are so good-looking (or thin, or well-built). I hate them"? When we compare ourselves to people who have the looks we want, we end up feeling worse about our own appearance and dislike these good-looking people for "making us feel unattractive."

◎ *Fact 7: Beauty can transform people into sex objects.* In song, Rod Stewart posed the question "Da ya think I'm sexy?" While most of us want our romantic partners to find us sexy, few of us enjoy being seen solely as a "sex object" by everyone we encounter. Good-looking people, especially women, are subjected to unwelcome sexual comments about their bodies. These remarks are often demeaning and harassing. Would you really want to be seen as *only* a sexy body or a pretty face?

◎ *Fact 8: Beauty engenders self-doubt.* Fact 7 gives rise to another problem for attractive people. Let me explain by conveying a conversation I once had with a longtime friend, Nancy, who is strikingly lovely. One day, I told her how beautiful I thought she was. To my surprise, she became very upset. "I thought you liked me for who I am. Now I'll never be sure that it's not just because of what I happen to look like." Nancy's point poses important questions. Wouldn't you rather know that people like you because you're a splendid person and not merely because you're nice to look at? Wouldn't you rather feel that you deserve the recognition you get than have to wonder if somebody's just being nice to you because of your looks?

◎ *Fact 9: Beauty is a weak foundation for self-esteem.* The more people put all their eggs in the "beauty basket," the more vulnerable is their self-worth. So, contrary to Appearance Assumption 1, good-looking people don't have it all if it all rests on being attractive. Time and life events can alter one's appearance—for better or worse. A foundation for self-worth built on beauty is a shaky foundation indeed.

◎ *Fact 10: Looks don't matter to everybody.* The early nineteenth century poet Robert Southey wrote, "How little do they see what is, who frame their hasty judgments upon that which seems." We all know "nearsighted" people who judge others solely on appearances. Fortunately, however, there are many people who aren't swayed by whether we're fat or skinny, "dressed to the nines" or wearing our comfortable "sloppy" clothes. They can see us and appreciate us for who we are. We should all try to become more like these terrific appearance-blind individuals. They make our world a fairer and more accepting place.

Changing a negative body image requires that you seriously question Assumption 1 and keep looks in perspective. Your New Inner Voice will remind you that beauty is a mixed bag that contains many false promises. In the absence of a positive body image and solid self-esteem, good looks aren't worth much. Relinquishing stereotypes and pursuits of physical perfection will free you to embrace many opportunities for appreciating yourself.

Assumption 2: The First Thing That People Will Notice about Me Is What's Wrong with My Appearance.

Again, this is a partial truth. Heads will turn if you have spiked orange hair, a pierced nose, or a likeness of Jerry Garcia tattooed on your forehead. But then, you probably want others to take notice. What about having physical characteristics that are not of your choosing? Here's what you must realize in questioning Assumption 2:

◎ If you're quite obese or have a pronounced physical disfigurement, few folks will fail to notice. That's the reality of human nature. But, so what? Just because others are aware of this doesn't mean that they'll despise or mistreat you, or that all is ruined. Your own actions are up to you. Your personality—your friendliness, kindness, and conversational skills, and so on—is much more influential than whatever might be "wrong" with your looks.

◎ Assumption 2 is wrong about most people most of the time. What is true is that *you* are the one noticing what you don't like about your appearance. Other people usually couldn't care less. They've got other things to think about. Of course, if they, too, have a negative body image, they're probably busy being self-conscious and worrying that you will notice *their* physical flaws.

◎ Your New Inner Voice will help you keep things in perspective: "So what if people notice that I'm short, or fat, or have a facial scar, or . . . whatever? What difference does that really make? Life goes on! I'm a pretty likable person. People tell me they like me because I'm . . . ."

Assumption 3: One's Outward Physical Appearance Is a Sign of the Inner Person.

This assumption goes back to the appearance stereotypes discussed previously. Both the scientific evidence and the experiences of daily life strongly contradict this assumption. We can't judge books by their covers with much accuracy; but we keep this false assumption alive by remembering a few instances when our initial impressions based on looks turned out to be correct, while forgetting all the times our impressions were mistaken. Here are some good arguments against Assumption 3:

◎ Think about your own personal experiences. Has somebody good-looking turned out to be thoughtful rather than egotistical? Do you know any blondes who aren't at all ditsy? Have big, muscular guys ever turned out to be coop-erative rather than coercive? Are you acquainted with any heavyset folks who are far from being lazy? I suspect you even know a few fellows with deep-set and penetrating eyes who actually aren't serial killers!

◎ Assumption 2 is an exaggeration. As the voice of reason, your New Inner Voice will say, "I know I pay too much attention to outer appearances, especially my own. I don't have to look perfect for people to see my inner qualities. People know me for who I am. Whenever possible, I need to remind myself that my actions, not my looks, tell people who I truly am."

Assumption 4: If I Could Look Just as I Wish, My Life Would Be Much Happier.

The trouble with Assumption 4 is its implication: Unless I can look the way I want to (that is, taller, thinner, more muscular, less wrinkled, or with my nose straightened), there's no way I can be happy. What makes you unhappy is not your physical appear-ance. It's your wish that sells you short and robs you of self-acceptance. Challenge this Appearance Assumption in these ways:

◎ Remember the scientific truth: Physically attractive people are not necessarily happier than less attractive people. Good-looking individuals have their body image wish lists too.

◎ Have you ever had experiences in which the more you desperately wanted something, the less you appreciated what you had? To justify your wishing for "the new" you have to denigrate "the old." Your burning desires destroy your ability to enjoy what you have. Wishing magnifies your discontent, which you believe can only be resolved by getting what you wish.

◎ Your New Inner Voice will put you in touch with reality. It reminds you that your goal is to achieve a better body image, not to have a different body. Listen to your New Inner Voice say "I realize that my appearance doesn't really pre-vent my being happy. I do. I make myself unhappy trying to look like my ideals. I cause myself despair by beating myself up for not having my wishes come true. Once I accept myself and learn to like my looks, my life will be much happier. That's up to me, not my body."

Assumption 5: If People Knew How I *Really* Look, They Would Like Me Less.

This is an assumption that fosters shame. Believing it will force you into hid-ing—concealing those aspects of your body that you think other people would find re-pulsive. You worry about what you assume to be the "naked truth." The problem with this assumption is that it becomes an "untested truth." Disproving Assumption 5 requires that you test it. Hiding only makes you feel worse.

One client of mine, Harriet, who completed this program, was ashamed of her "thick legs" and was convinced that anyone who saw them would stare in disgust. So she always wore long pants. Finally, Harriet was able to conjure up the courage to bring her legs out of hiding and wear shorts to school. She saw me walking across campus and approached me. "Look, I'm wearing shorts!" Harriet exclaimed. "So far, nobody's screamed and run in horror. I can't believe I refused to do this for so long."

◎ First try an indirect test. Ask yourself how often you stopped liking someone upon discovering some imperfection in their appearance. How often have you said something like, "I hadn't known that Jack had an appendectomy scar. I'll be sure to avoid him from now on"? Or, "Now that I've seen Joyce without her facial makeup on, I have no use for her"? Or, "Becky's breasts are smaller than I thought, so that's the end of our relationship"? Once we test the assumption, we typically find that we have been mistaken all along. People accept us, flaws and all. And that feels so much better than hiding.

◎ In Step 6, I'll help you come out of hiding and test this assumption directly, as Harriet did. For now, just let your New Inner Voice remind you that *you* are the one who is repulsed by some physical feature. It's your shame. If people knew how you really look, their opinions would not, in fact, change.

◎ Your New Inner Voice will coax you out of hiding: "I worried that I'd be rejected and hurt if people knew how I really look. I worried that if they see what I don't like about my body, they'd be ashamed of me and I'd feel bad. But all my worrying makes me feel bad. Could I really feel that much worse if I stopped concealing what I look like? Is it possible that I'm making this into a bigger issue than it really is?"

Assumption 6: By Controlling My Appearance, I Can Control My Social and Emotional Life.

You have tremendous control over your looks. Think about all the available tools for managing appearance—clothing, cosmetics, hairstyling, a healthy diet, and regular exercise. Proper grooming can certainly enhance your looks and make you feel attractive. The hazard, however, comes from relying excessively on these tools. As writer Northrop Frye noted, "The pursuit of beauty is much more dangerous nonsense than the pursuit of truth or goodness, because it affords a stronger temptation to the ego" (1957).

◎ In arguing with Assumption 6, you must start to see that you cannot effectively manage your self-esteem and your life by asking your appearance to do all the work. Just like a carpenter cannot construct a house with only a hammer, you cannot build a happy life using only your looks.

◎ Appearance management works only if it improves your body image. Stylish clothes are useless if you don't like how you look in them. Moreover, as you saw for Assumption 5, if all they do is cover what you hate, they aren't really helping your body image. Depending on them entirely for damage control only reinforces your belief that your unadorned body is objectionable.

◎ Review your own experiences for evidence that contradicts Assumption 6. If all your appearance-managing efforts to control your social and emotional life are so effective, then why do you still have a negative body image? We can reword Assumption 6 and make it truer: By changing my *body image*, I can better control my social and emotional life.

◎ What will your New Inner Voice say to help you modify this faulty assumption? It will say: "Spending too much effort trying to 'fix' my looks is misdirected effort. Constant repairs on my appearance are only a temporary Band-aid. I'm still unhappy with my looks. I want to feel better permanently. So I need to focus on changing my mind instead of my looks. That's a change that will give me more control over my life."

Assumption 7: My Appearance is Responsible for Much of What Has Happened to Me in My Life.

Yes, your appearance has affected some things in your life. There may have been times that it paid off and times it was a detriment. Nevertheless, most things that have happened in your life had absolutely nothing to do with your looks. Most were either the product of your personality, intelligence, decisions, and actions, or were simply the result of chance.

◎ History shows that attractiveness is not a prerequisite for success in most endeavors of life other than certain media, performance, and modeling roles. Abraham Lincoln, Winston Churchill, Mikhail Gorbachev, Henry Kissinger, and former New York Mayor Ed Koch wouldn't exactly qualify as handsome hunks. Golda Meir, Eleanor Roosevelt, Margaret Thatcher, and Mother Teresa would hardly win a beauty contest. What widely respected leaders from world history, the arts, or literature can you think of who were not, in your opinion, good-looking?

◎ Most of the people we've actually known who have touched our lives in significant ways aren't necessarily great looking. Can you think of individuals whom you loved, liked, or admired for reasons that had nothing to do with their looks?

◎ Your New Inner Voice will argue against Assumption 7 by realizing and saying: "My appearance may have influenced some things in my life. But I'm ultimately responsible for my life. I can make choices about how I deal with any effects that my looks have. My history has been written. But, my present and my future are up to me, not my appearance."

Assumption 8: I Should Always Do Whatever I Can to Look My Best.

The words "should" and "always" imply that looking your best is your *duty*. The statement also suggests that by not looking your best you have failed. Here are some questions to ask yourself about this assumption:

◎ First of all, why have you saddled yourself with this obligation? What do you expect will happen if you are able to look your best on all occasions? What would happen if you don't? Looking your best is extremely subjective, so how will you know you've performed your duty? Who can possibly look their best all the time? We can always think of ways we could look better; this assumption sets you up for failure by requiring the impossible!

◎ Do you require other people to have the best imaginable appearance at all times? Would you be so harshly judgmental if a friend wore less than perfectly flattering clothing, had a hair out of place, or got a zit? I hope not. Nor do I hope that you would tolerate such a demanding expectation from a friend. So why should you demand this of yourself? It's nice to feel that you look nice; it's not nice to feel that you always have to.

◎ Your New Inner Voice will speak out against perfectionism: "I enjoy liking how I look, but I could loosen up some. I don't have to look perfect all the time. When I look less than my best, nobody ever commands me to look better—nobody but me, that is. I'm the one pressuring myself. I'm the one giving myself grief. Instead, I need to do whatever I can to accept my looks. It's okay to look acceptable, rather than look exceptional."

Assumption 9: The Media's Messages Make It Impossible for Me to Be Satisfied with My Appearance.

With this assumption, you make yourself into a victim. Poor me! So you come to feel powerless. Then what's the use in trying to change your negative body image? Okay, it's true that the media convey strong and unhelpful images about physical appearance. They try to convince you there are only two ways that you can be happy and succeed in life. You either must be born with good looks or you must buy all the products and services needed to manufacture physical perfection. Let's take a look at Assumption 9:

◎ Genius isn't required to recognize how extreme and distorted these media messages are. As you learned in Step 2, if these messages were all-controlling, then no one would have a positive body image. But people do like their looks despite these unhelpful forces. That's because they see that personal fulfillment does *not* require physical perfection. Do you know what is certain to be much worse than not being a perfect 10? It's *worrying* about not being a perfect 10.

◎ The media and a huge appearance industry certainly make it difficult to accept your body, but difficult isn't the same as impossible. They are indeed a brainwashing force to be reckoned with, but they don't aim a loaded gun at you and command, "Believe and do everything we say, or else!" What you believe and what you do is entirely up to you. Think about it!

◎ So what do you do? A character in the 1976 movie *Network* proclaimed the media's injustices by yelling from a rooftop to the passive public below, "I'm mad as hell, and I'm not gonna take it anymore!" You don't have to take it anymore. Should you trash your television and cease reading magazines? Should you retreat to a nudist camp and boycott all appearance-altering products and services? Probably not. Our society could certainly use some improvements, but the best place to start is within yourself. Your own Private Body Talk does not have to echo the appearance-preoccupied voices of the media.

You can see and hear these voices without accepting them as your own inner voice. You don't have to be a victim.

◎ Your New Inner Voice will be assertive. It can empower you not to take it anymore: "I'm tired of expecting myself to look like all these perfect bodies in the media. Seeing them isn't believing them. I'm not them and I don't have to look like them. I'm going to work like hell to accept myself. The media don't make it impossible for me to accept my looks. I do."

Assumption 10: The Only Way I Could Ever Like My Looks Would Be to Change Them.

This is one self-defeating assumption! It drives people to try just about anything to alter their appearance. My new clients often want me to help them lose ten or fifteen pounds or to refer them to a cosmetic surgeon. Then they can have a positive body image. When I suggest that we *first* work on body image and *then* decide about weight loss or surgery, they look at me with disappointment and disbelief. Don't I understand what they need?

◎ I understand the basis and the power of Appearance Assumption 10. If something is broken, fix it. So, you go on a diet again, workout a lot, buy new clothes, get a new hairstyle, use the expensive wrinkle product, or have plastic surgery. Maybe you've done some of these things, and some even felt pretty good—for a while. But if all the fixes still haven't repaired how you feel about your looks, ask yourself the basic question, "What's really broken?" What's not working here is your body image, and that's what needs fixing.

◎ You learned from the research I described earlier in this workbook that you *can* improve your body image without altering your body. Here's the corrected version of Assumption 10: "The only way I could ever like my looks would be to change my *body image*."

◎ Let's tackle Assumption 10 head on! Your New Inner Voice will urge you to shift your emphasis: "I've spent too much of my life trying to change my looks. What I need to do is focus on the real problem and real solutions. Fixing my appearance feels good at the moment, but it doesn't last. I just keep looking for better ways to be better looking. The best way I can like my body is to work directly on my body image. That's really the problem I need to fix."

Your New Inner Voice Speaks Out

Establishing reasonable doubt of faulty Appearance Assumptions requires more than a casual commitment to "stop thinking those things." Change only comes from actively *doing* something to create a new attitude. A New Inner Voice will create a new attitude. This strong voice will speak realistically about appearance, in a language that enables you to take responsibility for how you think and feel, no matter what you look like. It is a voice of tolerance and reason. A New Inner Voice will understand that your body image affects the quality of life more than your body's actual appearance does.

Cultivating your own New Inner Voice is crucial to developing a more favorable body image. It's okay that right now this voice may be only a whisper in your mind. You can give it the words that it needs to speak more clearly and forcefully. And then you can listen to it and hear it! Here's how:

- ◎ The following Helpsheet, Questioning My Appearance Assumptions, will help you develop your New Inner Voice. Use your own words to talk to yourself about each arguable assumption listed, as I've done. Don't expect to believe totally everything you write. Write down what you want to believe—what makes rational sense.

- ◎ After putting your words on the Helpsheet, read them out loud. At an emotional level, your New Inner Voice may seem foreign to you—like somebody else talking. That's okay; that's understandable.

- ◎ Each day, take a few minutes to reread your words aloud. Soon this voice will begin to sound familiar. Increasingly, the wisdom of your New Inner Voice will become self-evident.

Final Words of Encouragement

A lot of people decide to change something in their lives—something they know they really need to change. Maybe it's their job, or a relationship, or a bad habit. They've even told their friends or loved ones that they need to change. They know they want to be happier, and they see the direction they need to take. They start on a path. They take the right steps. They're actually getting there. At about this point in the road, they wish they had already reached their destination. "Are we there yet?"

Impatience on a journey from a bad place to a good place is a normal human reaction. We've all felt this way. Use your impatience to be where you want to be. Step 5 is coming up and it will offer even more opportunities to exercise your New Inner Voice. By the end of the workbook you'll be fluent in this new language. And you'll have reached your destination.

Helpsheet for Change:
Questioning My Appearance Assumptions

Assumption 1: Physically Attractive People Have It All.

My New Inner Voice says:

_____

_____

_____

Assumption 2: The First Thing That People Will Notice about Me Is What's Wrong with My Appearance.

My New Inner Voice says:

_____

_____

_____

Assumption 3: One's Outward Physical Appearance Is a Sign of the Inner Person.

My New Inner Voice says:

_____

_____

_____

Assumption 4: If I Could Look Just as I Wish, My Life Would Be Much Happier.

My New Inner Voice says:

_____

_____

_____

Assumption 5: If People Knew How I Really Look, They Would Like Me Less.

My New Inner Voice says:

_____

_____

_____

Assumption 6: By Controlling My Appearance, I Can Control My Social and Emotional Life.

My New Inner Voice says:

_____

_____

_____

Assumption 7: My Appearance Is Responsible for Much of What Has Happened to Me in My Life.

My New Inner Voice says:

_____

_____

_____

Assumption 8: I Should Always Do Whatever I Can to Look My Best.

My New Inner Voice says:

_____

_____

_____

Assumption 9: The Media's Messages Make It Impossible for Me to Be Satisfied with My Appearance.

My New Inner Voice says:

_____

_____

_____

Assumption 10: The Only Way I Could Ever Like My Looks Would Be to Change Them.

My New Inner Voice says:

_____

_____

_____

Step 4
Your Path for Progress

★ Having identified your basic Appearance Assumptions, you're learning to recognize and challenge the ways in which these Appearance Assumptions command your Private Body Talk and, ultimately, your emotions. Increasingly, you can see that your assumptions are debatable and unhealthy.

★ You've begun to cultivate your New Inner Voice—a voice that does not passively accept your Appearance Assumptions. You're finding the right words for your New Inner Voice—words that challenge each assumption and words that support you in your efforts to change.

★ You're still practicing your Body-and-Mind Relaxation skills and using them to control distress in your daily life.

★ If you've not completed your Mirror Desensitization from Step 3, you're continuing to progress up your Ladder of Success.

★ Daily, you're recording the ABC Sequence of your negative body image experiences in your Body Image Diary.

Step 5: Critical Thinking

Correcting Your
Private Body Talk

Long ago, in the first century A.D., the philosopher Epictetus wisely asserted, "What disturbs people's minds is not events but their judgments on events." The essence of his wisdom is that our emotions depend upon our point of view as we try to make sense of our lives. Even earlier, the Roman poet Horace observed that "Nothing's beautiful from every point of view." His astute observation applies to homeliness as well.

Calvin is not only convinced that he's homely, he's also convinced that his looks are destroying his life. He believes that unless he can do something to fix his physical flaws, he's doomed to a life of rejection and unhappiness. He blames his looks for past disappointments. Calvin is certain that everybody he knows thinks he is one of the ugliest people in the world. He spends inordinate time mentally comparing himself with other guys who look like he wishes he could. Whenever he's stressed about work or relationships, his body image becomes even worse. Often, Calvin talks himself out of doing fun stuff because he might become self-conscious about his appearance. When you look at Calvin, you notice that he has some freckles. If you look closely, you can see that his teeth aren't perfectly straight. But you don't really care. These attributes are just an incidental part of who Calvin is. To Calvin, however, they are practically everything.

Like Calvin, you disturb your mind and your life with your viewpoint of your own looks. Epictetus and Horace were right!

In Step 4, you learned how your Appearance Assumptions lay out the basic roadmaps of your Private Body Talk. Your thoughts about your looks then travel these well-worn paths. Your Appearance Assumptions are joined by another force that steers your Private Body Talk—*Cognitive Distortions*. These are particular mental mistakes that drive your inner conversations down dead ends where it's impossible to turn around and along crooked paths that send you in the wrong direction.

How do Cognitive Distortions differ from Appearance Assumptions? Appearance Assumptions set the stage for the general focus of your attention and thinking in relation to your looks. Cognitive Distortions are the *specific* mental manifestations or contents of your thoughts. Appearance Assumptions set you up for faulty Private Body Talk, and your Distortions are the messengers that carry it out. The flowchart in Figure 5.1 describes the role of faulty thinking in how your body image experiences unfold in your daily life.

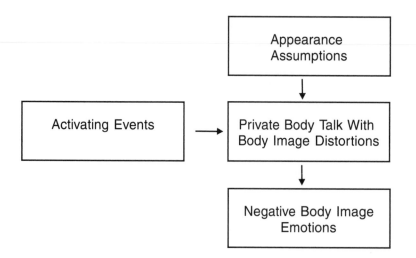

Figure 5.1. Your Unfolding Body Image Experiences:
The Role of Distorted Thinking

Discovering Your Body Image Distortions

Cognitive therapists teach their clients how to recognize and eradicate their mental mistakes from their inner conversations. Step 5 will teach you how to detect and eliminate your Cognitive Distortions. It will enable you to develop a more reasonable and rational Private Body Talk. As a result, negative feelings about your appearance will be less likely and less disruptive of your daily life.

As a therapist and a researcher, I've found that people with a negative body image tend to make the same mental mistakes. I have identified eight separate *Body Image Distortions*. For each of these thought patterns, you'll first take a self-test to find out how similar your thinking is. Afterward, I'll define each pattern for you and illustrate how it might show up in your Private Body Talk.

You may wish to review the thoughts you've recorded in your diary and compare them with the descriptions of the Body Image Distortions. Because they are the foes of a satisfying body image, you must come to know your own distortions well. Then, you'll be equipped to combat them later in Step 5.

Distortion 1: Beauty-or-Beast

❄ ❄ ❄ ❄ ❄

How characteristic of your thinking is each thought pattern?
Record your answers in the spaces to the left of the items.

0	1	2	3	4
Not at All Like Me	*Slightly Like Me*	*Moderately Like Me*	*Very Much Like Me*	*Extremely Like Me*

_____ Imagine that you weighed a few more pounds than your ideal weight. Would you think, "Until I lose these few pounds, I look really fat"?

_____ Imagine that on a particular day, you develop a few acne "zits" on your face. Would you think, "These zits make my face really ugly"?

_____ Imagine that on a certain day your hair doesn't look "right." Would you think, "I look awful today"?

_____ Imagine that you're out of town at a semiformal event and you realize that the outfit you packed doesn't go together as well as you'd like. Would you think, "This looks terrible; my appearance is ruined in this outfit"?

_____ Imagine that you leave for work or school one morning feeling that you don't look quite as good as you usually do. Would you think, "I really look terrible today"?

Put a check mark beside items you rated as 1 or 2 and an asterisk (*) beside those you rated as 3 or 4.

❄ ❄ ❄ ❄ ❄

❄ The Beauty-or-Beast Distortion occurs when you think about your appearance in extremes. This is called *polarized thinking*. Many people think in this way about their weight: "Either I'm at a perfect weight or I'm fat." A person fearful of becoming fat puts on a few pounds and concludes, "I'm such a blimp." Or, someone concerned with being too thin loses a few pounds and proclaims, "I'm just a bony rail." A less-than-ideal haircut leads one to decide that he resembles the lead creature in a horror movie.

❄ In a similar, but less extremely polarized, version of Beauty-or-Beast thinking, you consider a physical feature as either "okay, I guess" or "ugly." In this dichotomy, you're either apathetic to your appearance or you're hypercritical. When being neutral, your Private Body Talk is typically quieter, because you think, "My looks are nothing to notice, they're hardly worth thinking about."

✣ The undistorted truth is that reality is not a matter of either/or. Reality is on a continuum. In between black and white are many shades of gray. As you can see, Beauty-or-Beast thinking leads you to disregard the shades of gray, making exaggerated conclusions about your looks.

Distortion 2: Unfair-to-Compare

✢ ✢ ✢ ✢ ✢

How characteristic of your thinking is each thought pattern?
Record your answers in the spaces to the left of the items.

0	1	2	3	4
Not at All Like Me	Slightly Like Me	Moderately Like Me	Very Much Like Me	Extremely Like Me

_____ Imagine that you're thinking about an aspect of your appearance that you dislike. Do you then think about how you wish that aspect looked and how you don't measure up to your ideal?

_____ Imagine that you're trying on new swimsuits you've seen in newspaper ads. Would you think, "This suit doesn't look nearly as good on me as it does on the model in the ad"?

_____ Imagine that you're flipping through a magazine that has pictures of very attractive models of your gender. Would you compare your looks to theirs and think that you really don't look very good?

_____ Imagine that you're watching TV and on the commercials there are attractive people of your gender. Would you compare your attractiveness to theirs and find yourself inadequate by comparison?

_____ Imagine you see yourself and a group of friends and acquaintances in a photograph. Would you compare yourself with whomever looks best in the picture?

_____ Imagine that you go to a party where everyone is dressed up. Would you compare what you are wearing to that of the best dressed party-goers and conclude that they make you look less attractive?

_____ Imagine that you're at the beach or the pool. Would you notice all of the more "fit" bodies on the beach and compare your body to theirs?

_____ Imagine that you go to the gym or an exercise class and there are some "perfect bodies" in the room. Would you compare your body to theirs and think that these people make you look bad?

Put a check mark beside items you rated as 1 or 2 and an asterisk (*) beside those you rated as 3 or 4.

✢ ✢ ✢ ✢ ✢

The Unfair-to-Compare Distortion involves pitting your appearance against some unrealistic or extreme standard. When you compare yourself with these standards, you make yourself the loser. Let's look at this mental mistake closely:

※ In Step 2, you examined the various standards of appearance championed by our society—standards for weight, height, body shape, muscularity, and other physical attributes. Magazines, newspapers, movies, television, and now the Internet hit you so heavily with these ideal images that you cannot escape being aware of them. Mere awareness isn't the problem, however. You become vulnerable to the "unreal ideals" when you personally absorb these images—when you accept society's standards as your own.

※ To illustrate, I'd like to tell you about an experiment I once conducted in which research subjects viewed pictures of people in photo albums. Some participants saw a photo album filled with conventionally good-looking people; the rest viewed an album picturing average or less attractive people. Afterward, I asked the participants to evaluate their own appearance. And guess what? Those who had viewed photos of good-looking people reported feeling less attractive than did subjects who had viewed plainer looking people. Comparing provokes despairing!

※ The Unfair-to-Compare Distortion is one of the most common mental mistakes that people make. As the self-test items reflect, there are three basic types of unfair comparisons:

1. *Comparisons with your own personal physical ideals.* Your score on the Wishing Well Test in Step 1 is an index of how much you probably devalue your looks for not living up to these ideals. Gauging your physical worth by unrealistic ideals causes you to dwell on inadequacies. You focus on what you *don't* look like and on what you *don't* like about your looks. You engage in wishful thinking: "I wish I had thicker hair." "I really wish I were thin." "I wish I had a bigger chest." Your Private Body Talk will also be loaded with what I call "too" thinking. "I'm *too* short (or *too* fat or *too* this or *too* that)."

2. *Comparisons with media images.* Thumbing through certain magazines or seeing some ads on television may lead you to mentally compare your appearance with how the models look. Unless you're also airbrushed to perfection (and perhaps even if you are), chances are you'll conclude that you don't look as good as the models.

3. *Comparisons with real people.* This Unfair-to-Compare Distortion may take you beyond the media and mental images of perfection. You also compare your appearance with that of real people you encounter in everyday life. However, your comparison is skewed—made only with people you judge to have the physical qualities that you wish you had. Obviously, your thoughts are biased against you from the very start. You play the comparison game but, with the rules you choose, you always lose. If you always compare yourself to a taller standard, you can only come up short.

✲ The Unfair-to-Compare Distortion is unfair in another respect. Rarely do people pick just any physical characteristic for comparison. It's typically the one you like least, the one that bothers you most. In this way, you add insult to insecurity and make your insecurity that much worse.

✲ Which Appearance Assumptions instigate this distorted Private Body Talk? Assumption 4 maintains that "If I could look just as I wish, my life would be much happier." This underlying belief keeps you reviewing your ideals to see if you should be happy yet. Similarly, if Assumption 8 commands you always to look your best, you'll compare your looks to some notion of best and find ways you've not met the lofty expectation. Finally, there's Appearance Assumption 9, which complains, "The media's messages make it impossible for me to be satisfied with my appearance." You then empower these media images by comparing yourself to them.

✲ The ruminations on this mental mistake are terribly self-critical and use words such as *should*, *must*, and *ought*. For example, "I should have a clearer complexion." "I ought to have a smaller waist."

✲ Furthermore, when your comparisons are with actual people, not only do you have negative feelings toward your body, but you may also experience envy and jealousy toward the persons with whom you compare yourself. If you think, "They make me look bad," you become intimidated. You may try to avoid them, or gossip about them, or retaliate by giving them unwarranted grief. After all, if you could take them down a notch or two, you might be able to feel more adequate yourself. Obviously, the Unfair-to-Compare Distortion becomes unfair to everyone.

Distortion 3: The Magnifying Glass

✲ ✲ ✲ ✲ ✲

How characteristic of your thinking is each thought pattern?
Record your answers in the spaces to the left of the items.

0	1	2	3	4
Not at All Like Me	Slightly Like Me	Moderately Like Me	Very Much Like Me	Extremely Like Me

_____ Imagine that you're looking at your reflection in the mirror. Would you focus on your "flaws" more than you would your physical assets?

_____ Imagine someone comments favorably on your appearance. Would you then have thoughts about aspects of your appearance that you think would never be complimented?

_____ Imagine that you're with friends who are discussing what certain other friends look like. Would you privately begin to think about what's "wrong" with your physical appearance?

_____ Imagine that you're at the beach or in some other situation where you body is "on display." Would you dwell on your least favorite body area and how it looks?

_____ Imagine that you've done something that improves your appearance (e.g., weight control or a new hairstyle). Would you mentally disregard this change and think about other things that need improving in your looks?

_____ Imagine that you're getting ready to go out and you're looking at your appearance in the mirror. Would you ignore looking at or thinking about your best features?

_____ Imagine that an acquaintance compliments something about your appearance that other people have complimented before. Would you mentally dismiss the compliment because a compliment of your better features doesn't make up for the things about your appearance that you dislike?

Put a check mark beside items you rated as 1 or 2 and an asterisk (*) beside those you rated as 3 or 4.

❄ ❄ ❄ ❄ ❄

❄   The Magnifying Glass Distortion represents what psychologists call *selective attention*. You focus in on an aspect of your appearance that you dislike and then exaggerate it—as if you're putting your body under a magnifying glass. You commit this mental error when you can't contemplate your looks without zooming in on this one unsatisfactory feature. All you see is one huge flaw. You equate your entire appearance with your "squinty eyes," "flabby thighs," "chipmunk cheeks," or "knobby knees." Your Private Body Talk is defective because all it talks about are defects. Your inner dialogues repeat themselves like a broken record. You're certainly tired of hearing it, but you keep playing it anyway.

❄   The Magnifying Glass Distortion entails underemphasis as well as overemphasis. It involves a *blind mind*—as you ignore or minimize your positive physical qualities. Wouldn't you think that someone with a negative body image would want to feel a little better by thinking more about these assets. The Magnifying Glass mistake prevents you from appreciating the very features that others find most attractive about you. For example, in his Private Body Talk, a man with a handsome face says, "Oh, sure, my face is fine, but who the hell cares? Just look at this flabby mess of a body!"

❄   One reason that some people commit this distortion is a fear of vanity. As I discussed in Step 2, some folks fear that liking their own looks would mean that they are conceited. So, if they ever catch themselves having a positive perception of their looks, their Private Body Talk zaps them with guilt and commands them to change the subject.

✳   To understand this distortion, consider the following analogy: Imagine that you have bought a beautiful new car, the car of your dreams. You proudly care for it, keeping it spotless and running perfectly. One day you're driving behind a dump truck that spills some gravel, causing a dime-sized dent right in the middle of the hood. Understandably, you're quite upset. You don't have the funds to fix it. Whenever you look at your dream car, all you see is a nightmare. The slight dent takes on the dimensions of the Grand Canyon. Over the next few weeks, as you drive along, your eyes focus more on the dimple in your hood than on the road. When friends admire your new car, your reply is, "Yeah, but look at this awful dent." They hadn't noticed the minor blemish and probably never would have; but you can't seem to see anything else. As a Body Image Distortion, the Magnifying Glass keeps you staring at your body's "dents."

Distortion 4: The Blame Game

✻ ✻ ✻ ✻ ✻

How characteristic of your thinking is each thought pattern?
Record your answers in the spaces to the left of the items.

0	1	2	3	4
Not at All Like Me	*Slightly Like Me*	*Moderately Like Me*	*Very Much Like Me*	*Extremely Like Me*

_____   Imagine that you go on a job interview and the interview seems to go well, but you don't get hired. Would you think, "They probably hired someone who's better looking than I am"?

_____   Imagine that you're single and go out on a blind date. You both seem to have a pretty good time. Your date says "I'll call you in a couple of days," but never does. Would you think, "My looks probably messed things up"?

_____   Imagine that you're out with a group of people you don't know very well. You notice that some of these people are very friendly with others but not with you. Would you think that the reason they weren't attentive to you had something to do with your appearance?

_____   Imagine that you're single, go to a party, and meet someone you find attractive. This person leaves with another nice-looking person at the end of the night. Would you think, "My looks probably weren't good enough"?

_____   Imagine that you're shopping for new clothes and the salesclerk gives you rather poor service. Would you wonder if you would've been treated better if you looked better?

Put a check mark beside items you rated as 1 or 2 and an asterisk (*) beside those you rated as 3 or 4.

✻ ✻ ✻ ✻ ✻

❀ The Blame Game Distortion takes place when you incorrectly conclude that some disliked physical attribute is directly responsible for certain disappointments and difficulties that you experience. This psychological phenomenon is called *scapegoating*. You need to blame something for your troubles, and because you already see your appearance as offensive to you, it's the convenient target.

❀ Distorted Blame Game thinking goes like this: "If I didn't look so _____ , then (*something bad*) wouldn't have happened." If you don't get the job or the date or the social courtesy you wanted, you readily point the finger of blame at your appearance. Your Private Body Talk alleges that your looks have stolen something you had hoped for. Your appearance "stands accused," without a shred of solid evidence.

❀ In Step 2, I discussed that a person's looks *can* sometimes affect life events. Being 6'6" is likely to aid an individual in the basketball tryouts relative to someone who is 5'2". The pretty blonde might be shown favoritism in her bid to get the office receptionist job. Unfortunately, obese individuals are at times treated unfairly in our society. In the Blame Game, however, people scapegoat their appearance for problems that occur even in the absence of evidence. After some social disappointment, it's natural to try to figure out why things happen as they do. It's clearly wrong, however, to jump to the automatic conclusion that your appearance is responsible.

❀ Why are you so indicting of your looks? Well, in Step 4, did you endorse Appearance Assumption 7—the basic belief that your appearance is responsible for much of what has happened in your life? If so, then you probably play the Blame Game often. This Appearance Assumption falsely establishes a criminal record for your appearance and predisposes you to scapegoat your looks in your Private Body Talk.

❀ In the self-test of this distortion, I asked you to imagine going to a party and meeting someone you find attractive. This happened to Terri, who was disappointed when the "dreamboat" left the party with another woman. Terri's Private Body Talk blamed her own appearance: "It was my curveless body and dumb curly hair. Who'd be interested me. I look like a broccoli stalk?" She concluded, "It's my body's fault that he left with someone besides me. My looks aren't good enough." (Unbeknownst to Terri at the time, her "heartthrob" had left the party with his sister.)

Distortion 5: Mind Misreading

❊ ❊ ❊ ❊ ❊

How characteristic of your thinking is each thought pattern?
Record your answers in the spaces to the left of the items.

0	1	2	3	4
Not at All Like Me	Slightly Like Me	Moderately Like Me	Very Much Like Me	Extremely Like Me

_____ When you think about the aspects of your appearance with which you're dissatisfied, do you think that most other people also dislike those aspects of your looks?

_____ Imagine that you're wearing a new outfit and no one comments on it. Would you assume that people think the outfit doesn't look good on you?

_____ Imagine that your lover shows little interest in making love with you for a few weeks. Would you think that the reason for the disinterest is because your partner thinks you are physically unappealing in some way?

_____ Imagine that you are exercising in an aerobics class. Would you be convinced that those people that are watching you are doing so because they're noticing some flaw in your body as you exercise?

_____ Imagine that you're at a large social gathering and see someone staring at you. Would you think that person is staring at something he or she dislikes about your appearance?

_____ Imagine that you're showering at a gym and you notice another showerer glancing at your body. Would you suspect that the person is probably thinking about the imperfections in your body?

_____ Imagine that you get a different haircut and no one comments on it. Would you assume that people probably don't like it?

Put a check mark beside the items you rated as 1 or 2 and an asterisk (*) beside those you rated as 3 or 4.

❊ ❊ ❊ ❊ ❊

❊ Mind Misreading leads people with a negative body image to reason that, "If *I* think I look bad, then *others* must think I look bad too. Others see me exactly as I see myself." The truth is others may have entirely different ideas. Psychologists call this faulty mental process *projection*, because we project our own beliefs or thoughts into the minds of others. In the Blame Game section, Terri committed Mind Misreading by inferring that the fellow at the party had thought she was goofy looking. Those were her own evaluations of her appearance that she projected into his head.

❊ Have you already realized that Mind Misreading and Blame Game Distortions often go hand in hand? In order to blame your looks for how people react (or don't react) to you, you have to presume what those people "must be think-ing." Even without some disappointment to blame your appearance for, you may simply believe that others share your harsh judgments about your body. Without proof, you assume their thoughts are your thoughts.

✻ Appearance Assumption 3 may propel this distortion. By assuming one's out-ward appearance is a sign of the inner person, you're more likely to think others are constantly scrutinizing your looks. If you also buy into Assumption 2, that the first thing people will notice about you is what's wrong with your appearance, you're ready to misread their minds at a moment's notice. You're sure people are beholding your crooked teeth, baggy eyes, facial acne, protrud-ing ears, big buttocks, or whatever *you* are self-conscious about. If you're wor-ried about your weight for example, your Mind Misreading says, "They see how overweight I am and think I'm a fat slob."

Distortion 6: Misfortune Telling

✻   ✻   ✻   ✻   ✻

How characteristic of your thinking is each thought pattern?
Record your answers in the spaces to the left of the items.

0	1	2	3	4
Not at All Like Me	*Slightly Like Me*	*Moderately Like Me*	*Very Much Like Me*	*Extremely Like Me*

_____ Think about those aspects of your appearance that you've wished were different. Do you ever think that your future will be less satisfying because of how you look?

_____ Imagine that you've moved to a new area and are interested in meeting new friends. Would you have thoughts that your physical appearance could lead people to reject you as a possible friend?

_____ Imagine that you're single and down on your luck about dating. Would you think, "As long as I look as I do, no one will ever fall in love with me"?

_____ Imagine that you're invited to a party on the beach. Would you think that something about how you look will prevent you from having much fun?

_____ Imagine that you've been asked to join a club to plan community activities for the coming year. Would you have thoughts that because of something about your appearance you probably won't fit in or enjoy participating?

_____ Imagine that at work or school you have to give a speech. Would you think that because of your looks your speech won't go over very well?

Put a check mark beside the items you rated as 1 or 2 and an asterisk (*) beside those you rated as 3 or 4.

✻   ✻   ✻   ✻   ✻

✻ The Blame Game and Mind Misreading involve inferences about past and current events. The Misfortune Telling Distortion pertains to your predictions about how your appearance will affect your future. You predict that your physical shortcomings will have dreadful effects on your life. This may influence your expectations in short-term situations: "People in exercise class will stare at me and snicker." Misfortune Telling may deal with long-term expectations: "With my looks, I'll never be taken seriously in my workplace."

✻ Misfortune Telling uses extreme words such as *never* or *always* when you anticipate how your looks will be a detriment. For instance, you think, "With my homely face, I'll always be unloved." Or, "I look so old and wrinkled that I'll never get promoted." Or, "As long as I'm bald, people will never treat me with respect." Such sweeping expectations encompass what "all" or "most" people will think and do. "If I get any heavier, all my friends will tease me."

✻ What Appearance Assumptions fuel Misfortune Telling? The converse of Assumption 4 leads to the inference that unless you look exactly as you wish, your life will never bring you happiness. And of course, an implication of Assumption 7, which states that your appearance has adversely affected your past, is that your looks will mess up your future too. Assumption 10 requires that you change your appearance in order to accept your looks. Therefore, you conclude that the absence of that change means the absence of good things in your future. Misfortune Telling permeates your Private Body Talk with pessimism.

Distortion 7: Beauty Bound

✻ ✻ ✻ ✻ ✻

How characteristic of your thinking is each thought pattern?
Record your answers in the spaces to the left of the items.

0	1	2	3	4
Not at All Like Me	Slightly Like Me	Moderately Like Me	Very Much Like Me	Extremely Like Me

_____ Imagine that you hesitate to do something because of some shortcoming in your appearance. Would you think about all the reasons that you shouldn't do it and talk yourself into avoiding the situation?

_____ Imagine that you want to go work out at the gym. Would you think that you need to look more fit before you can go work out in front of others?

_____ Imagine that you're shopping for some new clothes. Do you talk yourself out of trying certain attractive styles or colors because they might call attention to parts of your body you don't like?

_____ Imagine that you're single and are dating someone you really like. Would you think that there are some "undesirable" parts of your body that you should hide from your partner?

_____ Imagine that some neighbors drop by unexpectedly and you have not yet worked on your appearance for the day. Would you think, "I can't answer the door and let them see me like this"?

_____ Imagine that you want to gain or lose a few pounds. Would you think that you can't buy any new clothes or a special outfit, until you've achieved those weight changes?

_____ Imagine that a nice-looking same-sex friend asks if you want to get together for dinner at a popular restaurant. Would you probably decline because you think the friend looks better than you do?

Put a check mark beside items you rated as 1 or 2 and an asterisk (*) beside those you rated as 3 or 4.

❈ ❈ ❈ ❈ ❈

❈   The Beauty Bound Distortion is reflected in Private Body Talk that says you *cannot* do certain things due to your looks. This distortion imprisons you. By limiting your activities and aspirations because of your negative body image, you become its prisoner.

❈   Beauty Bound thinking typically begins with the words "I can't." You forbid yourself to go places, do things, or be with certain people because you think you don't look good enough. You tell yourself you can't wear particular types or colors of clothing. You deny yourself certain social or recreational activities. Your "I can't" thinking usually takes the form of "I look too _____ to do that." Sometimes the prohibitions are temporary: "Until I get a tan, I can't go to the beach," or, "Until I lose ten pounds, I can't go dancing." Other times the Beauty Bound prohibitions are permanent: "With my hairy arms, I'll never be able to wear short-sleeved shirts," or, "With my ugly body, I'll never have a boyfriend and I'll never have sex."

❈   Notice how the various Body Image Distortions often team up to create your troubles. Beauty Bound seldom operates alone. For example, a woman who decides, "I can't go to the office picnic because my hair looks weird" is restricting her activities (Beauty Bound thinking) because she tells herself that people will snub her because of her looks (Misfortune Telling). A man whose Beauty Bound thinking dictates, "I'm too fat, so I can't eat in front of other people," is also Mind Misreading in concluding that others will judge him as fat and over-indulgent with food.

❈   Beauty Bound beliefs are fueled by several Appearance Assumptions. Return to Step 4 and reread Assumptions 5, 6, and 8. Can you see how each of these assumptions can lead you to constrain your freedom of choice in living a fuller life?

Distortion 8: Moody Mirror

❊　❊　❊　❊　❊

How characteristic of your thinking is each thought pattern?
Record your answers in the spaces to the left of the items.

0	1	2	3	4
Not at All Like Me	Slightly Like Me	Moderately Like Me	Very Much Like Me	Extremely Like Me

_____ Imagine that you're in a bad mood for some reason. Would you be apt to start mentally criticizing your appearance and find yourself unattractive?

_____ Imagine that you begin to think about one of your physical characteristics that you dislike. Would your thoughts then turn to other physical characteristics with which you're dissatisfied?

_____ Imagine that you're "stressed out" one day. Would you be more likely to have negative thoughts about what you believe is wrong with your looks?

_____ Imagine that you have a new haircut and aren't happy about how it looks. Would you then have critical thoughts about other aspects of your appearance, as well?

_____ Imagine that a friend has criticized something you've done and that it bothers you. Would you then find yourself being critical of yourself, including what you don't like about your appearance?

_____ Imagine that you had a large meal and feel overly full. Would your feeling full make you think that you're fat?

_____ Imagine that you're feeling particularly unattractive one day. Would you then attempt to justify these feelings by focusing on and thinking about all the things that are "wrong" with your looks?

_____ Imagine you feel that something is not quite right about your looks, and you ask a friend for feedback. Your friend reassures you that you look fine. Would you dismiss the reassurances because you *know* that how *you* feel must be the real truth?

_____ Imagine that you're wearing an article of clothing you don't particularly care for. Would you then tend to have negative, critical thoughts about other aspects of your looks?

Put a check mark beside items you rated as 1 or 2 and an asterisk (*) beside those you rated as 3 or 4.

❊　❊　❊　❊　❊

❀ The Moody Mirror Distortion involves what psychologists call *emotional reasoning*—reasoning based purely on feeling. You start with a strong emotion that you need to justify. You end up with a faulty conclusion that justifies and even strengthens the emotion.

❀ The Moody Mirror mistake can occur in three variations. In the first form, your initial emotion is a negative feeling about your looks. You notice it and you ask yourself, "Why do I feel so unattractive?" Then, with little thought, you readily answer the question, "It's because I *am* unattractive." This version of the Moody Mirror Distortion follows the not-so-brilliant logic that "because I *feel* ugly, I must *be* ugly."

❀ Here's an analogy: Imagine that you and a friend are on a leisurely walk through the park. Everything is lovely—that is, until your friend wonders aloud if any snakes might be strolling through the park as well. Not being especially enamored with such creatures, you notice your galloping heart rate. You also notice plenty of places where these reptiles might reside. There are logs where they could lie in wait for you. There are low-hanging branches from which they could launch an aerial assault. "This park is viper city," you conclude. "There must be hundreds slithering about. Let's get out of here!" Your fear leads you to decide that snakes must be there somewhere—despite having absolutely no evidence of them! You reasoned from your fear, inferring facts from feelings.

❀ Can you apply this analogy to the Moody Mirror Distortion? Your Private Body Talk is an emotional dialogue that confuses feelings with facts: "No wonder I feel so ugly, just look at me! Look how ugly and _____ (fat, or short, or beer-bellied, or disfigured . . .) I am!"

❀ This brings me to the second but related form that the Moody Mirror Distortion can take. It occurs when feelings of unattractiveness about one physical characteristic spill over to other features. Operating on the faulty principle of "guilt by association," your Private Body Talk searches for guilty parties. As it zeros in on some unacceptable attribute, you feel unattractive and dissatisfied. Then you ask yourself emotionally loaded questions: "Just *how* ugly am I?" or "What *else* is wrong with my looks?" In answering, your mind is like a bug-zapper that zaps anything coming its way. You annihilate one physical feature after another, feeling uglier each time. And the uglier you feel the more you notice any imperfection in order to justify your feelings.

❀ In the final manifestation of the Moody Mirror, you start with negative feelings about something unrelated to your looks—for example, being stressed out or in a bad mood. Then, the wildfire of your bad mood spreads and ignites your body image experiences. How can this happen? Your brain stores various Private Body Talk "tapes" that it plays and replays, producing predictable emotions. These tapes remain on pause until something switches them on. Negative emotions, such as anxiety, dejection, disgust, or shame, can set off these dormant dialogues, especially those tinged with a similar emotion. So your nasty mood seeks a ready target, and you unfairly malign your appearance. The Moody Mirror just looks for trouble—and really stirs it up!

The Undistorted Truth about Distorted Thoughts

Do you recall that in Step 4 I showed you a graph of the research evidence that Doubters of Appearance Assumptions have a much happier body image than do Assumers. This research further confirms that people's Body Image Distortions have a strong bearing on the nature of their body image experiences. Again, rather than asking that you accept this on faith, I'll show you what the research reveals.

Hundreds of people filled out a questionnaire comparable to the self-tests you answered in this chapter. They also completed the body image tests from Step 2. I divided participants into five groups based on how much they engaged in the various Body Image Distortions you've learned about. Then, out of each of these five groups, I determined the percentage of who had a negative body image on Appearance Evaluation, Body Areas Satisfaction, and Situational Distress tests.

Examine the bar graph in Figure 5.2. It indicates that as a person's distortion level increases (from Level 1 to Level 5) so do that person's body image problems. Body image discontent and distress are practically nonexistent for Level 1 scorers, whose Private Body Talk rarely reflects any of the distortions. In contrast, a negative body image is overwhelmingly prevalent among people at Level 5, who have inner conversations about their looks that are replete with mental mistakes.

At this point, you're probably wondering what level your own Body Image Distortions represent. Instead of translating your answers on the Step 5 self-tests into numerical scores and levels of distortion, let's do something that promises to be much more informative and helpful. Let's start to work to change the distorted Private Body Talk that you have, no matter how problematic it is. You'll use your self-test answers to direct and accomplish the changes. I'll teach you how.

Corrective Thinking: Start Talking Back

Your Old Inner Voice has hassled you too much for too long! By taking issue with your Appearance Assumptions in Step 4, you've already begun to take charge of problematic Private Body Talk. Now let's tackle your Body Image Distortions, so that you can change the unfair and self-defeating ways you think about your looks.

This is no "mission impossible." To combat your mental mistakes, you'll add a *D* to the ABC Sequence of your negative body image experiences. You've spent several weeks becoming more skilled in monitoring your Activators, Beliefs, and Consequences. This added *D* stands for *Disputing*—disputing the distortions of your Private Body Talk. In disputing your familiar "tapes," you'll learn to rethink yourself out of your distressing experiences.

Cognitive therapists refer to these highly effective strategies for changing your experiences as *cognitive restructuring* or *corrective thinking*. Because corrective thinking can be difficult to learn in the midst of a distressing episode, you'll develop your corrective thinking ahead of time. Then, with a little practice, you'll be ready to apply what you've learned to alter your Private Body Talk in your daily life.

On the following pages, I'm going to take aim at each Body Image Distortion, one at a time. I'll give you plenty of examples that show you exactly how to talk back to your distorted Private Body Talk. Here's how:

◎ Read about disputing the particular distortion.

◎ Then, go back earlier in the chapter to your self-test of that distortion. Read the specific items you flagged with an asterisk to indicate that these are quite characteristic of your own thought patterns.

◎ Next, read items you flagged with a check mark indicating that they are somewhat descriptive of your thought patterns.

◎ Then reread my suggestions on how to dispute that distortion. Underline or take note of anything that "hits home" or seems potentially valuable.

Afterward, it'll be *your* turn to take aim, with the aid of the Helpsheet at the end of the section on each specific distortion. Here's what you do:

◎ Based on your review of your self-test answers, pick a familiar scenario that causes you the most problems and reflects this particular Body Image Distortion.

◎ On the Helpsheet, write down the typical Activators of your body image distress.

◎ Write down the words of your Private Body Talk that commit this mental mistake. Include the self-statements, beliefs, and interpretations that reflect the distortion.

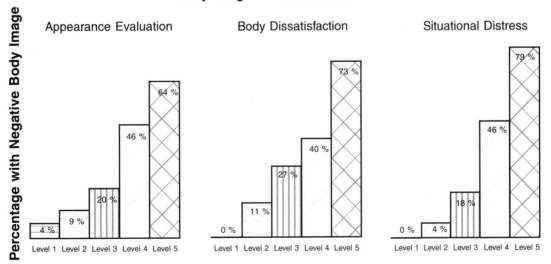

Figure 5.2.
How Does Distorted Private Body Talk Affect Your Body Image?

◎   Finally, talk back! Based on the discussion and examples of how to dispute the distortion, compose the narrative of your corrective thinking that will argue with your distortion.

Please understand that this shouldn't be osmosis therapy, in which you decide that just absorbing my words will be as helpful as finding your own voice. Your New Inner Voice must talk back with *your* chosen words. This means that you need to spend the small amount of time required to put your words on paper. Don't dismiss this opportunity for change by telling yourself, "Oh, this is that positive thinking stuff." It's not. This method of change is deeper and more complex than "thinking happy thoughts." You are discovering, dissecting, and disputing the personal inner causes of your body image difficulties. So if your Old Inner Voice is urging you not to use your Helpsheets, don't listen to it! It's been a misguiding advisor in the past, and you deserve better.

Correcting Your Beauty-or-Beast Distortions

Remember, Beauty-or-Beast thinking is "either-or" thinking: "Either I'm attractive or I'm homely." "Either I lose five pounds or I'm fat." "Some people have it and some don't; I don't." Here are some ways to dispute such polarized, black-and-white thinking:

◎   Force yourself to see things on a continuum. See the shades of gray. Remind yourself that not being a 10 on a 10-point scale of attractiveness doesn't necessarily make you a 1.

◎   Say to yourself: "Okay, so I'm not totally perfect; but I'm not totally imperfect either. I have features that enhance my appearance." Then, remind yourself of these physical assets.

◎   Ponder how you think about other people's looks. "Do I judge others with only two extreme categories? Or do I see them on a continuum?" If the latter, ask yourself, "Why should I view other people more fairly than I perceive myself?"

◎   Eliminate the loaded language of your thoughts by being more objective in your Private Body Talk. In your thoughts, replace "I'm a horse face" with "I have a long nose." "I have potholes for my facial complexion" is, more objectively, "My complexion isn't smooth." Replace "I'm a damned scarecrow" with "I have a thin physique." "Hippo hips" becomes "rounded hips." "I'm a Chrome Dome" should be "I have hair loss."

◎   Ask yourself, "Honestly, what is the evidence, other than my own harsh judgments, that I'm seen as extremely homely?" Ask, "What is the evidence to the contrary?" Think about compliments you receive. Think about occasions in which you felt pleased about some facet of your appearance.

Helpsheet for Change:
Correcting the Beauty-or-Beast Distortion by Talking Back

A typical activating situation or event is

_____

_____

_____

My distorted Private Body Talk often says

_____

_____

_____

_____

_____

_____

_____

To dispute this Beauty-or-Beast Distortion with corrective thinking, my New Inner Voice talks back and says

_____

_____

_____

_____

_____

_____

_____

Correcting Your Unfair-to-Compare Distortions

Remember that the Unfair-to-Compare Distortion comes in three forms. You pit your appearance against your own personal ideals, the media images of physical perfection, or people you find good-looking whom you encounter in everyday situations. So, you compare your appearance only with images of what you'd like to have. As a result, you spend a lot of time noticing others who you think look better than you do. And, not surprisingly, you end up feeling unattractive.

You focus on extreme images (or ideals, if you let them be) that few people can match. Don't overlook the fact that, by definition, professional models have an extreme and unusual appearance. Remember, from Step 2, that research confirms that individuals who have the looks that people idealize do *not* necessarily have a more positive body image. Happiness derives not from what you have but from how you regard what you have. Quite attractive people are often critical and worrisome about their looks.

This distortion fills Private Body Talk with words and phrases like *should, ought, must,* or *I have to be*. Envy and intimidation arise from Unfair Comparisons. Examples of faulty Private Body Talk here are: "I should be more attractive," or "I wish I were as attractive as that person is," or "That person makes me feel so ugly." Seldom do you notice that there are few people who come close to meeting your ideals for yourself.

Corrective thinking for this distortion first recognizes what you're doing. It catches you in the act of comparing yourself with somebody, leaving you upset about your looks. Use the following suggestions to let your corrective thinking set you straight:

- Replace your *shoulds, musts,* and *oughts* with less demanding language. Instead of saying, "I should be better looking, taller, thinner, or . . . ," correctively assert, "It might be nice if I lost a few pounds, but I look pretty good the way I am. I refuse to belittle myself for not looking like a cover model."

- Other helpful corrective thoughts are: "I don't have to have a perfect body to have an appealing appearance." Or, "Nobody's perfect; even models have imperfections that are airbrushed out of sight." Or, "Nobody (but me) expects me to look different. Nobody's complaining about me but me."

- Be adamant that "I refuse to continue to buy into this societal ideal of attractiveness; it's sexist and I refuse to treat myself that way."

- "The reality is that everybody is better looking than somebody else; everybody is less attractive than somebody else. I don't have to feel bad just because there's something about me that I don't like as much as what someone else has." .

- Recognize that your mental compliment of someone else doesn't have to be a mental criticism of you. "The fact that I like the way a person looks has nothing to do with how *I* look. That person doesn't make me look bad; he (or she) doesn't *make* me do anything."

- Your New Inner Voice says: "Okay, if I'm going to compare, then I need to be fair. So, who am I *more* attractive than?"

- Finally, "I'm going to take time now to think of something else about me (a special skill, talent, or personality trait) that compares quite favorably with other folks."

Helpsheet for Change:
Correcting the Unfair-to-Compare Distortion by Talking Back

A typical activating situation or event is

_____

_____

My distorted Private Body Talk often says

_____

_____

_____

_____

_____

_____

_____

_____

To dispute this Unfair-to-Compare Distortion with corrective thinking, my New Inner Voice talks back and says

_____

_____

_____

_____

_____

_____

_____

_____

Correcting Your Magnifying Glass Distortions

When you view your looks through the distorted Magnifying Glass, you over-emphasize the physical attributes you don't like and minimize the ones that don't cause a problem. You take a tunnel-visioned perspective on yourself. When you think about your friends and loved ones, do you think only about their weight, warts, or wrinkles? Of course you don't. You have a fairer, more balanced picture of their appearance and who they are as people. Freed of this distortion, your Private Body Talk reflects a more balanced view of your looks and yourself. Apply these helpful ideas:

- Begin by asking yourself, "Am I dwelling on what I don't like and forgetting about parts of me that are fine?" Think of two or three of your favorite features. Then, when you magnify, *un*blind your mind by saying to yourself, "I'm magnifying here and that's not the whole picture of my appearance. I'm just focusing on my dislikes. I do like (for example) my beautiful eyes and my smooth complexion, and I'm honestly pleased with my hairstyle."

- In addition, say to yourself: "I may not be fond of my _____ (hair, weight, nose, legs, or whatever), but other people see more to me than the characteristic that I keep hassling myself about."

- Just as you do to correct the Beauty-or-Beast Distortion, replace exaggerated, pejorative statements about magnified features with more objective, less demeaning descriptions. "Small chested" is more accurate than "flat as an ironing board." "I have long feet" is more accurate than "my clown feet."

- Any time you start criticizing your looks in front of the mirror, interrupt your thoughts and say, "There, I caught myself at it again—picking on myself. I'm going to stop, walk away from this mirror, and return only after I apologize to myself, give myself a smile, and say something considerate to myself."

- Make a promise to yourself. Promise to abide by the *Equal Time Rule:* Spend an equal amount of time on your unspoken likable features or traits whenever you catch yourself mentally harping on what you dislike about your body.

Helpsheet for Change:
Correcting the Magnifying Glass Distortion
by Talking Back

A typical activating situation or event is

_____

_____

My distorted Private Body Talk often says

_____

_____

_____

_____

_____

_____

_____

To dispute this Magnifying Glass Distortion with corrective thinking, my New Inner
Voice talks back and says

_____

_____

_____

_____

_____

_____

_____

Correcting Your Blame Game Distortions

The Blame Game makes the mistake of *misattribution*. You readily infer that your appearance is responsible for the occurrence of some disappointment or other undesirable event. Examples of Private Body Talk based on playing the Blame Game are: "I don't have a boyfriend because I'm so ugly," or, "People aren't friendly to me because of my balding," or, "I wasn't promoted at work because I'm overweight."

While correcting Blame Game thinking, you first must realize that blaming your looks for unfortunate events usually involves jumping to conclusions based on a guess—a biased guess. So what's the real evidence? If you objectively examine the facts, often the only evidence that indicts your appearance is your own discontent with your looks—hardly convincing proof. How can you use corrective thinking to dispute the Blame Game?

- ◎ Your New Inner Voice is a voice of reason and says, "I know I may be blaming my looks simply because I don't like them. That doesn't mean that my looks are actually causing anything bad to happen." In other words, blaming isn't convicting.

- ◎ Then, ask yourself, "Okay, what real evidence do I have that my appearance is to blame for this? What other likely explanations are there?"

- ◎ Talk back to your faulty Private Body Talk: "Here I go again, accusing my looks of ruining everything. Instead, I'm going to leave my appearance out of it and focus on what I can do to make things better."

- ◎ Sometimes all you need to do is catch yourself blaming your looks, see that you have no evidence for your conclusion, and tell yourself, "Stop blaming!" Then, move on to more important things—like being friendly or having fun.

- ◎ Suppose you do have reasonably good evidence that your looks really did cause the problem. For example, you asked somebody out for a date and the person declined, giving your looks as the reason. So what? Not everybody is going to like everything about your looks. For that matter, not every person you meet is going to like your car, your clothes, your politics, or your religious beliefs. One person's opinion is not everybody's opinion. If a few folks reject you because of such things, it may be their deficiency, their problem, and their loss! There are some judgmental and prejudiced people in this world. If you're overweight and somebody is hatefully biased against overweight people, this person is not rejecting *you*, he or she is rejecting an entire category of people. Do you really need to be concerned about what such a bigoted person thinks about you? Say "Adios" and move on!

Helpsheet for Change:
Correcting the Blame Game Distortion
by Talking Back

A typical activating situation or event is

_____

_____

My distorted Private Body Talk often says

_____

_____

_____

_____

_____

_____

_____

To dispute this Blame Game Distortion with corrective thinking, my New Inner Voice
talks back and says

_____

_____

_____

_____

_____

_____

_____

_____

Correcting Your Mind Misreading Distortions

Mind Misreading occurs when you project your own thoughts about your looks into the minds of others. You leap to the incorrect inference that other people see and judge your appearance in the same way that you do. You then worry that they have these negative opinions of your looks. You think, "Everybody who sees me is thinking about my _____ (large ears, acne, toupee, big breasts, short stature, or whatever)." Then you fill their heads with your own thoughts. "Anybody who walks behind me will be grossed out by my fat ass."

As I explained earlier, Mind Misreading often occurs in tandem with the Blame Game Distortion. Suppose, for instance, that your Private Body Talk is blaming: "My partner didn't want to have sex last week because he (or she) is turned off by my awful body." While you condemn your looks as the reason for sexual "rejection," you only reached your verdict by Mind Misreading. How do you know that your partner's thoughts about your looks led to a lapse of interest in sex? Could it be instead that your partner was simply not in the mood or was worn out or preoccupied with work? Besides, did you make it clear you were interested in sex? If not, why did you expect your partner to read *your* mind and know that you were feeling amorous?

The corrective strategies for handling Blame Game thinking are also useful in managing Mind Misreading. Here are some additional strategies to help you "keep your thoughts to yourself":

◎ First, recognize what you're doing—that you're thinking about what somebody else might be thinking about. If you're being presumptuous, admit this to yourself. Admit that you may be Mind Misreading.

◎ Next, ask yourself if the thoughts and opinions you suspect others are having about your looks strangely resemble your own opinions.

◎ Accept reality: "I'm fairly bright, but I can't read minds. The only mind I'm reading here is my own."

◎ Talk back assertively: "I need to stop thinking about what others may be thinking. Instead I need to change what *I* am thinking."

◎ do you have any evidence that contradicts what you presume another person is thinking? if the other person is someone you know well, has the person ever made positive or affirming comments about your looks? has the individual ever disagreed and reassured you when you complained about your appearance?

◎ Ask yourself, "If my appearance isn't what's bothering people, what else could it be?" In examining alternative explanations, consider several that are frequently true. People aren't likely to be warm and accepting if you are not friendly. Could you have been acting distant because of your fear that others won't like you or your looks? Also, others may be shy or merely having a bad day. Could their behavior mean that something is wrong with *them*—not with you?

Helpsheet for Change:
Correcting the Mind Misreading Distortion by Talking Back

A typical activating situation or event is

_____

_____

My distorted Private Body Talk often says

_____

_____

_____

_____

_____

_____

_____

To dispute this Mind Misreading Distortion with corrective thinking, my New Inner Voice talks back and says

_____

_____

_____

_____

_____

_____

_____

_____

Correcting Your Misfortune Telling Distortions

While the Blame Game charges your appearance with past or current offenses, Misfortune Telling looks ahead and distorts your thinking with pessimistic predictions. You convince yourself that bad things will happen because of your appearance. Your Private Body Talk often uses words like *always* or *never*. For example, "I look so over-the-hill, I'll *never* be asked out." "I'll *never* get a good job as long as I'm fat," or, "I'll *always* be a nobody because of my looks." Misfortune Telling can also distort expectations about some specific situation, such as, "I'll have a terrible time wearing this bathing suit at the beach," or, "Once George sees me naked, our relationship will be over." Did you detect the Mind Misreading that's going on here too?

In disputing this distorted thinking, you should again see that you are jumping to conclusions in the absence of clear evidence. How do you really know that your worst fears will come true? You need to separate your emotions from your judgments of your future. Here's how:

◎ Realize that your pessimism may actually emanate from the expectation that you'll feel self-conscious in some situation. In fact, your discomfort is probably the worst thing that will happen. So quit making dire predictions and start finding ways to lower your self-consciousness in the situation. Hint: Does the phrase Body-and-Mind Relaxation ring a comforting bell?

◎ Talk back to a thought like "I'll never be loved because of my appearance," by stating what's really happening here: "I'm *worried* that I won't be loved." By definition, your future hasn't occurred yet; it's your despondence or apprehension that's occurring. If you focus on feeling better about your appearance, you'll feel less apprehensive. Tackle any other worries separately.

◎ Analyze the evidence. Have your pessimistic predictions always come true? Think about experiences in which events turned out more favorably than you'd expected. What did you do to make a difference?

◎ Listen to your New Inner Voice say, "I'm going to quit worrying about the future and concentrate on now. What can I do now to prove my doom-and-gloom predictions wrong?" Instead of deciding that your future will be disappointing or even disastrous, figure out what you can do to make it more tolerable—perhaps even pleasant. Create a plan.

Helpsheet for Change:
Correcting the Misfortune Telling Distortion
by Talking Back

A typical activating situation or event is

_____

_____

My distorted Private Body Talk often says

_____

_____

_____

_____

_____

_____

_____

To dispute this Misfortune Telling Distortion with corrective thinking, my New Inner Voice talks back and says

_____

_____

_____

_____

_____

_____

_____

_____

Correcting Your Beauty Bound Distortions

You fall prey to the Beauty Bound Distortion when you think, "I can't do that because of my looks." This is a hazardous distortion because it can set in motion self-fulfilling prophecies. For example, suppose you tell yourself you're too fat to go to the pool party. Misfortune Telling and Mind Misreading drive you to make this Beauty Bound mistake in your thinking. So, you pass on the party and sit at home lamenting that your "loathsome looks" have robbed you of a good time—again! The Beauty Bound Distortion can also create Catch-22s like "I can't go to the gym and exercise to lose weight until I lose weight."

Guess what? In Step 6 I'll teach you some terrific behavioral techniques to prevail over the limits you allow Beauty Bound thinking to set for you. But first, here are some ways to talk back to this distortion:

◎ Ask yourself, "So *why can't I* do such-and-such?" For instance, "I can't go to the class reunion unless I lose twenty pounds." Why not? Will there be a sign posted that says "Heavy Folks Not Admitted under Penalty of Law"? Your answer is, "Because I am self-conscious about my weight and will worry about what others are thinking." Dispute your Misfortune Telling and Mind Misreading mistakes. It's your own discomfort stopping you, not your looks or what other people are truly thinking.

◎ Talk back to "I can't do it" by asking *"How can I* do it? What would make it easier to do?" For example, "I can't go to the mall with this haircut" becomes "I *can* go if I wear my favorite hat." Replace "I can't go to the gym until I lose more weight" with "I can go to the gym if I use Body-and-Mind Relaxation to put me in control and at ease."

◎ Face the fact that other people who are far from perfect physical specimens engage in the same activities that you deny yourself. Do they all really look better than you or do they refuse to be deprived of involvement in life simply because they aren't perfect? Will you really have the only imperfect body at the gym or the pool party?

◎ Remind yourself of other experiences in your life in which you've accomplished things that you first felt insecure about until you gave yourself a little push, took them on, and mastered them. How did it feel to prove to yourself that you can overcome obstacles and succeed?

◎ When you Beauty Bound yourself, how do you feel? Frustrated? Angry? Dejected? Imagine how you would feel if you stood up to "I can't" by saying, "I can too." Imagine that you face your apprehension and do it anyway. How would you feel? Relieved? More confident? More in control?

◎ Counter your pessimism with motivating experiences. Read the inspirational, not-just-for-children, book *The Little Engine That Could*. "I think I can! I think I can!"

Helpsheet for Change:
Correcting the Beauty Bound Distortion
by Talking Back

A typical activating situation or event is

_____

_____

My distorted Private Body Talk often says

_____

_____

_____

_____

_____

_____

_____

To dispute this Beauty Bound Distortion with corrective thinking, my New Inner
Voice talks back and says

_____

_____

_____

_____

_____

_____

_____

_____

Correcting Your Moody Mirror Distortions

Now let's work on the Moody Mirror mistake, which involves emotional reasoning. It can happen in several ways. When you are "feeling ugly," you take your negative emotion as proof that you *are* ugly. You search for any or all things about your looks that might justify your feelings. The Moody Mirror Distortion may also occur when you're in a bad mood or upset about something other than your appearance; your nasty mood contagiously infects your Private Body Talk. Moody Mirror thinking precipitates other mental mistakes, carrying you from one distortion to another and from one criticism to another, in feverish waves of distress.

Corrective thinking treats the spreading infection. The key is to realize that your bad mood came first, and you conveniently point to your looks to rationalize your distress. Other people with identical physical "flaws" do not necessarily feel as bad as you feel. An inferiority complex doesn't exist on the same genes that give you a short stature or a receding hairline or extra cushioning for your butt.

How often have you heard people find fault with their own looks, while your impression of their appearance is not as negative as theirs, perhaps not even negative at all? A friend says to you, "My hair looks terrible," yet objectively you can see that it looks fine. Or you hear a woman protest, "My hips are as big as a buffalo's," and knowing how big buffalo hips really are, you toss aside her comment as an exaggeration much larger than her hips. You're not that person, so you can be unemotionally objective. You see that the individual's actual appearance isn't really the problem—even if your friend's hair could look better or the woman's hips could be smaller. The problem is what the person believes and feels.

The following corrective thinking tactics can cure your Moody Mirror infections:

◎ Approach the Moody Mirror by thinking more objectively, as an unbiased observer would. Catch the distortion as soon as you notice your mood and before the discontent spreads. Like a snowball rolling down a hill, the farther it goes the larger and more forceful it becomes. Stopping it is much easier at the top of the hill than near the bottom. Realize that obsessing over your physical imperfections doesn't fix what's wrong. The obsessing itself is what's wrong.

◎ Use a mental *STOP* sign to halt your Private Body Talk. Listen to your New Inner Voice say, "I'm not feeling very attractive right now. This isn't a good time to contemplate my looks. I'm just making myself feel worse. So stop it!" Or you may say, "Here I go again, blasting my body when it's merely an innocent bystander." Step away from this Private Body Talk (after a brief apology, of course, to your body for the false accusations). Then follow the Equal Time Rule, and compliment yourself.

◎ Ask yourself this: "Was something else already bothering me before I started worrying about or criticizing my body?" Then say, "Okay, my appearance isn't really the issue here. I've had a really lousy day. That's what I've got to handle now. I'm going to leave my looks out of this." Suppose you've upset yourself by criticizing your face. Then you begin to insult your weight. Catch yourself

Helpsheet for Change:
Correcting the Moody Mirror Distortion
by Talking Back

A typical activating situation or event is

_____

_____

My distorted Private Body Talk often says

_____

_____

_____

_____

_____

_____

_____

To dispute this Moody Mirror Distortion with corrective thinking, my New Inner Voice talks back and says

_____

_____

_____

_____

_____

_____

_____

_____

and say, "Okay, I'm at it again. Being dissatisfied with my face is no reason to pick on other things about my looks."

◎   Replace "I *am*" thoughts with "I *feel*" thoughts. For example, replace "I *am* aw-ful-looking in this outfit" with "I *feel* less happy with this outfit than I'd like." Then deal with your feelings by correcting other distortions that caused your body image distress in the first place.

◎   Fixating on feelings often intensifies them, like dwelling on the sensations of a headache intensifies your pain. So *shift your attention* to something that can create different feelings. Pull yourself out of the emotional quicksand. Read the comics in the newspaper, watch a television sitcom, take a brisk walk, or im-merse yourself in Body-and-Mind Relaxation. If you're with other people, redi-rect the conversation to amusing or interesting topics.

◎   Your New Inner Voice repeats this variant of an old saying: "If I can't say any-thing nice about myself, I won't say anything at all." Then shift gears!

Making Corrective Thinking a Natural Part of Your Life

Using the Helpsheets for Change, you have helped your New Inner Voice find the right words to begin to create inner experiences that are free of painful distortions. This is such an important beginning. Still, I know that many of you aren't quite ready to carry out corrective thinking in the here-and-now Private Body Talk of everyday life. So, here's an intermediate routine to help you practice your corrective thinking:

◎   Look at the Helpsheet for Practicing Corrective Thinking on the next page. Photocopy the Helpsheet or just copy its format into your diary. For your most common distortions, use this Helpsheet to develop effective corrective think-ing. Complete a separate one for different episodes of body image distress.

◎   Review entries in your Body Image Diary to find real-life examples of your Private Body Talk that reflect the distortions you commit most frequently. Your diary captures these, of course, as the B (Belief) point in the ABC Sequences.

◎   Write out your faulty Private Body Talk on the Helpsheet and identify which distortions are evident.

◎   Reread my discussion and examples of how to dispute these mental mistakes. Then reread the Helpsheets for corrective thinking that you completed to begin to correct each of these distortions.

◎   Finally, write out your own corrective thinking. Talk back to your Private Body Talk with the New Inner Voice that works best for you. The strongest weapons in your arsenal are arguments that dispute more than one distortion.

Helpsheet for Change:
Practicing Corrective Thinking

My distorted Private Body Talk says:

_____

_____

This Private Body Talk contains these distortions:

_____

_____

_____

_____

_____

_____

To dispute my distortions with corrective thinking, my New Inner Voice talks back and says

_____

_____

_____

_____

_____

_____

_____

_____

Your Dress Rehearsal

Changing your painful Private Body Talk is a *learned skill.* The more often you speak with your New Inner Voice, the more effortlessly you'll be able to change your old mental "tapes." With this in mind, bolster your New Inner Voice as follows:

◎ Silently reread your "scripts"—the corrective dialogues you've written down using the previous Helpsheet. Make any adjustments you need.

◎ Read these aloud. Hear yourself say them in your own voice.

◎ Next, read your corrective dialogues aloud again, but this time tape-record them.

◎ Listen to your tape once a day for the next week. Soon you'll be able to anticipate exactly what you'll say next on the tape. What you're doing is internalizing your corrective thinking. You're hearing your New Inner Voice as your own voice.

Stop, Look, and Listen

Now you're prepared to change your problematic Private Body Talk in daily life. Whenever you have negative feelings about your looks, three words should immediately pop into your mind: *Stop, Look,* and *Listen.*

◎ First, *Stop* your Private Body Talk in midsentence. You literally think, "Stop!" as you flash a big, red, stop sign in your mind and interrupt your stream of thought.

◎ Then *Look* at the ABCs of your experience. What's the *A* (the Activating event) that triggered your distress? Then, jump to the *C* (the Consequences) to ask, "What emotions am I feeling right now?" Finally, what's the *B* (your Beliefs)? "What am I thinking here that's making me upset?" Be aware of familiar Appearance Assumptions and Body Image Distortions that lurk behind your distress. Thus, you *Look* at the precipitating situation, at your reaction, and at the Private Body Talk that fuels your emotions.

◎ Finally, you *Listen* to a more reasonable, realistic point of view. Right then and there, talk back to yourself with your New Inner Voice and correct your troublesome thinking. To undo your discomfort, take a minute or so listening to the better judgment of your New Inner Voice. Talk to yourself just as you would to a good friend who's said the same unfair, critical things about himself or herself that you've just privately said about yourself.

Treat Yourself

It's a fact of life that people are more likely to behave in ways that are *rewarded* and *rewarding* than ways that aren't. Rewarding yourself for corrective thinking is crucial. Mentally recognize your efforts and commend your successes.

For example, my former client Laurie was working on her most common mental mistake, the Unfair-to-Compare Distortion. She wanted to stop comparing herself with her more slender best friend when they shopped and tried on clothes together. Laurie's New Inner Voice reminded her that her friend wasn't really making her *look bad*. Laurie's own arbitrary comparisons were making her *feel bad*. She thought about the fact that she is actually more slender than many other people she knows. She shifted her attention to the real goals of the day—to buy a bra and, more importantly, to have fun with her dearest friend. Laurie recognized that her New Inner Voice had changed her experience. She had forestalled her usual Private Body Talk which, in the past, would have left her in tears and envious of her friend. So she said to herself, "I really took charge of my mind and my emotions. Good for me!" She bought a new compact disc to celebrate and reward her success.

A New Diary for a New Body Image

Rewarding your efforts concretely is important. However, the most important and immediate payoff of corrective thinking is the change in how you feel. It's so great to feel less anxious, despondent, frustrated, or ashamed about your appearance. These beneficial effects are essential to recognize explicitly. So you will! You should now add a final step to your ABCD Sequence of body image experiences. Add an *E* for the *Effects* of your corrective thinking, which will identify the emotional improvements that result from your active efforts in changing your Private Body Talk.

It's time to trade your old Body Image Diary in for a new and improved version—your *Corrective Thinking Diary*. From now on, use this version to record your Disputing of distortions and the Effects of this corrective thinking on your daily life. Turn to the following page and see how your new diary is laid out.

After a body image experience in which you successfully disputed your distressing Private Body Talk with corrective thinking, record the sequence of events in your new diary.

Final Words of Encouragement

There are some important things to keep in mind as you apply corrective thinking in your everyday life. Your first attempts at corrective thinking may seem odd or unnatural, like a new pair of shoes. That's certainly understandable. Your Old Inner Voice is so familiar that your New Inner Voice may not sound like you. Don't worry, it will soon. Moreover, don't expect that corrective thinking will cause your body image distress to disappear immediately and totally. Initially, it will mostly prevent your distress from getting out of hand, so appreciate that "less bad" is good. Because new events or situations may necessitate different words from your New Inner Voice, be flexible and be innovative.

Patience is a key virtue here. Human change is gradual. I remember a client who, after a couple of days of corrective thinking, complained that despite his efforts he still hated his body. He concluded, "Either this doesn't work or, if it does, I'm a hopeless case." Eventually, after becoming more patient with himself, he came to see that both

Helpsheet for Change:
My Corrective Thinking Diary

Date: _____

ABCDE Sequence

ACTIVATORS: _____

_____

_____

BELIEFS: _____

_____

_____

CONSEQUENCES: _____

_____

_____

DISPUTING by Corrective Thinking: _____

_____

_____

_____

_____

EFFECTS of My Corrective Thinking: _____

_____

_____

_____

Don't forget to reward your efforts and successes!

explanations were untrue. So be patient and be sure to applaud your accomplishments, but accept any tough times as expected "bumps in the road." Never give yourself a hard time for having a hard time. That only makes it worse. And you don't deserve worse!

Step 5
Your Path for Progress

★ You have discovered the Body Image Distortions that are typically evident in your episodes of body image distress.

★ You're finding the words with which your New Inner Voice can effectively challenge and dispute your faulty Private Body Talk. Using Helpsheets for Change, you have reviewed, rehearsed, and fine-tuned your corrective thinking. You are strengthening your New Inner Voice's ability to talk back and overpower your old, upsetting Private Body Talk.

★ You're applying corrective thinking in your everyday life. As you encounter a difficult situation, you are able to Stop, Look, and Listen and actively use corrective thinking to change how you feel.

★ With your new Corrective Thinking Diary, you're monitoring and recording the ABCDE Sequence of your daily body image experiences. In addition to the familiar ABC, you've added a *D* for Disputing your Body Image Distortions and an *E* for its effects in altering your body image emotions.

★ You're continuing to use your Body-and-Mind Relaxation to manage stress in your life, including the stress caused by your body image.

★ You continue questioning the Appearance Assumptions that set you up for a negative body image.

★ You're being realistic in your expectations and patient with yourself. Reward your efforts and enjoy your progress!

Step 6: Hide and Seek

Defeating Your Self-Defeating Behaviors

Jimmy does it in the morning before leaving home for work and again in the evening before heading out to his favorite night spots. When he's not doing it, he still thinks about it a lot. It consumes much of his time and his thoughts. Although it does help him feel better for a little while, it gives him no enduring pleasure. He feels trapped by it and tries to stop, but he can't seem to help himself.

What's Jimmy hooked on? Some bizarre and secretive sexual practice? Crack cocaine? Booze? Not at all. Like over thirty million other men in the United States, Jimmy suffers from androgenetic alopecia. Don't worry, it's not a disease: Jimmy has normal male pattern balding. And it drives him crazy. So what does he do? He counts the hairs lost forever as they swirl down his shower's drain. He mousses and meticulously combs the remaining strands over his visible scalp. He scrutinizes his scalp in the mirror from every possible vantage point. Jimmy's hooked on disliking his looks. His fix is fixing his hair.

Linda is quite a "fashion plate." Whatever she wears, it is always chic and well coordinated. Her hair and makeup are impeccable. Although her friends are a little envious of her striking appearance, they often tell her how terrific she looks. Most people would assume that Linda derives tremendous satisfaction from being so attractive. But she doesn't. In fact, Linda regularly ruminates that she doesn't look "right." Getting ready each morning takes up to two hours. Dressing for a social event requires that she change clothes three or four times. Each outfit somehow seems to reveal something "awful" about her body. Because Linda worries that her thighs are huge and that her stomach sticks out, she must find an outfit that won't betray her "ugly secrets." Terrified of gaining any weight, Linda diets constantly and she nervously weighs herself several times a day.

Self-Defeating Self-Defenses

With Steps 4 and 5, you began changing the faulty mental assumptions and distortions that provoke and perpetuate your painful body image experiences. Now, in Step 6, you'll learn how to change certain bothersome behavior patterns. As the stories about Jimmy and Linda illustrated, people engage in all kinds of behaviors to manage their appearance and to deal with their disturbing Private Body Talk. From monitoring the ABC Sequence of your own body image experiences, you probably see that you try to avoid certain Activators that set off discomfort. Among your Consequences, you may see specific self-protective actions you take to manage your misery once it's begun. Body image distress, whether actually experienced or merely expected, will usually set in motion behavior patterns for self-defense. These maneuvers are efforts to correct, conceal, or compensate for what you *think* is wrong with your looks. However, these habitual behavior patterns create their own problems. They stir up their own distress and then, paradoxically, are used to cope with the difficulties they've caused. Unfortunately, these well-learned patterns reinforce the conviction that your looks are somehow defective. Put simply, your self-defenses are self-defeating!

So why would you continue to do such things? The answer is self-protection: You want to avoid or escape feeling bad about your looks. You develop these behaviors to protect you, so that bad events either won't happen or, if they do, so that they won't be nearly as unpleasant. Psychologists call this *learning by negative reinforcement*. This is entirely different from *learning by positive reinforcement*, in which we do things because they reward us with positive outcomes and emotions.

Thus, self-protective actions are motivated more by preventing discomfort than by providing pleasure. With these actions, you either can try to hide (avoid, disguise, or flee) the problem, or you can compulsively seek to make it go away. These two patterns of behavioral self-defense—hiding and seeking—are called *Evasive Actions* and *Appearance-Preoccupied Rituals*. I want you to understand that such patterns of self-protection are really acts of self-rejection. You are rejecting the acceptability of your body, which worsens your body image and your self-esteem. Figure 6.1 shows how these self-protective patterns emerge in the flow of your body image experiences.

In Step 6, first you'll discover your own Evasive Actions. Then you'll identify your Appearance-Preoccupied Rituals. The remainder of this step will guide you in changing the patterns that are problematic for you. So, let's get going with self-discoveries.

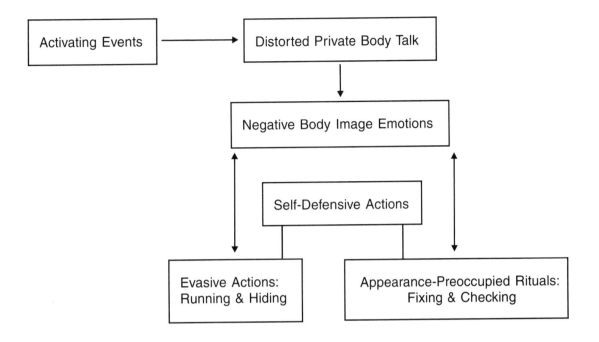

Figure 6.1. Your Unfolding Body Image Experiences:
The Role of Self-Defensive Actions

Discovering Your Evasive Actions

People with a negative body image will often go to great lengths to avoid displaying their "defects," not only to others but also to themselves. Let's closely examine two basic kinds of Evasive Actions—*Running* and *Hiding*.

Running

If you go back and review your Distressing Situations Test from Step 1 and the entries in your Body Image Diary, you'll probably find various situations and activities that you "run from." When you commit the Beauty Bound Distortion, you forbid yourself to do certain things because of your looks. You avoid them because they threaten you with feelings of self-consciousness, shame, anxiety, or embarrassment. What you avoid falls into one or more of four categories, the Four *P*s: *practices, places, people,* and *poses.*

The following self-tests list some common examples of each category, but these do not exhaust the possibilities. As you read a given self-test item, decide if *any one* of the item's examples or a comparable activity applies to you. On the blank line after each item, write down exactly what you avoid. Then, use the 0 to 4 numerical rating scale to indicate, to the left of the item, how often you avoid that practice, place, person, or pose in trying to protect yourself from body image discomfort.

✤ ✤ ✤ ✤ ✤

1. Do You Avoid Certain *Practices*?

Here are some activities commonly avoided by people with a negative body image. How often do you avoid any of them?

0	1	2	3	4
Never	Sometimes	Moderately Often	Often	Almost Always or Always

_____ Wearing clothes of a style, color, or fabric that might reveal your "flaws."
I avoid: _____

_____ Some physical activity that might call attention to your body's appearance—such as exercising, dancing, or playing certain recreational sports.
I avoid: _____

_____ Being photographed or videotaped.
I avoid: _____

_____ Some normal activity in which somebody might see you not fixed up—such as going to the grocery with sweats on, going to your mailbox or answering your doorbell without makeup on, or going for a walk without your hair fixed.
I avoid: _____

_____ Some activity that might "mess up" your appearance—for example, an activity like swimming that would wet your your hair or wash off your makeup.
I avoid: _____

_____ Eating heartily in the presence of others for fear they'll think you're fat—so you abstain, nibble, or order light.
I avoid: _____

_____ Paying attention to your body—for example, weighing yourself, viewing your mirror reflection or a photo of yourself—because "what you can't see can't hurt you!"
I avoid: _____

_____ Certain physical contact—such as giving or receiving hugs—that might disclose to others how your body feels.
I avoid: _____

_____ Allowing your partner to see you "in the buff."
I avoid: _____

_____ Physical exams at the doctor's office—because you must bare too much or because you don't want to find out how much you "officially" weigh.
I avoid: _____

✤ ✤ ✤ ✤ ✤

❅ ❅ ❅ ❅ ❅

2. Do You Avoid Certain *Places*?

If you have a poor body image, I'll bet we won't find you in some of the following locations. How often do you avoid these places?

0	1	2	3	4
Never	Sometimes	Moderately Often	Often	Almost Always or Always

_____ Any place where your body is relatively exposed—such as at the pool or beach, in dressing rooms or public showers.
I avoid: _____

_____ Places in which appearance is emphasized—such as dressy occasions or singles' gatherings.
I avoid: _____

_____ Certain clothing stores where your appearance is "on display" to sales clerks or other customers.
I avoid: _____

_____ Places with prominent mirrors—such as department-store dressing rooms or exercise classes in mirrored rooms.
I avoid: _____

_____ Places with conditions that might make your "flaws" more visible—for example, brightly lit environments.
I avoid: _____

❅ ❅ ❅ ❅ ❅

❅ ❅ ❅ ❅ ❅

3. Do You Avoid Certain *People*?

Being around particular types of individuals can be troublesome for folks with a negative body image. How often do you avoid these people?

0	1	2	3	4
Never	Sometimes	Moderately Often	Often	Almost Always or Always

_____ People who are good-looking in ways you'd like to be—for example, tall, thin, tanned, or well built.
I avoid: _____

_____ Good-looking members of the other sex.
I avoid: _____

_____ People who do a lot of things to "look good"—for example, people who diet, exercise regularly, or wear stylish clothes.
I avoid: _____

_____ Persons who talk a great deal about physical appearance—such as, what they or other people look like.
I avoid: _____

_____ People who might comment on your appearance—usually a friend or relative who's inclined to make unwanted comments about your weight, manner of dress, etc.
I avoid: _____

❉ ❉ ❉ ❉ ❉

❉ ❉ ❉ ❉ ❉

4. Do You Avoid Certain *Poses*?

You may try to avoid or be careful about particular poses or gestures, those that might accentuate disliked physical attributes and lead you to feel self-conscious. How often are you cautious about each of these?

0	1	2	3	4
Never	Sometimes	Moderately Often	Often	Almost Always or Always

_____ Where or how you sit or stand during social interaction—for instance, stances or profiles that might spotlight your disliked characteristics (e.g., body shape, height, posture, hair, or facial features).
I avoid: _____

_____ Gestures that may make your "defects" more pronounced—such as smiling (and exposing disliked teeth, dimples, or wrinkles) or hand gestures (which show short fingers or chipped nails).
I avoid: _____

_____ Particular positions during sexual relations—notably those that permit your partner to see areas of your body that you dislike.
I avoid: _____

❉ ❉ ❉ ❉ ❉

Hiding

In addition to Running, or avoiding, there is a second type of Evasive Action in which you attempt to protect yourself against negative body image feelings. This is Hiding, especially grooming to hide: people use various means to conceal or camouflage what they dislike about their looks. Certain Appearance Assumptions that you discovered in Step 4 can lead you to disguise what you despise. For example, if you assume that your actual, unadorned appearance is noticeably unacceptable and will taint others' impressions of you, you'll probably want to hide what you really look like.

The tools and materials of bodily adornment act as mood-altering substances. People wear certain clothing, jewelry, cosmetics, and hairstyles either to feel attractive ("positive reinforcement") or to feel less unappealing and shield their shortcomings from others ("negative reinforcement"). Of course, the latter is a self-protective way of grooming to hide.

How do people groom to hide? The heavy-hipped lady shrouds her shape with dark, loose-fitting attire. The thin guy wears long-sleeved shirts and long pants year-round to cloak his skinny arms and legs. The older woman conceals her wrinkled complexion with layers of makeup. She wears tinted glasses to camouflage the bags beneath her eyes. The balding man hides beneath his hat. The teenager with a birthmark on her neck keeps it covered with high-collared blouses. The man with protruding ears veils them with his long hair.

Think about your own physical characteristics that bother you. What do you do to hide them so they'll be less apparent to others? List these behaviors on the following Self-Discovery Helpsheet. Use the familiar rating scale to convey how often you engage in your acts of concealment.

Discovering Your Appearance-Preoccupied Rituals

Appearance-Preoccupied Rituals are repetitive efforts at body image "damage control." With these patterns, people compulsively seek remedies to fix whatever they suspect might be wrong with their appearance. Individuals trapped in such rituals spend inordinate amounts of time, money, and effort to "look right." Unlike the self-conscious avoiders of mirrors, these people may practically live in front of their mirrors, fussing over and fixing every perceived flaw. Their Private Body Talk constantly nags them about how they look. Appearance-Preoccupied Rituals come in two forms—*Fixing* and *Checking*.

Appearance Fixing

Fixing Rituals involve elaborate and meticulous efforts to manage or modify your appearance. You must do a lot of things with a lot of precision to be satisfied that you look okay. Special social situations may demand even more time and perfection in figuring out what to wear. If something doesn't appear (or feel) quite right, you may start your fixing all over again. How frustrating!

Self-Discovery Helpsheet:
How Am I Grooming to Hide?

List any of the ways in which you use clothes, cosmetics, or hairstyles to conceal or disguise what you consider to be your physical flaws. Then rate how often you do each one.

0	1	2	3	4
Never	*Sometimes*	*Moderately Often*	*Often*	*Almost Always or Always*

1. _____

2. _____

3. _____

4. _____

5. _____

6. _____

7. _____

8. _____

9. _____

10. _____

❀ ❀ ❀ ❀ ❀

Here are some telltale signs of Appearance-Preoccupied Fixing Rituals. Think about each one and decide how often you become fixated on fixing.

0	1	2	3	4
Never	*Sometimes*	*Moderately Often*	*Often*	*Almost Always or Always*

_____ At home, getting out of the bathroom and getting dressed on time is a rare feat.

_____ You primp and preen more than you want. Rationally, you know you look fine. Emotionally and behaviorally you just can't leave well enough alone.

_____ Different situations demand that you change what you're wearing. Otherwise, you worry that your looks might be inappropriate.

_____ Other individuals in your household have remarked on the amount of time you spend on your appearance. Their comments may range from friendly kidding to irritation at having to wait for you to get ready.

_____ You purchase clothing, jewelry, or grooming products that you seldom wear or use. At first, you were sure that they were what you needed to improve your looks. Ultimately, they didn't meet your expectations.

_____ Before going out, you change clothes or redo your hair several times until you're satisfied that you look okay.

_____ When you see yourself in a mirror, you reflexively adjust some aspect of your appearance—like your hair, your tie, or your dress—even though nothing was really amiss.

_____ You regularly make major modifications in your appearance—for example, changing hairstyles or hair colors, or getting cosmetic makeovers.

_____ Gaining a couple of pounds or the experience of feeling fat compels you to go on a dietary fast or to greatly restrict your eating for several days.

_____ Gaining a couple of pounds or the experience of feeling fat compels you to exercise more intensely for several days.

❖ ❖ ❖ ❖ ❖

Appearance Checking

The second type of pattern, Checking Rituals, usually coexist with Fixing Rituals. The recurrent thought that something might be unsatisfactory with your grooming preoccupies you and makes you ill at ease. Your Private Body Talk has an answer to its nagging notion that you might not look okay: "Better check it out!" So, to quiet your mind, you check it out.

Let me suggest an analogy. As you're tucked in bed and dozing off to sleep, has the question, "I wonder if I locked the door?" ever crossed your mind? You are 99.9 percent certain that you did. But the question lingers, and you can't seem to put it to rest. So what do you do? That's right, you get out of bed and go to check that the door is latched. It is. Now you can start counting sheep.

The principal aim of Checking Rituals is to *seek and obtain relief* from the unsettling worries about your appearance. Checking Rituals are sometimes willful, deliberate attempts to avoid worrying. At other times, they are mindlessly automatic reactions, because they've become well-practiced habits.

Check out the following signs of this pattern. To what extent does each example describe you?

❊ ❊ ❊ ❊ ❊

0	1	2	3	4
Never	Sometimes	Moderately Often	Often	Almost Always or Always

_____ You have intrusive thoughts that tell you to inspect your appearance. These thoughts are hard to push out of your head until you've acted on them.

_____ Whenever you pass by a mirror (or other reflecting surface), you check to see that your appearance is okay.

_____ You visit the restroom with the conscious intent of checking your appearance, even though you have no good reason to think that something is wrong with your looks.

_____ If concerned about your weight, you frequently weigh yourself to find out if you've gained or lost any small amount. Whenever scales are available, it's hard to resist weighing yourself.

_____ You routinely check out other people's opinions about your looks to seek reassurance that you look okay. Trusted loved ones or friends are typically asked: "Do you think I look okay? Are you sure? (Are you *really* sure?)"

_____ In social situations, you repeatedly check how your appearance compares with what others look like, so that you feel more certain that your appearance is acceptable.

❊ ❊ ❊ ❊ ❊

What Are Your Appearance-Preoccupied Rituals?

Review your self-tests. Identify the repetitive Fixing Rituals and the Checking Rituals that you engage in. Write down your Appearance-Preoccupied Rituals on the Helpsheet on the following page. For each type of ritual, first list the ones you rated as 4 on the self-tests, then list the 3s, next the 2s, and finally the 1s.

Avoiding Avoidance by Facing It

Having identified the self-defeating behavior patterns linked to a negative body image, it's time to learn how to control them, instead of letting them control you. Let's start with your Evasive Actions.

An effective way to control avoidance is to "avoid avoiding" by using an active strategy called *Facing It*. There is substantial scientific proof that people can overcome their anxieties by gradually exposing themselves to whatever they anxiously avoid. Here you apprehensively avoid looking bad or feeling bad about your looks.

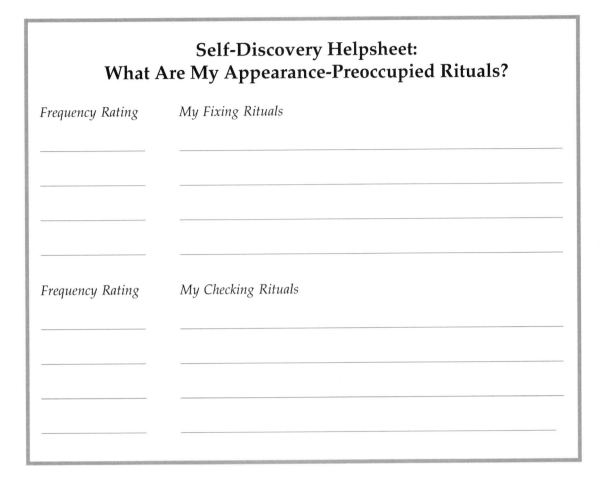

You've already acquired most of the skills you need to face down your Evasive Actions. You've learned Body-and-Mind Relaxation. You've learned how to construct Ladders of Success and how to do Mirror Desensitization. You've also cultivated your New Inner Voice—an essential ally for Facing It.

Building Your Ladder of Success for Facing It

Here's what you need to do to get ready for Facing It:

◎ Go back to the Evasive Actions self-tests on pages 146-148. Review the practices, places, people, and poses that you avoid due to the experience or expectation of discomfort.

◎ Make a simple judgment about each situation or activity that you avoid. This is a judgment that psychologists call *self-efficacy*. Self-efficacy is your degree of confidence that you could actually enter the situation or engage in the activity. For instance, let's suppose that you avoid going swimming at the community pool because you're self-conscious in a swimsuit and worry that you look unattractive with wet hair. Ask yourself, "How confident am I that I could actually go take a dip in the pool?" Your answer is your self-efficacy for this activity.

◎ Give each item on your list a self-efficacy rating from 0 to 100. A rating of 0 means "No way. Never in a zillion years would I be able to do that." A rating of 100 says, "I'm 100 percent certain that I can do that." A judgment of 50 means a fifty-fifty chance that you could face it. Write down your self-efficacy rating in the margin next to each self-test item you listed as avoided practices, places, people, or poses.

◎ Now design a Ladder of Success similar to what you did for Desensitization in Step 3. From all four self-tests, transcribe the items and their self-efficacy ratings to the new Helpsheet on the following page, your Facing It ladder. Put the hardest items (with the *lowest* self-efficacy ratings) at the top of the ladder and the easiest ones (with the *highest* ratings) at the bottom.

◎ Make sure your list contains a reasonable range of ratings, though most should be under 50 (that is, fairly difficult). If two or more items have the same numerical rating, decide which is really a little more difficult and list it on a higher rung. If an activity or situation is too general, be more specific. For example, "going to dance clubs" becomes "going to The Coconut Club with Karen." Drop any item that isn't practically feasible. You can't go to the beach if it's below freezing outside right now.

◎ If all or nearly all of your items are rated below 50, yours is a hard-to-do list. If most are rated above 50, it's an easy-to-do list. Try to even out a lopsided list, by adding a few more Evasive Actions, either easy or hard, or by modifying the ones you have to make them more or less difficult to do.

Learning to PACE Yourself

Next you will engage in the practices you avoid, go to the places you avoid, be with the people you avoid, and strike the poses you avoid. Don't worry, you'll do this gradually, a step at a time. You'll start out at the lowest rung on the ladder—the easiest one to do. Success at each step will take you up the ladder to master more difficult experiences.

I understand that you're apprehensive about facing these uncomfortable situations. Otherwise you wouldn't be avoiding them in the first place, right? So you may already be talking to yourself about what you're *not* going to do. Don't retreat! Together we'll formulate a positive plan of action so that you will be victorious over avoidance.

Facing It always has four fundamental steps: *Prepare*, *Act*, *Cope*, and *Enjoy*. The first letters of these four steps remind you to *PACE* yourself. Here's how it works:

◎ *Prepare*: You'll Prepare for Facing It by writing down your strategy in advance. This first step is crucial, as it involves your planning and rehearsing the remaining three steps. In this step, you decide exactly what you're going to do and when you're going to do it. You figure out how you'll talk back to your Old Inner Voice of avoidance that says, "No, I can't. Not now. I'll do it some other time." By anticipating what pessimistic thoughts will probably run

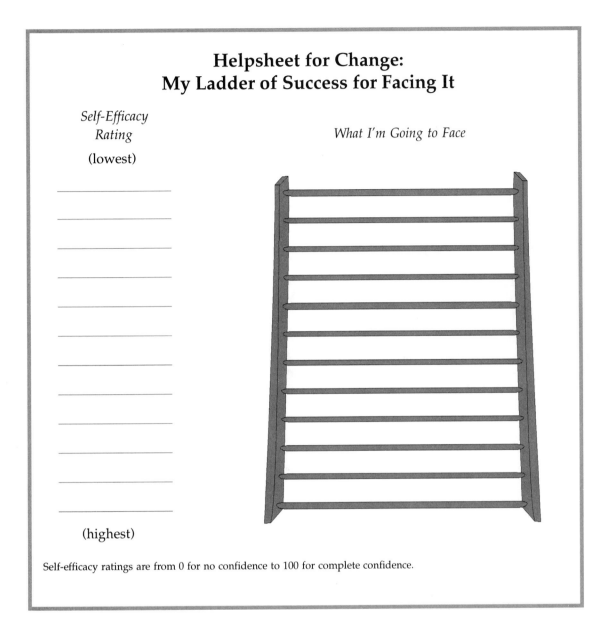

Helpsheet for Change:
My Ladder of Success for Facing It

Self-Efficacy
Rating

(lowest)

What I'm Going to Face

(highest)

Self-efficacy ratings are from 0 for no confidence to 100 for complete confidence.

through your mind and how you might feel, you can decide precisely how you'll handle them should they occur. Finally, promise to reward your efforts at Facing It. Determine ahead of time what your reward will be—a special treat, some affordable trinket, a cone of tasty frozen yogurt, or a relaxing moment with your favorite music. Having spelled out this detailed plan using the Helpsheet on page 158, rehearse it in your mind.

◎ *Act*: The time has arrived to Face It and carry out your plan. To warm up "cold feet," either give yourself the pep talk you've prepared, engage in a moment of Body-and-Mind Relaxation, or do whatever else will help you follow through. And off you go! As you begin confronting what you've so often avoided, encourage yourself and commend yourself. Good for you!

◎ *Cope*: Uncomfortable thoughts and feelings come as no surprise attack. You expected them, and you accept them. Just draw upon the coping skills you've learned and roll with any discomfort. For example, use planned corrective thinking or elements of Body-and-Mind Relaxation, like calming imagery or breathing techniques. Reassure yourself that you *can* handle this. Remind yourself that you *are* handling it.

◎ *Enjoy*: There, you Faced It! But don't forget the deal. Facing It earns a reward. Applaud your accomplishment, don't criticize it. Never "Yes, but" yourself by saying "Yes, I did it, but. . . . " Just Enjoy your success. Relish your reward. You deserve it.

Preparing Your PACE Plans

The My Plan for Facing It Helpsheet on page 158 is for developing your PACE plan of action for each item on your ladder. Make copies and fill them out as you climb each rung of your Facing It Ladder of Success. To assist your beneficial use of this Helpsheet, see the example on page 157, in which Jason is facing one of his Evasive Actions—avoiding being photographed. He always feels self-conscious and never thinks he looks good in pictures. Because his girlfriend really enjoys having photos of the two of them together, he would really like to get over this.

◎ Having seen Jason's plan for Facing It, create your first plan. Start at the bottom rung of your ladder, with the activity or situation that you're reasonably confident you can face. Prepare by drafting your plan for Facing It.

◎ Decide how you will Act. Specify the place, date, time, duration, and frequency of your action. For example, suppose your item reads, "I avoid standing anywhere that people are behind me and can see the shape of my rear." Your action plan might be, "Each day at work for the next five days, at 10 A.M. and 4 P.M., I'll spend five minutes at the file cabinets where my coworkers can see me from behind."

◎ Now write down your plans to Cope. Remember, your goal is not that you be totally free from discomfort while facing what you avoid. Your goal is just to carry out the activity and cope with any discomfort you feel. So, in my example, know that when you stand at the file cabinet you'll use pleasant imagery and certain corrective thinking to manage body image anxiety.

◎ What's the reward you'll Enjoy afterward? Be specific.

Implementing Your PACE Plans

Okay, you've prepared your plan by writing it out on the Helpsheet. Now what?

◎ Having scripted your plan, rehearse it. Mentally review exactly how will act, cope, and enjoy. Visualize yourself carrying out each step of your plan. Then . . . Ready . . . Set . . . Go execute your plan. Act . . . Cope . . . Enjoy!

Helpsheet for Change:
Jason's Plan for Facing It

Practice, Place, Person, or Pose Avoided:

The workout room at the gym.

Step-by-Step Plan for Facing It:

Prepare: Exactly what will I do?

First go when it's not crowded. Increase the length of my workout gradually. Eventually go when the "muscle guys" are there. I need to focus on how healthy I can be, not on other people's bodies.

Act: Where? When? For how long? What will I do if I get "cold feet"?

Weight room, 4 times per week, increments of five mins. until I do full workout. If I get cold feet I'll think of my hot tub reward.

Cope: What uncomfortable thoughts and feelings do I expect and how will I cope with them?

I'll be self-conscious, comparing my body with others around me.

Stay focused on the exercise, use my walkman to distract me from negative thoughts. Refuse to stare and compare!

Enjoy: How will I reward my efforts?

Soak in hot tub afterward.

What were the results of Facing It?

Did it. After three weeks I'm enjoying my workouts much more.

I'm getting better with free weights!

Helpsheet for Change:
My Plan for Facing It

Practice, Place, Person, or Pose Avoided:

_____

Step-by-Step Plan for Facing It:

Prepare: Exactly what will I do?

_____

_____

_____

_____

Act: Where? When? For how long? What will I do if I get "cold feet"?

_____

_____

Cope: What uncomfortable thoughts and feelings do I expect and how will I cope with them?

_____

_____

_____

Enjoy: How will I reward my efforts?

_____

_____

What were the results of Facing It?

_____

_____

◎ As you are moving up the ladder, if an item seems too hard to do, break it down into simpler steps. For example, the situation "having my partner see me naked" might begin with your partner seeing you in your underwear. No need to get naked until you're ready.

◎ Keep focused on the current rung of your ladder. Don't worry about rungs you haven't prepared for yet. You'll handle future concerns when you get there. Don't be like the guy who has trouble doing high school geometry because he starts worrying that he'll never be able to learn college calculus. Take one step at a time.

◎ After each accomplishment, however small, make a note of what worked best and record the results on your Helpsheet.

Onward and upward!

Coming Out of Hiding

With the second type of Evasive Action, you groom to hide what you dislike about your looks. The Facing It exercises to change these behaviors are identical to those used to confront the activities and situations that you avoid.

Building Your Facing It Ladder for Grooming to Hide

◎ Previously, on the Helpsheet on page 150, you listed your maneuvers for hiding what you don't like about your appearance. You know what to do next: Use this list to develop your next Ladder of Success for Facing It (on the following page).

◎ First rate your confidence in being able to *refrain* from using each particular action to conceal your looks.

◎ Next, organize and fine-tune your ladder from bottom (easiest item with the highest self-efficacy level) to top (hardest item with the lowest self-efficacy level).

◎ Because your grooming to hide takes place in a range of situations, pick specific contexts to work on. For example, suppose that you listed, "I always wear heavy cosmetics to conceal my freckles," or, "I usually wear long, baggy tops to hide my tummy," or "I wear baseball caps to hide my hair loss." For each of your behaviors, think of a couple of situations in which you could conceivably *not* do these things. Select common everyday situations such as going to class, walking around at the mall, or getting coffee at your local café. Choose situations in which *not* engaging in the behavior is reasonably acceptable for anyone. Nobody's asking you to wear a T-shirt that proclaims, "Look at My Huge Honker Nose" or to attend church in your bathing suit.

Helpsheet for Change:
My Ladder of Success for Facing It

*Self-Efficacy
Rating*

(lowest)

*How I Groom to Hide
(Specific Behaviors in Specific Situations)*

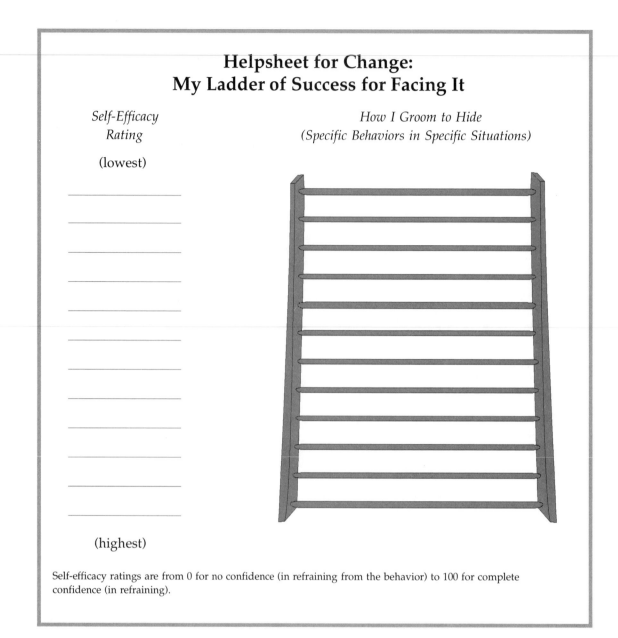

(highest)

Self-efficacy ratings are from 0 for no confidence (in refraining from the behavior) to 100 for complete confidence (in refraining).

Preparing and Executing Your Plans for Coming Out of Hiding

Having constructed your Ladder of Success, here's how you will "blow your cover" and come out of hiding:

◎ Start with the bottom item and PACE yourself. Use the Helpsheet format on page 162 to put down on paper how you will Prepare, Act, Cope, and Enjoy the success.

◎ Now rehearse each aspect of your plan.

◎ Afterward, carry out your plan, and acknowledge and write down the results.

◎ As usual, proceed to the next rung, and the next rung . . . , all the way to the top of the ladder.

◎ In halting your Evasive Actions, feel free to do a few items that entail facing avoided activities or situations, and then do some that involve coming out of hiding.

Before long, you'll see that your sense of self-efficacy and your ability to PACE yourself are much stronger. Avoiding and hiding are becoming patterns of the past. Facing It seems more like a game—a game of challenge and skill rather than one of chance and risk. And in the end, you'll be a winner!

Speaking of winners, I'd like tell you about Candice and Miguel, two people who successfully faced their Evasive Actions:

Candice would never leave home without layers of facial makeup. She was horrified that someone might see her and think she looked plain or unattractive. So Candice constructed her plan for Facing It. She started with something she felt she could do—go outside, without makeup, to her mailbox to retrieve her mail. She did this each day for five days. Next, she walked to a nearby park with less makeup than usual. Then, on three occasions with fewer and fewer cosmetics, she biked to a convenience store. Of course she felt somewhat nervous and self-conscious each time. But her discomfort diminished as she followed through with her plan. She used her mental imagery skills to calm her and relied on her New Inner Voice to control her Private Body Talk. Her corrective thinking countered thoughts that stemmed from the mental mistakes of Mind Misreading and Misfortune Telling. Candice capitalized on her love of exercise and focused on how invigorating the walk and the bike ride felt. After each trip, she rewarded herself by listening to Mozart. Ultimately, Candice freed herself from the necessity of hiding behind a mask of cosmetics. It felt so good to be able to be herself!

Miguel was intensely self-conscious, convinced that his penis was too small. When undressing or showering at the gym, he would always face a wall or wrap a towel around his waist to hide from potential embarrassment. Carrying out his Facing It plan, Miguel began by turning naturally in the direction of others during his shower. Soon, he could dress and undress in the locker room without having to shield himself with his towel. To manage self-consciousness, Miguel's New Inner Voice reminded him that nobody else really cared how big or small his penis was. He simply focused on how soothing the shower felt against his skin and on how well toned his abdominal muscles were. Later, he celebrated his courage with a frosted mug of his favorite imported beer. Cheers, Miguel!

Erasing Rituals

Now turn your attention to the other major self-defeating behavior pattern—Appearance-Preoccupied Rituals, in which you repeatedly fix and check your appearance. These time-consuming actions reinforce your body image discontent. After all, something must be wrong with your appearance if you must constantly make repairs.

I'm reminded of the story about the guy who regularly went out into his front yard, flapped his arms like a duck, turned in a circle, did a little dance, then spit three times over his left shoulder. A curious neighbor finally approached him to ask the fellow what he was doing. Somewhat nervously, he replied that he was keeping the elephants

Helpsheet for Change:
My Plan for Facing It

How I Groom to Hide:

_____

Step-by-Step Plan for Facing It:

Prepare: Exactly what will I do?

_____

_____

_____

_____

Act: Where? When? For how long? What will I do if I get "cold feet"?

_____

_____

Cope: What uncomfortable thoughts and feelings do I expect and how will I cope with them?

_____

_____

_____

Enjoy: How will I reward my efforts?

_____

_____

What were the results of Facing It?

_____

_____

away. Perplexed, the neighbor said, "But there are no elephants around here." The fellow smiled proudly and said, "I know. What I do really works!"

Appearance-Preoccupied Rituals also sustain false assumptions—that if you don't look perfect all the time, bad things will happen or people won't like you. To eliminate these habitual patterns, you either prevent yourself from initiating them or interrupt them once you've begun the ritual. I call this solution *Erasing It*. Several successful strategies exist for Erasing It. I'll describe each and illustrate its effective use.

Obstructing Your Rituals

Most Appearance-Preoccupied Rituals occur whenever the "right" opportunity arises. Given certain triggers, or Activators in your ABC Sequence, you carry out the behavior before you know it. Therefore, you may need to obstruct its opportunity to occur. You block its path.

* Think about one Appearance-Preoccupied Ritual for which you need certain "tools" or conditions to carry out. For example, you require a mirror for rituals in which you repeatedly scrutinize your looks. Compulsive weighing would be impossible without scales. How could you make trouble for your ritual by altering the environment? Developing this strategy is a challenge to your creativity. So be creative!

* This obstructive technique for change is usually a short-term, stopgap approach. You don't want to avoid one thing in order to avoid another. It can be helpful, especially at first, but you'll want to use additional strategies to remove most rituals.

Let me illustrate: Louis felt compelled to weigh himself almost every time he ate anything. He was distracted until he confirmed that he had not put on several pounds. So Louis applied masking tape to the weight-displaying window of his scale. In this way, he weakened his compulsion to weigh himself. He had obstructed his ritual's path. He combined this technique with the By Appointment Only tactic (which I'll discuss later), weighing only on Saturdays when he changed the tape. His innovative strategy helped him change his preoccupying mental tape as well.

Delaying Your Rituals

Another method for Erasing It is really simple. You learn to wait a while before commencing your ritual. This works quite well for Checking Rituals.

* Appearance checking is usually preceded by an inner urge to check. For example, you have a gnawing feeling that you "need" to weigh yourself, inspect your hair or makeup, or seek reassurance about your looks. Your urge is typically narrated by Private Body Talk that asks "What if?" and conjures up distressing scenarios. "What if I've gained weight and I look fat?" "What if my hair is out of place and looks really stupid?" "What if my makeup is wearing

thin and my big pores are showing?" "What if my husband thinks this outfit looks dumb and he's embarrassed to be seen with me?"

✳ Checking Rituals serve several self-protective purposes: They interrupt your preoccupied thoughts and your discomfort. They offer a clear answer to your "What if?" question. If you learn that you look fine, you feel relief. And if something was slightly amiss, fixing it brings relief.

✳ By postponing your checking for a brief while, you sap the power of your anxious urge. Instead of succumbing to the urge and letting it immediately dictate your actions, *you* become the decision maker. You take control of the deciding when to check on your looks. This usurps both the urge that instigates your ritual as well as the ritual itself.

You can learn from this success story: Robin is a sales representative for a pharmaceutical firm. She's on the road a lot, calling on doctors and clinics. During the course of a typical day, she used to check her appearance often. Each time she stopped at a traffic light, she would inspect her hair and face in the rearview mirror. At her office, she checked her appearance once or twice per hour, using a mirror in her makeup compact or the one in the ladies' room. When Robin decided to delay her rituals, she put off checking her reflection in the rearview mirror until she'd reached her destination. Whenever she had this urge at the office, she deferred checking for twenty minutes. At first the wait was worrisome to her—what if she looked awful all that time? However, she spent a few moments with diaphragmatic breathing and her encouraging New Inner Voice. Then, she more easily shifted her attention to her work. Eventually, Robin kept in check her urge to check.

Restricting Your Rituals

Fixing Rituals can be exasperating. Each fixing episode usually continues until you are either momentarily content with its results or you run out of time. An alternative to allowing your ritual to run its course is to place specific limits on it. Here are three ways to weaken your rituals through limits:

Playing Beat the Clock

Tackle a form of Fixing in which you take too long readying your appearance to face the world.

◎ First establish how long your Fixing usually takes.

◎ Then make a fair estimate of how long would be reasonable for you to take if you didn't get so compulsively caught up in it. For example, suppose your morning grooming regimen takes two hours. You know that you should be able to get ready in an hour. Set your initial goal generously—to be ready in one hour and fifty minutes.

◎ Set your alarm clock or kitchen timer to this limit and play Beat the Clock.

◎ After a few days of success, lower the limit, say to one hour and forty minutes, and Beat the Clock for several more days.

◎ Continue in this fashion, shaving off ten minutes at a time until you've reached the reasonable amount of time that is your goal.

◎ Reward your progress by using the time saved for something enjoyable. Then you'll appreciate the change even more.

Kyra liked her hair, but she insisted that it always look perfect. It's the "saving grace" she relied on to make up for the physical features she disliked. Dreading a bad hair day, each morning Kyra would style and restyle her hair for an hour, until her ride for work arrived. For two weeks, Kyra played Beat the Clock by setting her timer for a gradually shorter interval—forty-five minutes, then thirty, then twenty, and finally a reasonable fifteen minutes. Her goal was to be finished with her hair, out of the bathroom, and enjoying her juice before the timer alarm went off. By making a challenging game of it, Kyra eliminated her morning preoccupation with her hair, which looks just as attractive as it did back in the days of one-hour fixing sessions. Now if she has a bad hair day, she sticks to her new abbreviated schedule anyway. She knows that the world won't come to an end!

Rationally Rationing Rituals

This method sets a limit on the number of times you engage in a ritual within a certain period. How does this work?

◎ Suppose that whenever you go out to dinner with a friend or loved one, your requests for reassurance that you look okay begin to sound like a broken record. The more you ask, the more insecure you feel, especially if you begin to sense your companion's annoyance.

◎ So you set a quota and allow yourself only two reassurance requests during an entire evening. You may use your allocation whenever you wish, but having used up your ration, your requests are over.

◎ Of course, over time the goal is to set your ration progressively lower until it reaches zero.

By Appointment Only

Here's the third method of restricting your rituals:

◎ An urge often dictates when your rituals occur. So instead, put your rituals on a schedule. In effect, you make an appointment with yourself to carry out your ritual.

◎ Like any appointment, the one for your ritual begins and ends on time.

◎ Because you're permitted to have the ritual "by appointment only," it cannot occur at unscheduled times.

◎   If you miss your appointment, you must wait for the ritual's next scheduled occasion.

Here's an example of the effective use of this strategy: Ever since adolescence, Chuck's face has been prone to have blackheads. Many times each day, he would get his magnifying mirror and peruse his pores in search of blackheads and blemishes, squeezing them and picking at them. Not only did his search-and-destroy missions take a lot of time, they took their toll on his complexion as well. To gain control, Chuck scheduled an appointment for his ritual, allowing it only during ten-minute visits to the mirror at 7 A.M., noon, and 10 P.M. Thus, he restricted its duration and frequency. Much to the relief of his dermatologist, Chuck eventually reduced his unhealthy practice to once a week.

Resisting by Rebellion

This last strategy for Erasing It can be rather difficult, yet it is sometimes the most successful. You rebel against your ritual by resisting it "cold turkey." You face the temptation and exercise restraint. You ride out the urge without the ritual. Controlling a ritual despite the conditions being ripe for its occurrence can greatly boost self-confidence.

◎   You may first want to try this approach on weaker rituals. For stronger ones, you'll probably graduate to this approach after successfully delaying, restricting, or obstructing your behavior pattern.

◎   With Body-and-Mind Relaxation and corrective thinking as your allies, you force yourself to remain in the situation without enacting your ritual—the longer the better.

◎   If you try this and don't succeed, give yourself the deserved credit for trying. Never give yourself a hard time for having a hard time!

◎   Often a gradual approach is most helpful. Schedule your rebellions for progressively longer periods. In this way, you are building up your resistance.

◎   In other instances, it may be effective for you to remain in the situation until the urge to perform your appearance-preoccupied pattern has subsided. Like a former smoker who chews gum, busy yourself with other activities.

Take inspiration from Jessica who resisted two self-defeating patterns: Whenever she was on a date, Jessica spent almost as much time in the restroom checking and fixing her appearance as she spent with her companion. She would end up stuck to the mirror like a magnet, brushing her hair, freshening her makeup, and adjusting her clothes. Jessica planned her resistance. On several occasions when she was at a restaurant, she allowed herself to visit the restroom only to use the toilet, not to primp. When washing her hands, she made a point of looking down at the sink instead of up at the mirror. For her next step, Jessica required that, on each visit, she look at herself in the mirror but not fix anything. She progressed to longer periods between "check-ups." Relying on her coping skills to get her through the initial discomfort, Jessica was ultimately able to break her pattern of checking and fixing.

Building Your Ladder of Success for Erasing It

Now it's your turn to weaken your Appearance-Preoccupied Rituals. Erasing It requires creative planning on your part to devise a strategy appropriate for you. Execute it often to erase the old pattern.

- ◎ Go back to the Helpsheet on page 153, where you listed your Checking and Fixing Rituals. Read through your list and evaluate your confidence that you could refrain from the behavior if you were in the situation where it normally occurs. Assign each entry on your list a self-efficacy rating from 0 to 100.

- ◎ Arrange these rituals in order of self-efficacy on the following Ladder of Success, going from the highest rating at the bottom to the lowest rating at the top.

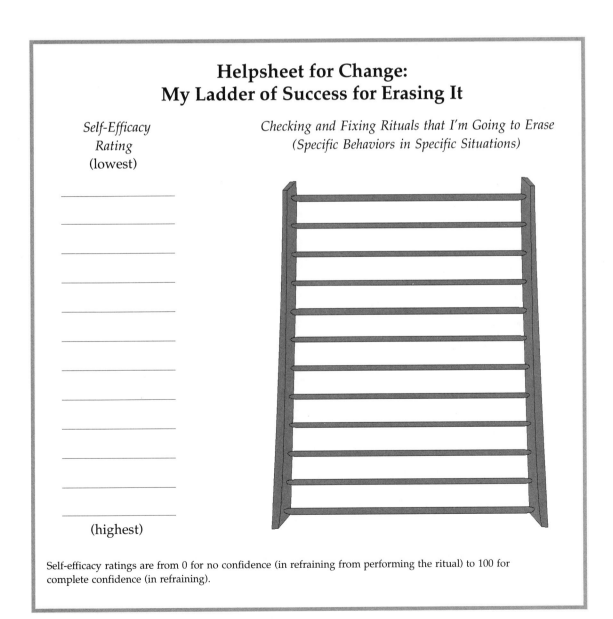

Helpsheet for Change:
My Ladder of Success for Erasing It

Self-Efficacy
Rating
(lowest)

Checking and Fixing Rituals that I'm Going to Erase
(Specific Behaviors in Specific Situations)

(highest)

Self-efficacy ratings are from 0 for no confidence (in refraining from performing the ritual) to 100 for complete confidence (in refraining).

Preparing and Executing Your Plans for Erasing It

◎ Start with the ritual at the bottom—the easiest one to eliminate. Write out your plan for Erasing It, following the Helpsheet format on page 169.

◎ PACE yourself, just as you do in facing your Evasive Actions. As you plan, anticipate and specify each step—Prepare, Act, Cope, Enjoy. Visualize yourself carrying out your plan, coping effectively with any troubling thoughts or feelings, and affirming your achievement.

◎ You've made and rehearsed your plan for Erasing It. Now go for it!

◎ One rung at a time, just keep climbing your ladder. When you've made headway, go ahead and begin Step 7 of this workbook.

Final Words of Encouragement

Depending on how many behaviors you've targeted for change, Facing It and Erasing It will take some time—a few weeks, at least. Right now you should take a few minutes at least to remind yourself of what's been helpful and how far you've come. The encouraging words at the end of this step of the program are yours. Think about the ways that you've improved your body image thus far. On the Helpsheet on page 170, write down your achievements. Savor your successes!

Step 6
Your Path for Progress

★ You have identified your Evasive Actions and Appearance-Preoccupied Rituals and have constructed Ladders of Success to combat them. On Helpsheets, you are drawing up the battle plans to face and erase these troublesome patterns, one at a time.

★ To conquer each pattern, you're learning to PACE yourself—to Prepare, Act, Cope, and Enjoy. For each Evasive Action, you are systematically Facing It. For each Appearance-Preoccupied Ritual, you are systematically Erasing It. You are patiently accepting that these important changes take time. So you're taking the time, climbing your Ladders of Success, and recording your progress.

★ You have written your key accomplishments so far in the program. Well done!

★ Body-and-Mind Relaxation should be second nature by now. You are using it successfully to prepare for and handle difficult situations in your daily life.

★ You're keeping up with your Corrective Thinking Diary, recording how you actively apply corrective thinking in your daily life. With your New Inner Voice, you are making progress in anticipating and altering your faulty Private Body Talk. You are talking back!

Helpsheet for Change:
My Plan for Erasing It

The Appearance-Preoccupied Ritual that I'm Going to Change:

_____

Step-by-Step Plan for Erasing It:

Prepare: Exactly what will I do?

_____

_____

_____

_____

_____

Act: Where? When? For how long? What will I do if I get "cold feet"?

_____

_____

Cope: What uncomfortable thoughts and feelings do I expect and how will I cope with them?

_____

_____

_____

Enjoy: How will I reward my efforts?

_____

_____

What were the results of Erasing It?

_____

_____

Self-Discovery Helpsheet:
My Proudest Moments of Body Image Change

Think about what you've done so far in your *Body Image Workbook.* What are your most satisfying accomplishments? What are some of your experiences from which you realize that your efforts to change are paying off?

_____

_____

_____

_____

_____

_____

_____

_____

_____

_____

_____

_____

_____

_____

_____

_____

_____

_____

_____

_____

_____

_____

Congratulations!

Step 7: The Good Times

Treating Your Body Right

All human relationships involve something quite fundamental—an exchange of actions and reactions between persons. We exchange both positive and negative giving and receiving. In satisfying romantic relationships or friendships, we feel that the giving and the getting are balanced fairly. Positive, rewarding exchanges greatly exceed and overshadow negative, punitive exchanges. Good times can redeem bad times. In unhappy relationships, giving and receiving are out of balance, and negative exchanges outweigh the few good times. The common complaints are, "I'm not being treated right. I deserve better than this!" Discontent ranges from resigned disappointment to raging resentment. Whether in self-protection or in protest, each person tends to react in ways that make the relationship deteriorate even further. Quietly withdrawing and avoiding or ignoring one's partner won't restore troubled relations. Angrily demanding better treatment and punishing the partner for not providing it only make matters worse.

So what does all this have to do with body image? Well, your body image does involve a relationship—between you and your body. If it's an unsatisfying one, the "gives and gets" seem unjust, and the exchanges are distressing and demeaning. You then react in ways that worsen rather than affirm and enhance your relations with your body. Seeing how you mistreat your "body-partner" is essential to turning this relationship around.

Thus far in *The Body Image Workbook*, the principal emphasis has been on changing your negative interactions with your body. By correcting your distorted Private Body Talk, you de-escalate the critical assaults and accusations of your body-partner. You are also working on being less demanding of perfection and more accepting of your body-partner's shortcomings. By Facing and Erasing your self-defeating patterns of behavior, you're getting less wrapped up in frustrating and resentful efforts to fix or control your body-partner.

These are necessary changes, but they aren't enough. As in human relationships, a successful body-partnership requires something more than the absence of bad times. Have you ever felt fulfilled by a friendship solely because the friend didn't belittle you? How many people do you know who are happily married only because their spouses *don't* beat or berate them? The truth is that good things happen in good relationships. They thrive as the result of affirming and rewarding experiences, not just because of a lack of distressing ones. In Step 7, you'll add good times to your relationship with your body.

Taking Affirmative Actions

If you wanted to resolve a troubled relationship with a friend or relative, I would counsel you to create new shared experiences. You would put aside complaints about the past and concentrate on the present. Both of you would commit to do what you know you have to do to make things better—to take *Affirmative Actions*—even if you don't feel like it. You stop the mutual finger-pointing and say to one another, "I'm truly sorry. I know I haven't treated you well. I want to start anew. I want to be as good to you as I can." Then each of you affirms, "Rather than being so fault-finding, I'm going to remind you and myself of what I value in you."

If you were in an unfulfilling relationship, you would be understandably skeptical of the other person's promises. But what if your friend or partner actually began to behave in affirming ways toward you? You would start relinquishing the past and enjoying the present. You would have growing optimism that the future could bring good times.

Affirmative Actions are also essential for improving your relationship with your body. These actions involve doing special things to foster positive body image thoughts and feelings. With conscious effort, you can counteract the quagmire of your past negative experiences and start fresh.

So let's get started. I'm giving you four Affirmative Actions for your body image.

Writing Wrongs

Thinking of your body as you would a friend, you can only reach one conclusion: You've mistreated your friend. In this first exercise, you will write your "body-partner" a letter expressing your wish to set the relationship on a better course. Here are some suggestions:

◎ In your letter, apologize to your body-partner for prior mistreatment, express assurances that you want to change, and thank your body-partner for the good things it has given you.

◎ Right now you may be thinking, "You want me to do *what*? Write a letter to my body? That's weird!" Yes, it is a little unusual. But that's okay, do it anyway. Suspend judgment and see what happens.

◎ With the following Helpsheet, compose your Writing Wrongs letter to your body. Write it as you would to an estranged friend with whom you want to restore relations. Keep your letter nearby, perhaps taped to your bathroom mirror. It's a reminder of your new attitude.

To help you draft your letter, here's a thoughtful one that Yvonne wrote:

Dear Body of Mine,

First, I want to say I'm sorry. For years, I've done nothing but criticize you. I can't believe the unkind things I've said about you. I apologize! It's an apology I've owed you for a long time.

We've had some great times together and you've done a lot for me. Still, I never gave you the credit you really deserve. If it weren't for you, I wouldn't have been on my high-school soccer team. I wouldn't have excelled at ballet. And, oh yes, I wouldn't have been able to enjoy my first kiss! You've managed to get me terrific compliments. People often say how warm your smile is and how nice you look in a new outfit. Rather than see your assets, I dwelled on how much you weigh. I know it's not fair for me to eat tacos, cheesecake, and the other stuff, and then to blame you for gaining a few pounds.

Body of Mine, the truth is you're not that fat. Because I'm so scared you'll get fat, I exaggerate sometimes. Sorry! I promise to be kinder. See you in the mirror soon!

Love,
Yvonne

Face-to-Face Affirmations

Accepting compliments can be difficult for people with a negative body image. While they may privately yearn for social compliments to counter their insecure view of their looks, words of praise are foreign to their Private Body Talk. If your New Inner Voice will speak affirmatively about your appearance, your body image will rely less on other people's judgments. At the same time, you'll be able to accept others' favorable

Helpsheet for Change:
Writing Wrongs

Dear Body of Mine,

_____

_____

_____

_____

_____

_____

_____

_____

_____

_____

_____

_____

_____

_____

_____

_____

_____

Love,

comments more easily. Face-to-Face Affirmations are compliments to yourself, in recognition of your physical assets. Why do I call these *Face-to-Face* Affirmations? Because you will face yourself in the mirror as you carry out this exercise. Here's how:

◎ Once a day, stand in front of your mirror, make eye contact with your reflection, and mentally express a positive statement about your body.

◎ Draw your affirmations from many sources. You can repeat the compliments that others have given you or state the favorable remarks that you wish others would give you. Affirmations may be corrective revisions of old Appearance Assumptions or your faulty Private Body Talk. Your affirmations can celebrate your efforts to improve your body image.

◎ Write out your affirmations ahead of time on the Helpsheet given on the next page. Eventually, you'll be able to conceive more impromptu affirmations.

◎ Allow your New Inner Voice to repeat the affirming words confidently and genuinely several times *for one full minute*. Your affirmations are statements that you want to believe and to feel, even though you may not be entirely convinced of them just yet.

◎ Don't worry if you feel slightly foolish "talking to yourself" in front of the mirror. After all, you've been doing this for years. What's foolish is that you never had much nice to say. Feeling silly will soon subside. And who knows, after a while you may even start saying your one-minute affirmations out loud. Speak up, I can't hear you!

Here are examples of Face-to-Face Affirmations from past program participants:

❖ "What a nice smile! People love to see me smile."

❖ "I don't have to have a perfect complexion to like myself."

❖ "I really like my bright eyes. I like how they sparkle."

❖ "Being athletic feels great!"

❖ "I look so vibrant in red. I love wearing this outfit."

❖ "I don't have to be thin to be happy."

❖ "I'm so glad to be working on my body image. I'm really making changes!"

❖ "I don't need to be perfect; I can accept myself as I am."

❖ "There's much more to me than meets the eye."

❖ "I love the energetic feeling in my body when I work out."

❖ "I'm looking good. I'm feeling good. Go get 'em!"

❖ "This is your New Inner Voice talking! You look really nice today."

Helpsheet for Change:
One-Minute Face-to-Face Affirmations

List ten morale-boosting statements or compliments that you want to believe and feel about your body and about your new and improved body image.

1. _____

_____

2. _____

_____

3. _____

_____

4. _____

_____

5. _____

_____

6. _____

_____

7. _____

_____

8. _____

_____

9. _____

_____

10. _____

_____

Feature Attraction Days

This Affirmative Action creates and celebrates more good times for your body image. One day each week, on Feature Attraction Day, you give special recognition and treatment to a specific aspect of your body. It could be some aspect of your appearance, such as your physique, or your hair, or a facial feature. It could be a physical capability, like being a good dancer or a fit runner. On this day, you devote efforts to experience an affirming attitude toward this aspect of your body. A fulfilling relationship with your body requires that you give credit where credit is due. And credit is due!

For example, LaToya celebrated her hands on Feature Attraction Day. She began the day in the mirror complimenting how pretty her fingers are and how pleasantly smooth her hands feel. From her jewelry box, LaToya chose and wore a special birthstone ring that her grandmother had given to her. She had her nails manicured and wore her favorite rose-colored polish. Later, she "handily" played the guitar for a while. That evening, LaToya asked her boyfriend to come over—just to hold hands!

Plan several Feature Attraction Days on the Helpsheet on the following page. At the end of each day, jot down the results of the exercise. How did it feel to treat your body right?

I Am Becoming

The fourth Affirmative Action is an imaginative exercise called I Am Becoming. Back in Step 5, you learned that the Unfair-to-Compare Distortion leads you to devalue yourself by comparing your looks to some lofty ideal. You also learned about the Beauty Bound Distortion, in which you curb your activities because of not living up to some physical ideal. Instead of insulting and restricting yourself for not measuring up to your ideals, I want you to *become* them—in your mind's eye. Here's how:

◎ First, turn back to Step 1 in the workbook and review your answers to the Wishing Well Test.

◎ If you could wave a magic wand and immediately transform yourself to match your physical aspirations, how would you think, feel, and act differently than you do now?

◎ On your Helpsheet on page 179 describe your ideals and then write down how you expect things would be if you looked this way.

◎ Each week, pick one day and live that day as you would if you embodied your ideals. Read your description and vividly imagine that this is exactly how you look. Your visualization skills from Body-and-Mind Relaxation can help create this experience. Allow your Private Body Talk and your actions to flow from the images of being your ideals.

◎ At the day's end, record the fruits of your experience.

Helpsheet for Change:
Feature Attraction Days

Date   *Featured*   *Activity*
               Asset

_____   _____   Plans: _____

                                   _____

                                   _____

                                   _____

                                   _____

                                   _____

                                   Results: _____

                                   _____

_____   _____   Plans: _____

                                   _____

                                   _____

                                   _____

                                   _____

                                   _____

                                   _____

                                   Results: _____

                                   _____

_____   _____   Plans: _____

                                   _____

                                   _____

                                   _____

                                   _____

                                   _____

                                   _____

                                   Results: _____

                                   _____

Your I Am Becoming exercise can be emotionally and behaviorally liberating. It does have two potential hazards that you will need to ward off:

- Don't slip into Unfair-to-Compare thoughts in which you start hassling yourself for not *really* looking like your ideal.
- Especially if you espouse Appearance Assumption 4 (from Step 4) that you would be much happier if you looked the way you wish, this exercise can sometimes trigger faulty thinking: "Gosh, imagining being my ideals felt so good that it's depressing that I don't actually look that way so that I could *really* feel good." The flaw in such logic is that with the exercise *you really did feel good*. You did not have to *look* different to *be* different.

Helpsheet for Change: I Am Becoming

Description of my body ideal:

____

____

____

____

How I expect to think, feel, and act:

____

____

____

____

How did I think, feel, and act?

____

____

____

____

Self-Discovery Helpsheet:
Survey of Positive Physical Activities

For each activity listed below, rate how often you engaged in the activity during the past year. Then rate how much mastery you experienced and how much pleasure you felt. If you did not engage in the activity, rate the mastery and pleasure you would expect to feel.

Frequency during the past year (**Freq**):
 0 = I never did this.
 1 = I did this once or only a few times.
 2 = I did this fairly often.
 3 = I did this often.

The experience of mastery (**M**) refers to your sense of accomplishment or achievement felt when engaging in the activity.
 0 = None
 1 = Somewhat
 2 = Moderate
 3 = A lot

The experience of pleasure (**P**) refers to feeling enjoyment or having fun when engaging in the activity.
 0 = None
 1 = Somewhat
 2 = Moderate
 3 = A lot

Freq	**M**	**P**	
___	___	___	1. Taking a long or brisk walk
___	___	___	2. Waterskiing or surfing
___	___	___	3. Wearing fashionable or formal clothes
___	___	___	4. Playing a team sport (baseball, softball, football, soccer, volleyball, basketball, etc.)
___	___	___	5. Hiking or rock climbing
___	___	___	6. Playing golf
___	___	___	7. Playing tennis or racquetball
___	___	___	8. Taking a relaxing shower or bath
___	___	___	9. Downhill skiing
___	___	___	10. Cross-country skiing

___	___	___	11. Wearing favorite casual clothes
___	___	___	12. Brushing hair in a soothing manner
___	___	___	13. Soaking in a hot tub or Jacuzzi
___	___	___	14. Playing pool or table tennis
___	___	___	15. Putting on makeup
___	___	___	16. Having sexual relations
___	___	___	17. Bowling
___	___	___	18. Gardening or doing lawn work
___	___	___	19. Wearing new or colorful clothes
___	___	___	20. Social dancing
___	___	___	21. Scuba diving or snorkeling
___	___	___	22. Sunbathing
___	___	___	23. Riding a bicycle
___	___	___	24. Having a manicure
___	___	___	25. Getting a body massage or backrub
___	___	___	26. Canoeing, rowing, or rafting
___	___	___	27. Getting a facial or a cosmetic makeover
___	___	___	28. Lifting weights
___	___	___	29. Masturbating
___	___	___	30. Horseback riding
___	___	___	31. Playing lawn sports (badminton, croquet, etc.)
___	___	___	32. Wearing favorite jewelry
___	___	___	33. Wearing cologne or perfume
___	___	___	34. Wearing your hair in a different style on occasion
___	___	___	35. Doing aerobic dance exercise
___	___	___	36. Giving massages or backrubs
___	___	___	37. Doing yoga or Body-and-Mind Relaxation
___	___	___	38. Roller-skating, rollerblading, or ice-skating
___	___	___	39. Doing heavy outdoor work

continued on next page

Freq	**M**	**P**	
——	——	——	40. Having a scalp massage
——	——	——	41. Brushing your teeth
——	——	——	42. Swimming
——	——	——	43. Running or jogging
——	——	——	44. Doing calisthenics (push-ups, sit-ups, etc.)
——	——	——	45. Being naked at home
——	——	——	46. Rubbing your own body with lotion
——	——	——	47. Individual dancing (ballet, expressive)
——	——	——	48. Performing martial arts
——	——	——	49. Bouncing on a trampoline
——	——	——	50. Working out on exercise machines
——	——	——	51. Doing gymnastics
——	——	——	52. Having a pedicure
——	——	——	53. Relaxing in a "flotation tank"
——	——	——	54. Bungee jumping
——	——	——	55. Sailing or windsurfing

Now you add to the list!

Other Health/Fitness Activities:

——	——	——	_____
——	——	——	_____

Other Sensate Activities:

——	——	——	_____
——	——	——	_____

Other Appearance-Related Activities:

——	——	——	_____
——	——	——	_____

On his I Am Becoming day, Chen imagined being taller. This mental image overrode his usual self-conscious Private Body Talk—giving him permission to act more assertively, exchange more eye contact, and smile more often. His game of pretend gradually led to very real and satisfying experiences. He felt better about himself and interacted with others more comfortably. Chen began to see how his old image of himself prevented him from being the person he was capable of being.

Body Image Enhancement: Achieving and Pleasing

George Sand, a nineteenth century French novelist, observed that "The beauty that addresses itself to the eyes is only the spell of the moment; the eye of the body is not always that of the soul" (1872). Bodies are more than what they look like; they are instruments of action and sensation. People with a negative body image often neglect to derive satisfaction from their bodies in ways that have nothing to do with appearance. Preoccupied with loathing, hiding, and repairing their looks, they also fail to find opportunities to enjoy their appearance.

In addition to Affirmative Actions, there is a another important way to treat your body right—activities for *Body Image Enhancement*. These activities fall into three categories of bodily experience: (1) physical health and fitness, (2) sensate experiences, and (3) physical appearance.

Two psychological experiences that enhance your relationship with your body are mastery and pleasure. *Mastery* produces gratifying feelings of accomplishment from reaching a set goal. For example, setting and achieving the goal of running two miles or swimming ten laps can provide a satisfying sense of mastery. *Pleasure* simply means having fun. It doesn't require reaching a goal, only enjoying an activity because it inherently feels good. For instance, getting a massage or relaxing in a hot tub brings about soothing sensations. Some activities furnish both mastery and pleasure. While aerobic dance involves mastering new moves and achieving improved fitness, it also gives a pleasing, invigorating sense of bodily freedom.

Realizing Your Potential for Positive Physical Activities

The preceding Helpsheet lists possible sources of physical mastery and pleasure. Answer this survey to discover potential ways to enhance your relationship with your body.

◎ Let's review your answers to the survey. Regardless of how often you engaged in the activities, circle those that you rated as 2 or 3 on pleasure or mastery.

◎ Now classify the activities you circled as relating either to physical appearance, to health and fitness, or to sensate experience. Beside each circled activity, write an *A* for appearance, *H* for health and fitness, or *S* for sensate experience. If some fall into more than one category, you may mark them more than once, but think about which category that activity fits best. Each activity has the potential to yield different experiences for different people. For example, although most people would regard "putting on makeup" as an appearance activity, someone might regard it as sensate because of the tactile pleasure enjoyed while applying the makeup. Similarly, an activity like lifting weights can enhance feelings about appearance, promote the experience of being strong or fit, or evoke certain bodily sensations during the workout.

◎ Tabulate your results. Count the number of activities circled in each category. Exclude any that aren't feasible to do in the next month. For example, don't count "sexual relations" if you're not in a sexual relationship. Forget about "rock climbing" if your arm is in a cast. For activities that relate to multiple categories, only count them in one primary category. How many health/fitness activities did you circle? How many sensate activities? And appearance-related activities?

◎ Choose at least four activities from each of the three categories. If you have less than four, here are some ideas for coming up with more: Look for circled items that you can break down into more specific activities. For example, "playing team sports" lists six sports. "Wearing favorite casual clothes" could be split into "wearing my favorite jeans" and "wearing my red bow tie." Find activities you initially placed in multiple categories but counted only in one primary category. Reassign a few of these to a secondary category that needs more activities. Finally, ask yourself, "What have I done or considered doing that could lead me to feel physical mastery or pleasure?"

◎ Write down these twelve activities on the following Helpsheet. Soon you will use your chosen activities to build a better relationship with your body.

The next three sections of your workbook focus on the ways that you will use these activities for body image enhancement. By committing some quality time to these experiences, your relationship with your body has a good chance for positive change.

Having Good Times with Health and Fitness Enhancement

Health and Fitness Enhancement nurtures your experiences of physical competence and well-being. Routine exercise can benefit your body image, as well as your overall mental health. Compared to "couch potatoes" whose only workouts are with the remote control for the television set, regular exercisers feel better about their fitness, their health, and also their appearance.

The most formidable obstacles to Health and Fitness Enhancement pertain to motivation. Studies of people's motives for exercise reveal these four basic reasons:

❖ To be more attractive or to lose weight

❖ To improve physical competence, fitness, and health

❖ To improve mood and manage stress

❖ To meet, socialize with, and have fun with others.

Helpsheet for Change:
My Positive Physical Activities

List at least four Health/Fitness Activities that you will carry out soon:

1. _____

2. _____

3. _____

4. _____

List at least four Sensate Activities that you will carry out soon:

1. _____

2. _____

3. _____

4. _____

List at least four Appearance Activities that you will carry out soon:

1. _____

2. _____

3. _____

4. _____

People with the first motive exercise to achieve a certain look—to *look* fit. Good health is incidental. Women are somewhat more likely than men to exercise primarily to manage their appearance and weight. Research has shown that a negative body image is more prevalent among people who exercise for this reason. However, neither the mirror nor the scale measures your body's capabilities.

Physical exercise is most psychologically rewarding if done for the right reasons. Fitness reflects what your body can *do*—its dexterity, agility, strength, stamina, and endurance. This mastery component of exercise reflects the second motivation that I mentioned above. This is certainly a healthy reason for exercise, unless taken to the extreme.

Pushing themselves harder and harder, compulsive exercisers' pursuit of physical mastery becomes dangerously consuming, or addictive. Driven to achieve perfect control over their body, they ultimately feel that their body controls them. They exercise more but with less enjoyment. Illness, injury, and other interferences with exercise are exasperating.

In contrast, regular physical activity in sensible moderation can benefit your emotional life *and* your body image. In 1994, psychologists at the University of South Florida discovered that a program of aerobic activity and weight training fostered body image improvements. At Old Dominion University in 1995, Dr. Sherri Hensley Crosson and I evaluated the effects of regular participation in an aerobic dance class. Not only did the exercisers enhance their cardiovascular fitness, they also developed a more satisfying body image than did their sedentary peers. If you're thinking that body images got better because exercisers lost weight, you'd be wrong. The gains in body image were *not* the result of losses in weight.

Remember in Step 1 of this workbook you discovered your extent of Appearance Orientation and Fitness/Health Orientation. What were your scores? If your Appearance Orientation is quite high, you may exercise mostly to manage your looks. To get more out of exercise, you should shift your attention away from issues of appearance or weight control and focus more on your satisfying experiences of physical mastery and pleasure.

The pleasure of exercise arises from the third and fourth motives. Exercise can greatly contribute to improving mood and managing stress. It can offer opportunities to enjoy the company of others. Good times represent good reasons to be physically active.

What is your Fitness/Health Orientation score from Step 1? If it's below average, you probably resist regular exercise. Please just give yourself a chance to feel good. I'm not asking that you run a marathon or try out for the Olympics. If your Fitness/Health Orientation score is quite high, get in touch with your motives for exercise. Are you so demanding and judgmental of your physical competence that you take the fun out of exercise? If so, you need to exercise restraint and emphasize enjoyment!

- ◎ This week, set aside time for two of the Health and Fitness Activities you selected.

- ◎ As you engage in these activities, monitor your feelings of mastery and pleasure. On the Helpsheet that follows, rate your experiences.

- ◎ Each week, do at least two activities. Instead of always doing the same ones, try new activities.

- ◎ And, of course, if you've been inactive for a while or have certain health problems, consult your physician about your exercise plans.

Having Good Times with Sensate Enhancement

Your body has millions of specialized cells that enable you to experience your body and the world around you. You can take in the visual beauty of a colorful sunset or a baby's smile. You can sense the essence of fragrant flowers. You can savor your favorite flavor. You can experience the symphonic sounds of an orchestra or the melody of a distant

---

Helpsheet for Change:
My Positive Health and Fitness Activities

Date	Health/Fitness Activity	Ratings (0–3) Mastery	Pleasure
_____	_____	_____	_____
_____	_____	_____	_____
_____	_____	_____	_____
_____	_____	_____	_____
_____	_____	_____	_____
_____	_____	_____	_____
_____	_____	_____	_____
_____	_____	_____	_____
_____	_____	_____	_____
_____	_____	_____	_____

Ratings of mastery and pleasure: 0 = None, 1 = Somewhat, 2 = Moderate, 3 = A lot

---

meadowlark. You can feel your body move rhythmically to music. You can feel your skin luxuriate in the sun's gentle warmth and the coolness of a soft breeze. You can be soothed by the caring touch of a loved one. If you're like most people, you take for granted such wonderful, sensate experiences. With all that your body endows you, why dwell unappreciatively on what your body looks like? Follow these suggestions for satisfying your senses:

◎ Each week from now on, create opportunities to enjoy at least two of the Sensate Activities from your Positive Physical Activities Helpsheet. Schedule them and carry them out.

◎ Immerse yourself in the pleasurable feelings. Let your sensate pleasure fill your consciousness.

◎ As enjoyable as these experiences may be, don't always schedule the same ones (like having sex!). Expand your sensory horizons.

◎ Use the following Helpsheet to record the enjoyment you harvest each time. You need not rate mastery, of course. Sensate activities are treats of pleasure, not achievement.

**Helpsheet for Change:
My Positive Sensate Activities**

Date	*Sensate Activity*	*Ratings of Pleasure (0–3)*
_____	_____	_____
_____	_____	_____
_____	_____	_____
_____	_____	_____
_____	_____	_____
_____	_____	_____
_____	_____	_____
_____	_____	_____
_____	_____	_____

Ratings of pleasure: 0 = None, 1 = Somewhat, 2 = Moderate, 3 = A lot

---

Having Good Times with Appearance Enhancement

In Step 6, you began chiseling away at the various self-protective behaviors you use to manage your looks. You realize now that your Evasive Actions and your Appearance-Preoccupied Rituals undermine your body image. Many of these problematic patterns of behavior pertain to appearance management or grooming. But grooming doesn't have to be a problem. It can enhance your feelings of mastery and pleasure. Whether your grooming affirms a positive body image or perpetuates a negative one depends on which type of groomer you are. There are three basic types:

The person who grooms to hide and is repeatedly checking and fixing is called the *Insatiable Groomer*. You recognize this pattern from Step 6. Primping, preening, fussing, and fretting are incessant. Satisfaction is fleeting.

A second grooming pattern also brings few good times. Unlike Insatiable Groomers, *Gloomy Groomers* have given up on their looks. As an Evasive Action, they largely neglect their appearance, believing either that nothing could ever improve their looks or that they lack the ability to do so. Most Gloomy Groomers fear doing anything to call attention to their body and invite self-consciousness. Therefore, they cling to a narrow range of "safe" ways to look. Some rationalize their pattern with a conviction that grooming is somehow bad—self-absorbed or provocative.

Consider Zelda, who's worn the same swimming-pool–blue eye shadow and thick black mascara for over fifteen years. Her hair has been up in a bun for at least as long. She always wears sacklike, ankle-length dresses, usually solid black or dark gray. Zelda "doesn't care for" her appearance. She's unwilling to attempt even simple grooming changes that could allow her to enjoy her looks more. To her, that would seem vain. Besides, she hasn't a clue of what she would do.

The first two types of grooming are clearly self-defeating. Insatiable Groomers stir up trouble. Gloomy Groomers want to leave bad enough alone. Both types have an inflexible relationship with their body's appearance.

The third type of groomer has the best attitude. This *Flexible Groomer* is neither preoccupied with compulsive grooming nor neglectful of appearance. The Flexible Groomer has adaptively discovered a happy medium between unhappy extremes. My own research findings confirm the advantages of being a Flexible Groomer. For example, we found that women who are versatile in their use of facial makeup feel more in control socially than women who are rigid in their cosmetics use. Further, women who inflexibly wear lots of makeup no matter what situation they're in underestimate their unadorned attractiveness. Their makeup is more a mask of self-required concealment than an optional and enjoyable adornment. Flexible grooming offers you choices and the affirming experience that you are acceptable with a variety of looks. It provides opportunities for pleasure and playfulness. It is not a self-imposed duty.

As a Flexible Groomer, Michelle's basic goal is to enhance her appearance in ways that express her individuality. She uses cosmetics in moderation, but she isn't reluctant to explore a new look from time to time. In selecting clothing colors and styles, Michelle wears what delights *her* eye—rather than conforming to the fiats of fashion or what camouflages the thighs that she's not so fond of. About once a year, she changes her hairstyle somewhat, simply because she knows this will be a refreshing change. Michelle doesn't depend on other people's compliments to enjoy her appearance. She doesn't aspire to be a flawless beauty, nor does she try to neutralize her looks. A Flexible Groomer like Michelle isn't afraid to look less than perfect and isn't afraid to experiment some.

Becoming a Flexible Groomer is possible through two parallel paths of action: First, keep using the lessons from Step 6 to lessen your self-defensive grooming. Keep on Facing It and Erasing It! Second, carry out positive activities for Appearance Enhancement. Learn to use mood-altering tools of adornment—like clothing styles, fabrics, colors, cosmetics, hair care, jewelry, and fragrances—to *enjoy* your appearance. Don't work at it; play at it!

Deriving personal enjoyment from your grooming activities doesn't mean you are vain or self-centered. It means you accept the body that's yours. What could be so terrible about that? The creation of mastery experiences might involve figuring out how to put clothing together to achieve a certain style you like. It might involve learning how to apply makeup more efficiently or how to do your hair in an easier-to-manage style. Be attuned to your motives though. Mastery at concealing "defects" or at emulating some movie star is not healthy mastery. Follow this routine to groom your way to good times:

◎ Examine the Appearance Activities that you chose and listed on your Positive Physical Activities Helpsheet.

◎ Schedule and carry out a couple of these each week. Enjoy the good times!

◎ Remember to note your experiences on the following Helpsheet.

Helpsheet for Change:
My Positive Appearance Activities

Date	Appearance Activity	Ratings (0–3)	
		Mastery	*Pleasure*
_____	_____	_____	_____
_____	_____	_____	_____
_____	_____	_____	_____
_____	_____	_____	_____
_____	_____	_____	_____
_____	_____	_____	_____
_____	_____	_____	_____
_____	_____	_____	_____
_____	_____	_____	_____
_____	_____	_____	_____
_____	_____	_____	_____
_____	_____	_____	_____

Ratings of mastery and pleasure: 0 = None, 1 = Somewhat, 2 = Moderate, 3 = A lot

Final Words of Encouragement

So often in life our views of reality hold us back, preventing us from becoming everything we can be. In the blockbuster movie *Forrest Gump*, Forrest didn't know he wasn't supposed to be able to do all the things he imagined. So he lived his dreams. He happily became his aspirations, despite his imperfections.

Improving your relationship with your body is ultimately up to you. What innovative activity can you dream up that would enhance and affirm your body image? Sorry, no suggestions from me on this one. Your final words of encouragement in Step 7 are these: Challenge your creativity. Do some brainstorming and then put your ideas into action.

Use a little imagination, and just let the good times roll!

Step 7
Your Path for Progress

★ You've learned how to create good times and improve your relationship with your "body-partner." You're taking Affirmative Actions by creatively engaging in special exercises to appreciate and celebrate your physical being.

★ You're making conscious efforts to treat your body right—to bolster your body image with experiences of mastery and pleasure. Based on self-test results, you're regularly carrying out three types of Body Image Enhancement activities: Health and Fitness Enhancement, Sensate Enhancement, and Appearance Enhancement.

★ You're learning to be a more Flexible Groomer, instead of an Insatiable Groomer or a Gloomy Groomer.

★ In your diary, you're continuing to record your daily body image experiences—your triumphs as well as your troubles. You learn from both.

★ You're listening to your New Inner Voice, which guides you in the right direction and supports your efforts to improve your body image.

★ You're following through with your Facing It plans to halt Evasive Actions and your Erasing It strategies for freeing your life from Appearance-Preoccupied Rituals.

Step 8: From This Day Forward

Preserving Your
Positive Body
Image for Life

Can you believe it? You've reached the final step of your program. The principal purpose of Step 8 is to help you ensure that your future brings the best for your body image. How can you progress even further and preserve your positive changes? How can you prevent discouraging setbacks? How will you handle tough times for your body image? Rather than leave your future to fate, we're going to look ahead to what tomorrow might bring. By starting now and devising your plans for the future, your body image remains forever in your control.

How Far Have You Come?

First, let's take stock of your changes since you began *The Body Image Workbook*. Taking stock simply means retaking the five body image tests from Step 1. People are often pleasantly surprised when they compare their "Before" and "After" test scores. Because people become accustomed to their positive changes, their memories of past problems fade and they don't realize how much they've actually improved.

Clearly Picturing the Present

To see how far you've come, this is what I want you to do:

◎   Get five sheets of lined paper, and title each with the name of the self-test.

◎   Follow the original instructions from Step 1, number each sheet with the number of items on the particular test, and write down your answers as you go along. Looking at your previous test answers could color your current judgment, so please cover your earlier responses as you retake the five tests.

◎   Answer the test questions when you won't be interrupted and when you feel as you typically do. For each question, think about your recent experiences and respond honestly and accurately.

◎   After completing all the self-tests, score them exactly as you did in Step 1.

◎   Following, you'll find the new Personal Body Image Profile forms. Using the form for your gender, record and categorize your test results.

The Personal Body Image Profile for Women

Score the tests as explained in the text. Enter each test score in the blank provided below. Then, to classify your score, from "very low" to "very high," circle the appropriate results.

Body Image Self-Test	Score	Very Low	Low	Average	High	Very High
1. Body Areas Satisfaction Test	_____	8–22	23–25	26–27	28–32	33–402
Wishing Well Test	_____	0–8	9–17	18–26	27–50	51–90
3. Distressing Situations Test	_____	0–50	51–72	73–80	81–110	111–192
4. Body Image Thoughts Test						
A. Negative Thoughts	_____	0–8	9–17	18–21	22–39	40–120
B. Positive Thoughts	_____	0–16	17–26	27–32	33–39	40–60
5. Body/Self Relationship Test						
A. Appearance Evaluation	_____	7–17	18–23	24–25	26–29	30–35
B. Appearance Orientation	_____	12–40	41–46	47–48	49–53	54–60
C. Fitness/Health Evaluation	_____	11–33	34–40	41–42	43–47	48–55
D. Fitness/Health Orientation	_____	14–41	42–49	50–52	53–59	60–70

The Personal Body Image Profile for Men

Score the tests as explained in the text. Enter each test score in the blank provided below. Then, to classify your score from "very low" to "very high," circle the appropriate numbers.

Body Image Self-Test	*Score*	*Very Low*	*Low*	*Average*	*High*	*Very High*
1. Body Areas Satisfaction Test	_____	8–25	26–28	29–30	31–33	34–40
2. Wishing Well Test	_____	0–8	9–17	18–26	27–50	51–90
3. Distressing Situations Test	_____	0–24	25–43	44–49	50–65	66–192
4. Body Image Thoughts Test						
A. Negative Thoughts	_____	0–7	8–15	16–17	18–32	33–120
B. Positive Thoughts	_____	0–13	14–21	22–25	26–34	35–60
5. Body/Self Relationship Test						
A. Appearance Evaluation	_____	7–19	20–24	25–26	27–29	30–35
B. Appearance Orientation	_____	12–36	37–42	43–44	45–50	51–60
C. Fitness/Health Evaluation	_____	11–36	37–42	43–44	51–55	45–50
D. Fitness/Health Orientation	_____	14–41	42–49	50–52	53–59	60–70

Computing Your Earnings

Now discover how much progress you've made. Just compare your present test results with those you had at the beginning of the program. On the next page is a special Helpsheet called Taking Stock of My Body Image Changes. Use it to transfer all your Before and After scores and their classifications (from "very low" to "very high").

As you examine your scores and review your progress, take pleasure in your well-earned gains! What about scores that didn't change much? Don't unrealistically expect huge improvements in *every* facet of your body image. Please don't shortchange your achievements by declaring your glass half empty. Scores showing slight or no change are *not* a final verdict on your body image potential. Appreciate that these scores are informative feedback about paths for future improvement.

Self-Discovery Helpsheet:
Taking Stock of My Body Image Changes

Enter your "Before" scores (from Step 1) and your current "After" scores. Beside each score, indicate how it was classified on your Body Image Profile:

Very Low = VL, Low = L, Average = A, High = H, Very High = VH

Body Image Self-Test	*Before* Score	Category	*After* Score	Category
1. Body Areas Satisfaction Test	_____	_____	_____	_____
2. Wishing Well Test	_____	_____	_____	_____
3. Distressing Situations Test	_____	_____	_____	_____
4. Body Image Thoughts Test	_____	_____	_____	_____
A. Negative Thoughts	_____	_____	_____	_____
B. Positive Thoughts	_____	_____	_____	_____
5. Body/Self Relationship Test	_____	_____	_____	_____
A. Appearance Evaluation	_____	_____	_____	_____
B. Appearance Orientation	_____	_____	_____	_____
C. Fitness/Health Evaluation	_____	_____	_____	_____
D. Fitness/Health Orientation	_____	_____	_____	_____

Learning from Your "Before" and "After" Pictures

Clinical studies have proven that most participants in this program become significantly more satisfied, particularly with those aspects of their appearance that they'd previously disliked the most. Let's take a look at your scores on the Body Areas Satisfaction Test:

❧ Did your "After" score increase compared to what it was before? If so, does this shift your level of satisfaction to a higher category—for example, from "low" or "very low" to "average" or better?

❧ Now let's get specific. Compare your satisfaction ratings of the specific body areas to see exactly where the changes occurred. What happened with those areas with which you were most displeased before the program?

The Wishing Well Test shows how you think you resemble your physical ideals. Improvement on this test would mean that your "After" score is lower than your "Before" score:

⁕ Did your Wishing Well score decline? If so, that's great. But let's figure out why it did. There are three explanations for improvement: First, you may now perceive your body in a more objective, undistorted manner. Second, you may have become more moderate and realistic in your ideals. Third, you may place less importance on attaining your ideals and regard them as mere preferences, not necessities. Think about these three explanations. Which are the reasons for your changes?

A central purpose of this program is to relieve you of negative body image emotions that are reactions to various activating events and situations. Research on the effectiveness of the program has confirmed that most people lower their scores on the Distressing Situations Test. How about you?

⁕ Did you reduce the occurrence of unwanted emotions in previously upsetting situations?

⁕ Now compare your "Before" and "After" answers item by item. In which situations are you now more free of distress? Which ones still bother you?

The Body Image Thoughts Test samples some of the possible content of your Private Body Talk. There are negative body image thoughts as well as positive ones. How have your thoughts changed?

⁕ Have negative thoughts become less prevalent in your Private Body Talk?

⁕ Have your positive thoughts increased?

⁕ Even if you have appreciably purged your Private Body Talk of self-criticisms, take note of any negative thoughts that are still popping up more than you would like.

On the Body/Self Relationship Test, your Appearance Evaluation score indicates how you see your overall appearance. Improvement means you have a better "big picture" of your looks. Did you raise your Appearance Evaluation score?

⁕ If it hasn't advanced as much as you'd like, think about why. Is there some physical attribute that you continue to allow to obscure your view of your looks? It's important that you figure out why and how you let this one characteristic spoil your overall body image.

Your Appearance Orientation score reflects your investment in your looks. It shows how much mental and behavioral effort you direct toward your appearance. How did you do?

⁕ If you began the program with a very high score, I hope that it's decreased some and that you've become less of an Insatiable Groomer.

⁕ Of course, some of you, the Gloomy Groomers, probably started out with low scores. A slight increase in Appearance Orientation might actually be a good sign. It could mean that you're beginning to make attempts to derive pleasure from your appearance.

Your two Fitness/Health scores are indicators of a relationship with your body that goes beyond its looks. Because you just began Health and Fitness Enhancement activities in Step 7, your Fitness/Health scores may not have gone up yet. Take a look at how you did:

* Increased Fitness/Health Evaluation scores reveal improved feelings that come with a more physically active lifestyle.

* Continued nurturance of this lifestyle will lead low Fitness/Health Orientation scores to grow. If your score didn't budge because it was high to begin with, keep your healthful habits going!

Rediscovering Your Needs, Resetting Your Goals

Changes in your test scores are only one way to gauge your gains. Another yardstick takes your own goals into consideration. This approach to understanding your progress is more personalized than comparing "Before" and "After" scores. Here's how you do it:

◎ At the end of Step 1, you listed your goals on your Needs for Change Helpsheet. Go back and look at each goal you set.

◎ How much progress do you feel you've made on each of your personal goals? What changes do you still want to make?

◎ Now turn to the new Helpsheet that follows, How I Need to Help Myself Now. Record your gains and update your goals.

◎ In the coming weeks, apply the know-how you've acquired in this program. Target each new goal and work toward it, one planned step at a time.

◎ Be sure to appreciate the positive accomplishments you've already made. Sustained improvement needs sustained nourishment.

Preparing for Tomorrow: For Better or Worse

The rest of Step 8 will help you nourish your changes and reach the new goals you've set. There are two obstacles to continued growth: First, certain self-defeating attitudes can stagnate progress. Second, neglecting to think ahead, anticipate challenges, and troubleshoot can leave you vulnerable to ambush by adversities. The forward-looking solution affords strength by the "power of prevention."

Helpsheet for Change:
How I Need to Help Myself Now

Physical characteristics I need to feel better about:

How I have improved: _____

_____

I still need to _____

_____

Negative body image emotions I need to control and reduce:

How I have improved: _____

_____

I still need to _____

_____

Physical ideals I need to emphasize less:

How I have improved: _____

_____

I still need to _____

_____

Negative thoughts I need to eliminate:

How I have improved: _____

_____

I still need to _____

_____

Positive thoughts I need to have more of:

How I have improved: _____

_____

I still need to _____

_____

continued on next page

Situations I need to learn to handle better:

How I have improved: _____

_____

I still need to _____

_____

Self-defeating Evasive Actions I need to change:

How I have improved: _____

_____

I still need to _____

_____

Appearance-Preoccupied Rituals I need to change:

How I have improved: _____

_____

I still need to _____

_____

Fitness/health-oriented behaviors I need to change:

How I have improved: _____

_____

I still need to _____

_____

Other things I still need to change to improve my body image:

I need to _____

_____

_____

I need to _____

_____

_____

Be Aware of and Beware of Stagnating Attitudes

Do you have any of the following four "stagnating attitudes" that could impede your improvements?

◎ The "Now Is Forever" attitude is a nasty notion that goes something like this: "Now that I've completed this workbook and I like my looks better, I'll never have to work on my body image again." This is like the attitude of some students I've taught, who think, "Now that I've taken the final exam, I can forget everything I've learned." What you have learned in this program will continue to be useful only if you continue to *use* it.

◎ The "Good Things Never Last" attitude espouses the opposite extreme. For example, some people become apprehensive when good things happen—if they are promoted at work or if they find themselves falling in love. Because they now have something valuable to lose, they start to worry and search for signs that their job or their romance may not be secure. Their actions then slowly sabotage their success and happiness, and they conclude, "I knew it all along. Good things never last." But, it's actually that the attitude set in motion a self-fulfilling prophecy. With effective efforts, good things surely do last.

◎ The "My Best Isn't Good Enough" attitude is self-blaming for unattained changes or some episode of body image distress. As a result of completing this workbook, should you now have a perfectly positive, problem-free body image? Absolutely not! Learning new skills well enough to make them a natural part of your life takes time and practice. Furthermore, perfection is a myth—an unreasonable standard against with to judge whether or not you've "done your best." Improvement builds on itself and on continued effort, which is good enough. Tough times mean tough times, and that's all. They do challenge your coping skills, but they are not some ultimate proof of your abilities or your character.

◎ The "Some Things Will Never Change Attitude" is similar to the notion that your best isn't enough. Both attitudes can cause what psychologists call *learned helplessness*. This happens when people give up because they decide that they have no control over events. If you resolve that some facet of your body image is unalterable, then you'll throw up your hands and do nothing to change it. So obviously nothing will change. On the other hand, if you put your pessimism on hold, set your goal, and work toward it, change has a real chance. Have you ever achieved things you once believed you couldn't?

Troubleshooting

Although you cannot foresee every body image difficulty on the horizon, many problems can be anticipated. So take a few minutes and constructively look for trouble.

◎ What events and situations still evoke your negative body image emotions? What do these troublesome triggers have in common? For example, do they involve reactions of certain people? Do they entail others seeing particular parts of your body? Are they situations that spotlight your weight or body shape? Do they pertain to how your clothes look?

◎ Whenever you expect to enter one of your "risky situations," don't start contemplating how to avoid it. That's the Beauty Bound mistake. Relying on skills you've developed in this program, here are two ways to ready yourself and steady yourself.

　✣ The first solution is to schedule a Desensitization session, without the mirror. Apply what you learned in Step 3. Create a Ladder of Success that breaks down the situation into elements that are progressively more difficult for you. Then practice dissolving your anticipated discomfort with Body-and-Mind Relaxation while visualizing these elements or events one at a time.

　✣ The second strategy applies what you learned in Step 6. PACE yourself. *Prepare* for the anticipated situation. Imagine being in the situation. Mentally rehearse how you want to deal with the worst-case scenario. Picture yourself effectively handling it. *Act* on your plan for confronting the situation. *Cope* as planned by using relaxation and corrective thinking. Your New Inner Voice can support you through this tough time and help keep your Private Body Talk free of mental mistakes. Stop, Look, and Listen! Your goal is simply to survive the situation, not to feel totally wonderful. *Enjoy* the fact that you stood up to adversity. Reward your courage.

Dealing with Provocative People

For most individuals, the troublesome situations pertain to other people. There are at least three ways that people can provoke problems for your body image: (1) Their looks are intimidating. (2) They don't give you the body image strokes that you want. (3) They say things that give you the body image despair that you don't want. Let's see how to deal with these people.

The "Beautiful" People

Some people "have no right to look so good." Their mere presence "makes" you feel unhappy with your appearance. Their looks remind you that you don't "measure up." You already know how to deal with these all-too-perfect-looking people:

◎ Stop committing the Unfair-to-Compare Distortion. Comparing yourself to them is unfair to both of you.

◎ Take them off the pedestal you've built for them. Just relate to them like regular folks, not like lofty kings or queens.

◎ Judge them based on what they say and do, instead of on how they look. If they're nice people, enjoy them. If they're clods, move on!

The "Inattentive" People

Your spouse or romantic partner may sometimes be inattentive to your looks—not critical, but not complimentary either. "Gee, you look so nice!" are words they seldom express. As a result, you become insecure about what your partner privately thinks about your appearance. So, what can you do?

◎ First, recognize your own mental mistakes. Are you Mind Misreading and projecting your own negative thoughts in the other person's head? What factual proof do you have that the person has a negative opinion of your looks? What other explanations exist to account for the person's inattentiveness? Consider these possibilities:

❉ Understand that some people never give compliments to anybody about anything. Obviously, the deficiency is theirs, not yours.

❉ Some people are completely "appearance blind"—oblivious to how others look *and* to how they themselves look. They don't comment on your appearance simply because it never crosses their mind to do so. "No news" isn't bad news. That's just the way these people are—apathetic about appearances.

❉ Another reason for their inattentiveness could be that they've "grown accustomed to your face" (and other aspects of your looks). They take your appearance for granted, assets and all. If their silence and your uncertainty compel you to ask, "Do you find me attractive?" they usually reply, "Sure. You know that." Familiarity doesn't breed contempt, it breeds complacency—about many things.

❉ A final, likely reason that a particular person doesn't comment favorably on your appearance is the "can of worms" explanation. As I explained previously, a negative body image can lead some individuals to be vocally critical of their own looks and to seek excessive reassurance. If the topic of your appearance is a well-worn subject, it's no wonder that this other person might be reluctant to reopen such a can of worms.

◎ As you can see, there are abundant reasons that certain people rarely compliment your looks. If you feel you want strokes from these folks, your best chances are with the Golden Rule; so, "do unto others." Behavioral scientists refer to this as the *norm of reciprocity*, which means that inattentiveness begets inattentiveness and that compliments beget compliments. So change channels. Give sincere positive feedback when you notice that they look especially nice. If they reciprocate your compliment, accept it and tell them you appreciate it. If they don't, give them compliments anyway. After all, being positive is its own reward!

◎ Don't expect miracles. People don't change overnight, and some won't change at all. Don't depend on strokes from others in order to appreciate your looks. Punch your own ticket!

The "Insensitive" People

Do particular friends, loved ones, or acquaintances seem intent on making insensitive remarks that stir up your body image distress? Their comments come in various forms:

* ❧ "Friendly" teasing: "You know I only kid you about your 'fuzzy' hair because we're good friends. If I didn't like you, I wouldn't kid you that way!"

* ❧ "Caring" concerns: "It's because I care about you that I can be honest about how terrible you look in shorts."

* ❧ And, of course, "helpful" advice: "I don't mean to hassle you about how chunky you've become. I'm just worried about your health. I only want what's best for you."

Short of buying them all a one-way fare to a faraway place, how can you handle these insensitive people? Before I tell you, I want you to recognize three common but definitely unproductive approaches. You've probably already tried them, with no success. With the *passive*, or unassertive, approach, you don't want to "cause trouble" so you hide your hurt or annoyance and quietly sustain the insults—maybe even believing you deserve them. With an *aggressive* approach, you blow your cool and retaliate with hostile threats or insults. In the *passive-aggressive*, or indirect, approach, you sulk or become cranky or oppositional, without ever telling the offender why you're acting this way.

The best way to deal with insensitive people is to take a rational, *assertive* course of action. Assertiveness is made easier if you better understand the other person, which can help neutralize their unwelcome words. Perhaps they truly are trying to be friendly, or caring, or helpful. On the other hand, maybe they act insensitively because of their own body image insecurities. For example, parents who have struggled with their own weight may shift their weight-watching burden onto their children. So they pass the misery along by nagging, "Why don't you go on a diet and lose weight?," or, "With your weight, you shouldn't be eating that cookie."

Are there other plausible motives for insensitivity? Jealous partners or friends may worry that if you look too good, you'll have chances for other relationships. Their jabs at your appearance may be unconscious efforts to diminish your self-confidence and prevent losing you to someone else. Moreover, did you ever stop to consider that critical people may be envious of you or your looks? You are the focus of their own Unfair-to-Compare Distortions, and your appearance makes them feel unattractive. Perhaps because you intimidate them in some other way, they try to even the score by pointing out your physical imperfections.

After gaining insight into possible motives for their insensitivity, lay out a plan for direct and thoughtful communication. Rational assertion has six sensible steps that you can readily remember with the acronym *RIGHTS:*

* ◎ *Review* the situation in advance. Identify what the problem is, how you feel about it, and how you're going to approach the offending person about it. Know exactly what you want to accomplish with assertive action. Because you want to be prepared and confident when you talk with the person, plan your words, write them down, and even practice them beforehand.

◎ *Initiate* conversation with the person at a time and place that's mutually convenient. Don't just sit around and wait until you're offended again. It's preferable to talk without the pressure of time or the presence of distractions.

◎ *Get specific* about the problem. Calmly and confidently tell the person the particular remarks or behaviors you find objectionable. Stay focused on the facts. Be descriptive, without being accusatory. For instance, you might say something like: "Recently you've often mentioned that you think I ought to lose weight. I want to talk with you about your comments and how I feel about them." *Don't* take the passive path, meekly muttering, "I'm really sorry to bring this up. It's probably petty and I'm just being overly sensitive, but. . . . " *Don't* exaggerate or use aggressive, inflammatory words—for example, "You are always bitching at me about being fat!" *Don't* stray off-course into other issues—like, "I'm tired of your insults about my weight. I'm sick of your total inconsideration of me. You've never really been in my corner when I needed you. Like last year when you. . . . "

◎ *How you feel* is an essential aspect of what you will want to communicate. Use "I" statements to express how the objectionable behavior feels to you. For instance, "When you make jokes about my being short, *I* feel hurt." Casting blame about how the person makes you feel will put him or her on the defensive. Keep the focus on your feelings, without tossing in opinionated conclusions. The statement, "I felt embarrassed when we were at the beach and you criticized how I looked in my swimsuit," properly expresses an emotion. The proclamation, "I feel you are a rude and insensitive scoundrel who takes great pleasure in humiliating me," is an opinion. The person can toss aside your opinion with, "You're wrong!" It's harder to dismiss your feelings.

◎ *Target the change* you want. Propose a specific solution, firmly stating what you want. For example, "I'm asking that from now on you stop calling me 'Jelly Butt' in front of our children." That's a more precise request than "I wish you'd quit being so damned hateful."

◎ *Secure an agreement* from the person. Mention the inherent advantages to each of you that cooperation with your request would bring. Propose a win-win solution. "If you stop asking me whether I've lost weight, I'll take less time getting dressed before we go out, and I know I'll be more fun to be with." To negotiate change, offer positive consequences: "If you promise to refrain from criticizing my appearance today, I'll give you a back rub tonight." Of course, sometimes serious sanctions are called for—when the unwanted behavior is longstanding or when the offender has been unresponsive to previous requests for change. Under these circumstances, you may need to stipulate punitive outcomes for noncompliance with your assertive request. "I do want you to know in advance that if you make your usual jokes about my body tonight, I will leave the party without you."

Follow the six steps of rational assertiveness—your RIGHTS—to take charge of how insensitive people affect your body image. On the following Helpsheet, lay out your

Helpsheet for Change:
Rationally Asserting My RIGHTS with
Insensitive People

Review the problem: What is the problem you want to change?

_____

_____

Initiate discussion: When and where will you assert yourself?

_____

_____

Get specific: Exactly what will you say about what you object to?

_____

_____

How you feel: What "I" statements express your feeling about the person's insensitivities?

_____

_____

Target the desired changes: Exactly what do you want from the person?

_____

_____

Secure an agreement: What are the proposed consequences to the person's complying or not complying?

_____

_____

assertive plan. If it doesn't work at first, refine it and try again. Don't give up. You have a right to assert yourself and be treated with respect!

Surviving Surprise Attacks

It's one thing to deal with the "known enemies" of your body image—the people, events, or situations that predictably attack your satisfaction with your looks. Sometimes, however, you may be assaulted by a "surprise attack" of body image distress. How could you even plan for the unexpected? The answer is that you can plan for setbacks in general. Here are some of your allies in defending yourself during an ambush:

- You've learned to turn on Body-and-Mind Relaxation. So when ambushed by adversity, concentrate on modifying your mood. Pause for a moment, close your eyes, release distress, picture pleasant images, repeat soothing self-instructions, and create a body-and-mind experience of contentment and control.

- During a surprise attack, put your New Inner Voice in command. "Right now I'm upset. I'm in a mode of self-criticism. This is only temporary. I know I won't always feel this way because I don't always feel this way. This isn't the time for passing judgment on my appearance. I can think about this later, when I'll be able to make unemotional sense out of this."

- Remind yourself that everybody experiences bad days and bothersome events. You're just as human as everyone else. Accept that you are having difficulties. Refuse to give yourself a hard time for having a hard time.

- Think about what you can do to feel better. Then do it!

Metamorphoses

One thing that never changes is the fact that things will always change. Your body certainly has and will change.

Several years ago I went to my twenty-fifth high-school reunion. Many of us hadn't seen one another since graduation. Our reacquainting conversations often touched upon how our current looks matched our recollections of each other, aided by circulating copies of our yellowed yearbook. "Wow, you look just the same!" was typically reserved for average- or better-looking classmates. "You look terrific, you really do!" was seemingly remarked to those whose attractiveness had improved over time. "So how have you been?" may have been the socially sensitive equivalent of "The aging process hasn't been too kind, has it?"

The former basketball team captain and dreamboat to most girls in the class was now paraplegic—his body altered forever while fighting in Vietnam. The prettiest cheerleader, whose body had been ravaged by a deadly disease, felt obliged to explain her appearance repeatedly over the course of the reunion. More than a few of the guys had substantial scalp to show for the quarter century that had passed. "Hair today, gone tomorrow," they quipped. And the woman with gray hair warned us not to call her

"Grandma." Classmates who'd added inches to their "love handles" groaned about how they had "grown" over the years. Some women displayed photos taken during pregnancy and sought reassurances that they were no longer "as big as a beached whale." Some smooth faces had weathered with wrinkles. And speaking of faces, where was Larry? We wondered if his cystic acne, for which he'd been so terribly teased, had scarred his life.

Time truly transforms everyone—psychologically *and* physically. With nutrition, exercise, and other healthful practices, we can exert some control over the extent and rate of unwanted physical changes. But we can never look like kids again. This reality, however, doesn't seem to stop many of us from trying. We search for fountain-of-youth products. We chase the promises of "take it off fast and forever" diets. We hire cosmetic surgeons to erase time with a scalpel or laser. What would happen if we devoted to physical self-acceptance half of the effort we invest in trying to turn back the clock or have the perfect body? The answer is profoundly simple: We would live happier lives.

Additional Roads to Self-Acceptance

As you learned in Step 2, it's difficult to like yourself if you dislike your body. The converse is true as well: Disliking yourself makes it hard to accept what you look like. Poor self-esteem sends people on a fault-finding mission that doesn't spare what they see when they look in the mirror.

Becoming the best that you can be is a journey involving many roads. Beyond body image, there are other aspects of yourself and your life that you may need to work on. You can apply what you have learned from *The Body Image Workbook* to *self*-acceptance, just as you did to improve your body acceptance. Following are some excellent self-help workbooks to guide you in your quest for a more favorable relationship with yourself:

Burns, D. 1980. *Feeling Good: The New Mood Therapy*. New York: Morrow.

———. 1989. *The Feeling Good Handbook: Using the New Mood Therapy in Everyday Life*. New York: Morrow.

———. 1993. *Ten Days to Self-Esteem*. New York: Morrow.

Copeland, M. E. 1992. *The Depression Workbook: A Guide for Living with Depression and Manic Depression*. Oakland, CA: New Harbinger.

Davis, M., E. R. Eshelman, and M. McKay. 1995. *The Relaxation and Stress Reduction Workbook, fourth edition*. Oakland, CA: New Harbinger.

McKay, M., and P. Fanning. 1992. *Self-Esteem: A Proven Program of Cognitive Techniques for Assessing, Improving, and Maintaining Your Self-Esteem*. Oakland, CA: New Harbinger.

McKay, M., and P. Fanning. 1991. *Prisoners of Belief: Exposing & Changing Beliefs that Control Your Life*. Oakland, CA: New Harbinger.

As a scientist and a practitioner, I understand the power of professional therapy to help people make positive life changes. If you suffer from more than your share of stress, anxiety, depression, relationship problems, or other difficulties that threaten your self-esteem and happiness, please get the help you need. Obtaining professional help doesn't mean that you are a weak person or a failure. It means that you want things to be better. You are entitled to seek a happy life.

Final Words of Encouragement

Everything you've learned in *The Body Image Workbook* constitutes a new lifestyle and relationship between you and your body. This relationship will continue to grow and give you gratification as long as you stay active in your efforts. There will be times you'll want to reread parts of this workbook as fuel for thought and action. Your personal Body Image Diary remains an essential avenue for you to communicate with yourself about your troubles and to plan your triumphs. Once in a while, reread your journal of experiences and see just how far you've come. Every several months, take the self-tests again and review and revise your goals, just as you did earlier in Step 8.

In this workbook's preface, I began by saying that the human condition is inherently one of embodiment. Indeed, in the wise words of the philosopher Plato, "We are bound to our bodies like an oyster is to its shell." Yes, but we are not bound to be unhappy with our bodies. My sincerest wishes to you for a satisfying body image throughout your life.

Step 8
Your Path for Progress

★ To take stock of your progress, you have retaken the body image self-tests and compared the results with those obtained in Step 1.

★ You have evaluated how well you've met the goals you set at the beginning of the program.

★ Having identified your specific needs for further body image changes, you have reset your goals.

★ You're now aware of various "stagnating attitudes" that could erode your progress and hinder your continued improvement.

★ Using the techniques and skills you've acquired in this program, you are preventatively preparing for potentially difficult situations that challenge you and your body image.

★ You're applying rationally assertive strategies, using the RIGHTS approach, in dealing with people who are troublemakers for your body image.

★ To maintain your positive body image for life, you're examining other facets of your self-acceptance and well-being.

References

Special Credits

The Body Image Workbook relies substantively on these previous versions of the author's body image therapy program:

Cash, T. F. 1995. *What Do You See When You Look in the Mirror?: Helping Yourself to a Positive Body Image*. New York: Bantam Books.

———. 1991. *Body-Image Therapy: A Program for Self-Directed Change*. New York: Guilford Publications.

Other Sources

Alberti, R. E., and M. Emmons. 1974. *Your Perfect Right* (rev. ed.). San Luis Obispo, CA: Impact Press.

American Psychiatric Association. 1994. *Diagnostic and Statistical Manual of Mental Disorders* (4th ed.). Washington, D.C.: American Psychiatric Association.

Bandura, A. 1977. Self-efficacy: Toward a unifying theory of behavior change. *Psychological Review*, 84:191–215.

———. 1977. *Social Learning Theory*. Englewood Cliffs, NJ: Prentice-Hall.

Beck, A. T. 1976. *Cognitive Therapy and the Emotional Disorders.* New York: International Universities Press.

Beck, A. T., and G. Emery. 1985. *Anxiety Disorders and Phobias: A Cognitive Perspective.* New York: Guilford Press.

Benson, H. 1975. *The Relaxation Response.* New York: Morrow.

Bernstein, N. R. 1990. Objective bodily damage: Disfigurement and dignity. In T. F. Cash and T. Pruzinsky (eds.), *Body Images: Development, Deviance, and Change* (131–148). New York: Guilford Press.

Berscheid, E., E. Walster, and G. Bohrnstedt. 1973. Body image. The happy American body: A survey report. *Psychology Today*, 7:119–131.

Bower, S. A., and G. H. Bower. 1976. *Asserting Your Self.* Reading, MA: Addison-Wesley.

Brooks-Gunn, J., and M. P. Warren. 1985. Effects of delayed menarche in different contexts: Dance and nondance students. *Journal of Youth and Adolescence*, 14:285–300.

———. 1988. The psychological significance of secondary sexual characteristics in nine- to eleven-year-old girls. *Child Development*, 59:1061–1069.

Brown, T. A., T. F. Cash and R. J. Lewis. 1989. Body-image disturbances in adolescent female binge-purgers: A brief report of the results of a national survey in the U.S.A. *Journal of Child Psychology and Psychiatry*, 30:605–613.

Brown, T. A., T. F. Cash, and P. J. Mikulka. 1990. Attitudinal body image assessment: Factor analysis of the Body-Self Relations Questionnaire. *Journal of Personality Assessment*, 55:135–144.

Brown, T. A., T. F. Cash, and S. W. Noles 1986. Perceptions of physical attractiveness among college students: Selected determinants and methodological matters. *Journal of Social Psychology*, 126:305–316.

Brownell, K. D. 1991. Dieting and the search for the perfect body: Where physiology and culture collide. *Behavior Therapy*, 22:1–12.

Brownell, K. D., and C. G. Fairburn. 1995. *Eating Disorders and Obesity: A Comprehensive Handbook.* New York: Guilford Press.

Brownell, K. D., and J. Rodin. 1994. The dieting maelstrom: Is it possible and advisable to lose weight? *American Psychologist*, 49:781–791.

Bull, R., and N. Rumsey. 1988. *The Social Psychology of Facial Appearance.* New York: Springer-Verlag.

Burns, D. 1989. *The Feeling Good Handbook: Using the New Mood Therapy in Everyday Life.* New York: Morrow.

Butters, J. W., and T. F. Cash. 1987. Cognitive-behavioral treatment of women's body-image dissatisfaction. *Journal of Consulting and Clinical Psychology*, 55:889–897.

Cash, T. F. 1985. Physical appearance and mental health. In J. A. Graham and A. Kligman (eds.), *Psychology of Cosmetic Treatments.* (196–216). New York: Praeger Scientific.

———. 1987. The psychology of cosmetics: A review of the scientific literature. *Social and Behavioral Sciences Documents*, 17(1):Manuscript 2800.

———. 1989. Body-image affect: Gestalt versus summing the parts. *Perceptual and Motor Skills*, 69:17–18.

———. 1990. The psychology of physical appearance: Aesthetics, attributes, and images. In T. F. Cash and T. Pruzinsky (eds.), *Body Images: Development, Deviance, and Change* (51–79). New York: Guilford Press.

———. 1991. Binge-eating and body images among the obese: A further evaluation. *Journal of Social Behavior and Personality*, 6:367–376.

———. 1992. Body images and body weight: What is there to gain or lose? *Weight Control Digest*, 2(4):169–176.

———. 1992. Psychological effects of androgenetic alopecia among men. *Journal of the American Academy of Dermatology*, 26:926–931.

———. 1993. Body-image attitudes among obese enrollees in a commercial weight-loss program. *Perceptual and Motor Skills*, 77:1099–1103.

———. 1994. Body image and weight changes in a multisite comprehensive very-low-calorie diet program. *Behavior Therapy*, 25:239–254.

———. 1994. Body-image attitudes: Evaluation, investment, and affect. *Perceptual and Motor Skills*, 78:1168–1170.

———. 1994. The situational inventory of body-image dysphoria: Contextual assessment of a negative body image. *The Behavior Therapist*, 17:133–134.

———. 1994. *The Users' Manual for the Multidimensional Body-Self Relations Questionnaire.* Available from the author, Old Dominion University, Norfolk, VA.

———. 1995. Developmental teasing about physical appearance: Retrospective descriptions and relationships with body image. *Personality and Social Behavior: An International Journal*, 23:123–130.

———. 1995. The psychosocial effects of adolescent facial acne: Its severity and management in a medically untreated sample. Technical report to the Neutrogena Corporation, Los Angeles, CA.

———. 1996. Body image and cosmetic surgery: The psychology of physical appearance. *The American Journal of Cosmetic Surgery*, 13:345–351.

———. 1996. The psychosocial effects of adolescent facial acne: Investigation of a clinical sample. Technical report to the Neutrogena Corporation, Los Angeles, CA.

———. 1996. Remembrance of things past: A scientific investigation of the vestigial psychological effects of adolescent acne in early adulthood. Technical report to the Neutrogena Corporation, Los Angeles, CA.

———. 1996. The treatment of body image disturbances. In J. K. Thompson (ed.), *Body Image, Eating Disorders, and Obesity: An Integrative Guide for Assessment and Treatment* (83–107). Washington, D.C.: American Psychological Association.

Cash, T. F., and T. A. Brown. 1987. Body image in anorexia nervosa and bulimia nervosa: A review of the literature. *Behavior Modification*, 11:487–521.

———. 1989. Gender and body images: Stereotypes and realities. *Sex Roles*, 21:361–373.

Cash, T. F., and D. W. Cash. 1982. Women's use of cosmetics: Psychosocial correlates and consequences. *International Journal of Cosmetic Science*, 4:1–14.

Cash, T. F., D. W. Cash, and J. W. Butters. 1983. "Mirror, mirror, on the wall . . .?": Contrast effects and self-evaluations of physical attractiveness. *Personality and Social Psychology Bulletin*, 9:351–358.

Cash, T. F., B. Counts, and C. E. Huffine. 1990. Current and vestigial effects of overweight among women: Fear of fat, attitudinal body image, and eating behaviors. *Journal of Psychopathology and Behavioral Assessment*, 12:157–167.

Cash, T. F., K. Dawson, P. Davis, M. Bowen, and C. Galumbeck. 1989. The effects of cosmetics use on the physical attractiveness and body image of college women. *Journal of Social Psychology*, 129:349–356.

Cash, T. F., and E. Deagle. In press. The nature and extent of body-image disturbances in anorexia nervosa and bulimia nervosa: A meta-analysis. *International Journal of Eating Disorders*.

Cash, T. F., and N. C. Duncan. 1984. Physical attractiveness stereotyping among Black American college students. *Journal of Social Psychology*, 122:71–77.

Cash, T. F., and J. R. Grant. 1996. The cognitive-behavioral treatment of body-image disturbances. In V. Van Hasselt and M. Hersen (eds.), *Sourcebook of Psychological Treatment Manuals for Adult Disorders* (567–614). New York: Plenum.

Cash, T. F., and P. E. Henry. 1995. Women's body images: The results of a national survey in the U.S.A. *Sex Roles*, 33:19–28.

Cash, T. F., and K. L. Hicks. 1990. Being fat versus thinking fat: Relationships with body image, eating behaviors, and well-being. *Cognitive Therapy and Research*, 14:327–341.

Cash, T. F., and L. Jacobi. 1992. Looks aren't everything (to everybody): The strength of ideals of physical appearance. *Journal of Social Behavior and Personality*, 7:621–630.

Cash, T. F., and L. H. Janda. 1984. Eye of the beholder. *Psychology Today*, 18:46–52.

Cash, T. F., and A. S. Labarge. 1996. Development of the Appearance Schemas Inventory: A new cognitive body-image assessment. *Cognitive Therapy and Research*, 20:37–50.

Cash, T. F., and D. M. Lavallee. 1995. *Cognitive-behavioral body-image therapy: Extended evidence on the efficacy of a self-directed program.* Unpublished manuscript, Old Dominion University, Norfolk, VA.

Cash, T. F., R. J. Lewis, and P. Keeton. 1987. *Development and validation of the Body-Image Automatic Thoughts Questionnaire.* Paper presented at the annual meeting of the Southeastern Psychological Association, Atlanta, GA.

Cash, T. F., J. Muth, P. Williams, and L. Rieves. 1996. Assessments of body image: Measuring cognitive and behavioral components. *AABT 30th Annual Convention Proceedings*, Association for Advancement of Behavior Therapy.

Cash, T. F., P. Novy, and J. Grant. 1994. Why do women exercise?: Factor analysis and further validation of the Reasons for Exercise Inventory. *Perceptual and Motor Skills*, 78:539–544.

Cash, T. F., V. Price, and R. Savin. 1993. The psychosocial effects of androgenetic alopecia among women: Comparisons with balding men and female controls. *Journal of the American Academy of Dermatology*, 29:568–575.

Cash, T. F., and T. Pruzinsky. (eds.). 1990. *Body Images: Development, Deviance, and Change.* New York: Guilford Press.

———. 1996. The psychosocial effects of androgenic alopecia and their implications for patient care. In D. B. Stough and R. S. Haber (eds.), *Hair Replacement: Surgical and Medical* (1–8). St. Louis, MO: Mosby.

Cash, T. F., J. Rissi, and R. Chapman. 1985. Not just another pretty face: Sex roles, locus of control, and cosmetics use. *Personality and Social Psychology Bulletin*, 11:246–257.

Cash, T. F., and M. L. Szymanski. 1995. The development and validation of the Body-Image Ideals Questionnaire. *Journal of Personality Assessment*, 64:466–477.

Cash, T. F., M. Szymanski, A. Labarge, and J. Grant. 1994. New assessments of cognitive components of body image: Schemas, errors, and ideals. *AABT 28th Annual Convention Proceedings*, Association for Advancement of Behavior Therapy, p. 209.

Cash, T. F., B. A. Winstead, and L. H. Janda. 1985. Your body, yourself: A Psychology Today reader survey. *Psychology Today*, 19:22–26.

———. 1986. The great American shape-up: Body image survey report. *Psychology Today*, 20:30–37.

Ciliska, D. 1990. *Beyond Dieting: Psychoeducational Interventions for Chronically Obese Women, A Nondieting Approach.* New York: Brunner/Mazel.

The Columbia Dictionary of Quotations. 1995. New York: Columbia University Press.

DeJong, W., and R. Kleck. 1986. The social psychological effects of overweight. In C. P. Herman, M. P. Zanna, and E. T. Higgins (eds.), *Physical Appearance, Stigma, and Social Behavior: The Ontario Symposium, Vol. 3* (65–87). Hillsdale, NJ: Erlbaum.

Dermer, M., and D. I. Thiel. 1975. When beauty may fail. *Journal of Personality and Social Psychology*, 31:1168–1176.

Dion, K., E. Berscheid, and E. Walster. 1972. What is beautiful is good. *Journal of Personality and Social Psychology*, 24:285–290.

Downs, A. C. 1990. The social biological constructs of social competency. In T. P. Gullotta, G. R. Adams, and R. Montemayor (eds.), *Developing Social Competency in Adolescence* (43–94). New York: Sage Publications.

Drewnowski, A., and D. K. Yee. 1987. Men and body image: Are males satisfied with their body weight? *Psychosomatic Medicine*, 49:626–634.

Dworkin, S. H., and B. A. Kerr. 1987. Comparison of interventions for women experiencing body image problems. *Journal of Counseling Psychology*, 34:136–140.

Eagly, A. H., R. D. Ashmore, M. G. Makhijani, and L. C. Kennedy. 1991. What is beautiful is good, but . . .: A meta-analytic review of research on the physical attractiveness stereotype. *Psychological Bulletin*, 110:226–235.

Elam, P., and D. Kimbrell. 1995. Sex, lies, and measuring tape. *Cognitive and Behavioral Practice*, 2:233–248.

Ellis, A. 1977. *Techniques for Disputing Irrational Beliefs*. New York: Institute for Rational Living, Inc.

Ellis, A., and R. Grieger. (eds.) 1977. *Handbook of Rational Emotive Therapy*. New York: Springer.

Fairburn, C. G., R. C. Peveler, R. Jones, R. A. Hope, and H. A. Doll. 1993. Predictors of 12-month outcome in bulimia nervosa and the influence of attitudes to shape and weight. *Journal of Consulting and Clinical Psychology*, 61:696–698.

Fallon, A. E. 1990. Culture in the mirror: Sociocultural determinants of body image. In T. F. Cash and T. Pruzinsky (eds.), *Body Images: Development, Deviance, and Change* (80–109). New York: Guilford Press.

Fallon, A. E., and P. Rozin. 1985. Sex differences in perceptions of body shape. *Journal of Abnormal Psychology*, 94:102–105.

Fallon, P., M. A. Katzman, and S. C. Wooley. (eds.). 1994. *Feminist Perspectives on Eating Disorders*. New York: Guilford Press.

Feingold, A. 1988. Matching for attractiveness in romantic partners and same-sex friends: A meta-analysis and theoretical critique. *Psychological Bulletin*, 104:226–235.

———. 1990. Gender differences in effects of physical attractiveness on romantic attraction: Comparison across five research domains. *Journal of Personality and Social Psychology*, 59:981–993.

———. 1992. Good-looking people are not what we think. *Psychological Bulletin*, 111:304–341.

Fisher, E., and J. K. Thompson. 1994. A comparative evaluation of cognitive-behavioral therapy (CBT) versus exercise therapy (ET) for the treatment of body image disturbance. *Behavior Modification*, 18:171–185.

Fisher, S. 1986. *Development and Structure of the Body Image*. Hillsdale, NJ: Erlbaum.

Freedman, R. 1986. *Beauty Bound*. Lexington, MA: Lexington Books.

Garner, D. M. 1997. The 1997 body image survey results. *Psychology Today*, 30(1):30–44, 75–84.

Garner, D. M., P. E. Garfinkel, D. Schwartz, and M. Thompson. 1980. Cultural expectations of thinness in women. *Psychological Reports*, 47:483–491.

Garner, D. M., and S. C. Wooley. 1991. Confronting the failure of behavioral and dietary treatments for obesity. *Clinical Psychology Review*, 11:729–780.

Gillen, H. B. 1981. Physical attractiveness: A determinant of two types of goodness. *Personality and Social Psychology Bulletin*, 7:277–281.

Goldfried, M., and G. C. Davison. 1976. *Clinical Behavior Therapy.* New York: Holt, Rinehart and Winston.

Gould, R. A., and G. A. Clum. 1993. The meta-analysis of self-help treatment approaches. *Clinical Psychology Review,* 13:169–186.

Grant, J. R., and T. F. Cash. 1995. Cognitive-behavioral body-image therapy: Comparative efficacy of group and modest-contact treatments. *Behavior Therapy,* 26:69–84.

Guidano, V. F., and G. Liotti. 1983. *Cognitive Processes and Emotional Disorders.* New York: Guilford Press.

Hangen, J. D., and T. F. Cash. 1991. Body-image attitudes and sexual functioning in a college population. Paper presented at the annual meeting of the Association for Advancement of Behavior Therapy, New York.

Hatfield, E., and S. Sprecher. 1986. *Mirror, mirror . . . The importance of looks in everyday life.* Albany, NY: SUNY Press.

Heinberg L. J., and J. K. Thompson. 1992. Social comparison: Gender, target importance ratings, and relation to body image disturbance. *Journal of Social Behavior and Personality,* 7:335–344.

———. 1995. Body image and televised images of thinness and attractiveness: A controlled laboratory investigation. *Journal of Social and Clinical Psychology,* 14:325–338.

Hensley-Crosson, S. L., and T. F. Cash. 1995. The effects of aerobic exercise on state and trait body image and physical fitness among college women. *AABT 29th Annual Convention Proceedings,* Association for Advancement of Behavior Therapy, p. 299.

Huddy, D. C., and T. F. Cash. In press. Body-image attitudes of male marathon runners: A controlled comparative study. *International Journal of Sport Psychology.*

Irving, L. M. 1990. Mirror images: Effects of the standard of beauty on the self- and body-esteem of women exhibiting varying levels of bulimic symptoms. *Journal of Social and Clinical Psychology,* 9:230–242.

Jackson, L. A. 1992. *Physical Appearance and Gender: Sociobiological and Sociocultural Perspectives.* Albany: SUNY Press.

Jacobi, L. and T. F. Cash. 1994. In pursuit of the perfect appearance: Discrepancies among self-and ideal-percepts of multiple physical attributes. *Journal of Applied Social Psychology,* 24:379–396.

Kanfer, F., and A. Goldstein. 1980. *Helping People Change.* New York: Pergamon Press.

Keeton, W. P., T. F. Cash, and T. A. Brown. 1990. Body image or body images?: Comparative, multidimensional assessment among college students. *Journal of Personality Assessment,* 54:213–230.

Kleck, R. E., and A. Strenta. 1980. Perceptions of the impact of negatively valued physical characteristics on social interaction. *Journal of Personality and Social Psychology,* 39:861–873.

Krueger, D. W. 1989. *Body Self and Psychological Self: Developmental and Clinical Integration in Disorders of the Self.* New York: Brunner/Mazel.

Lavallee, D. M. 1996. The comparative efficacy of two self-help programs for a negative body image. Unpublished doctoral dissertation, Virginia Consortium for Professional Psychology, Virginia Beach, VA.

Lazarus, A. A. 1977. *In the Mind's Eye: The Power of Imagery for Personal Enrichment.* New York: Rawson.

Lazarus, R. S., and S. Folkman. 1984. *Stress, Appraisal, and Coping.* New York: Springer.

Lerner, R. M., and J. Jovanovic. 1990. The role of body image in psychosocial development across the life span: A developmental contextual perspective. In T. F. Cash and T. Pruzinsky (eds.), *Body Images: Development, Deviance, and Change* (110–127). New York: Guilford Press.

Lerner, R. M., S. A. Karabenick, and J. L. Stuart. 1973. Relations among physical attractiveness, body attitudes, and self-concept in male and female college students. *The Journal of Psychology,* 85:119–129.

Lewis, R. J., T. F. Cash, L. Jacobi, and C. Bubb-Lewis. In press. Prejudice toward fat people: The development and validation of the Anti-fat Attitudes Test. *Obesity Research.*

Mahoney, M. J., and C. E. Thoresen. 1974. *Self-Control: Power to the Person.* Monterey, CA: Brooks/Cole.

Major, B., P. I. Carrington, and P. J. Carnavale. 1984. Physical attractiveness and self-esteem: Attributions for praise from an other-sex evaluator. *Personality and Social Psychology Bulletin,* 10:43–50.

Major, B., and K. Deaux. 1981. Physical attractiveness and masculinity and femininity. *Personality and Social Psychology Bulletin,* 7:24–28.

Markus, H. 1977. Self-schemata and processing information about the self. *Journal of Personality and Social Psychology,* 35:63–78.

Markus, H., R. Hamill, and K. P. Sentis. 1987. Thinking fat: Self-schemas for body weight and the processing of weight relevant information. *Journal of Applied Social Psychology,* 17:50–71.

Marlatt, G. A., and J. Gordon. 1984. *Relapse Prevention: A Self-Control Strategy for the Maintenance of Behavior Change.* New York: Guilford Press.

Marrs, R. W. 1995. A meta-analysis of bibliotherapy studies. *American Journal of Community Psychology,* 23:843–870.

Marsella, A. J., L. Shizuru, J. Brennan, and V. Kaneoka. 1981. Depression and body image satisfaction. *Journal of Cross-Cultural Psychology,* 12:360–371.

McMullin, R. E. 1986. *Handbook of Cognitive Therapy Techniques.* New York: Norton.

Meichenbaum, D. 1985. *Stress Inoculation Training.* Elmsford, NY: Pergamon Press.

Mitchell, K. R., and F. F. Orr. 1976. Heterosexual social competence, anxiety, avoidance, and self-judged physical attractiveness. *Perceptual and Motor Skills,* 43:553–554.

Muth, J. L., and T. F. Cash. In press. Gender differences in body-image attitudes: Evaluation, investment, and affect. *Journal of Applied Social Psychology.*

Nash, J. D. 1995. *What Your Doctor Can't Tell You about Cosmetic Surgery*. Oakland, CA: New Harbinger.

Neimark, J. 1994. The beefcaking of America. *Psychology Today*, 27:32–72.

Noles, S. W., T. F. Cash, and B. A. Winstead. 1985. Body image, physical attractiveness, and depression. *Journal of Consulting and Clinical Psychology*, 53:88–94.

Novy, P. L., and T. F. Cash. 1995. Exercise involvement of college women and men: Motivational and body-image implications. Unpublished manuscript, Old Dominion University, Norfolk, VA.

Phillips, K. A. 1991. Body dysmorphic disorder: The distress of imagined ugliness. *American Journal of Psychiatry*, 148:1138–1149.

———. 1996. *The Broken Mirror*. New York: Oxford University Press.

Pliner, P., S. Chaiken, and G. L. Flett. 1990. Gender differences in concern with body weight and physical appearance over the life span. *Personality and Social Psychology Bulletin*, 16:263–273.

Podolsky, D. with B. Streisand. 1996. The price of vanity. *U.S. News and World Report*, 14 October.

———. 1996. Read this first. *U.S. News and World Report*, 14 October.

Polivy, J., and P. Herman. 1983. *Breaking the Diet Habit*. New York: Basic Books.

———. 1992. Undieting: A program to help people stop dieting. *International Journal of Eating Disorders*, 11:261–268.

Pruzinsky, T. and T. F. Cash. 1990. Medical interventions for the enhancement of adolescents' physical appearance: Implications for social competence. In T. P. Gullotta, G. R. Adams, and R. Montemayor (eds.), *Developing Social Competency in Adolescence* (220–242). New York: Sage Publications.

Pruzinsky, T., and M. Edgerton. 1990. Body-image change in cosmetic plastic surgery. In T. F. Cash and T. Pruzinsky (eds.), *Body Images: Development, Deviance, and Change* (190–236). New York: Guilford Press.

Ramirez, E. M., and J. C. Rosen. 1995. A comparison of dieting vs. dieting plus body image therapy in the treatment of a negative body image in obese individuals. *AABT 29th Annual Convention Proceedings*, Association for Advancement of Behavior Therapy, 290.

Rieves, L., and T. F. Cash. 1996. Reported social developmental factors associated with womens' body-image attitudes. *Journal of Social Behavior and Personality*, 11:63–78.

Rodin, J. 1992. *Body Traps*. New York: Morrow.

Rodin, J., L. R. Silberstein, and R. H. Striegel-Moore. 1985. Women and weight: A normative discontent. In T. B. Sonderegger (ed.), *Nebraska symposium on motivation: Psychology and gender* (267–307). Lincoln: University of Nebraska Press.

Rosen, G. M., and A. O. Ross. 1968. Relationship of body image to self-concept. *Journal of Consulting and Clinical Psychology*, 32:100.

Rosen, J. C. 1990. Body-image disturbance in eating disorders. In T. F. Cash and T. Pruzinsky (eds.), *Body Images: Development, Deviance, and Change* (190–216). New York: Guilford Press.

———. 1995. The nature of body dysmorphic disorder and treatment with cognitive behavior therapy. *Cognitive and Behavioral Practice*, 2:143–166.

Rosen, J. C., S. Cado, N. T. Silberg, D. Srebnik, and S. Wendt. 1990. Cognitive behavior therapy with and without size perception training for women with body image disturbance. *Behavior Therapy*, 21:481–498.

Rosen, J. C., and T. F. Cash. 1995. Learning to have a better body image. *Weight Control Digest*, 5:409, 412–416.

Rosen, J. C., P. Orosan, and J. Reiter. 1995. Cognitive behavior therapy for negative body image in obese women. *Behavior Therapy*, 26:25–42.

Rosen, J. C., J. Reiter, and P. Orosan. 1995. Cognitive-behavioral body-image therapy for body dysmorphic disorder. *Journal of Consulting and Clinical Psychology*, 63:263–269.

Rosen, J. C., E. Saltzberg, and D. Srebnik. 1989. Cognitive behavior therapy for negative body image. *Behavior Therapy*, 20:393–404.

Rozin, P., and A. Fallon. 1988. Body image, attitudes to weight, and misperceptions of figure preferences of the opposite sex: A comparison of men and women in two generations. *Journal of Abnormal Psychology*, 97:342–345.

Schulman, A. H., and C. Kaplowitz. 1977. Mirror-image responses during the first two years of life. *Developmental Psychobiology*, 10:133–142.

Scogin, F., J. Bynum, G. Stephens, and S. Calhoon. 1990. Efficacy of self-administered treatment programs: Meta-analytic review. *Professional Psychology: Research and Practice*, 21:42–47.

Segal, Z. V., and S. J. Blatt. (eds.) 1993. *The Self in Emotional Distress: Cognitive and Psychodynamic Perspectives.* New York: Guilford Press.

Seligman, M. E. P. 1975. *Helplessness: On Depression, Development, and Death.* San Francisco, CA: Freeman.

Shontz, F. C. 1990. Body image and physical disability. In T. F. Cash and T. Pruzinsky (eds.), *Body Images: Development, Deviance, and Change* (149–169). New York: Guilford Press.

Sigall, H., and J. Michela. 1976. I'll bet you say that to all the girls: Physical attractiveness and reactions to praise. *Journal of Personality*, 44:611–626.

Silberstein, L. R., R. H. Striegel-Moore, C. Timko, and J. Rodin. 1988. Behavioral and psychological implications of body dissatisfaction: Do men and women differ? *Sex Roles*, 19:219–232.

Silverstein, B., L. Perdue, B. Peterson, and E. Kelly. 1986. The role of the mass media in promoting a thin standard of bodily attractiveness for women. *Sex Roles*, 14:519–523.

Steinem, G. 1992. *Revolution from Within: A Book of Self-Esteem.* Boston, MA: Little, Brown and Company.

Steketee, G., and K. White. 1990. *When Once Is Not Enough: Help for Obsessive-Compulsives.* Oakland, CA: New Harbinger.

Strauman, T. J., J. Vookles, V. Berenstein, S. Chaiken, and E. T. Higgins. 1991. Self-discrepancies and vulnerability to body dissatisfaction and disordered eating. *Journal of Personality and Social Psychology*, 61:946–956.

Striegel-Moore, R. H., L. R. Silberstein, P. Frensch, and J. Rodin. 1989. A prospective study of disordered eating among college students. *International Journal of Eating Disorders*, 8:499–509.

Striegel-Moore, R. H., L. R. Silberstein, and J. Rodin. 1986. Toward an understanding of risk factors for bulimia. *American Psychologist*, 41:246–263.

Stunkard, A. J., and V. Burt. 1967. Obesity and body image II. Age at onset of disturbances in the body image. *American Journal of Psychiatry*, 123:1443–1447.

Stunkard, A. J., and M. Mendelson. 1967. Obesity and body image I. Characteristics of disturbances in the body image of some obese persons. *American Journal of Psychiatry*, 123:1296–1300.

Szymanski, M. L., and T. F. Cash. 1995. Body-image disturbances and self-discrepancy theory: Expansion of the Body-Image Ideals Questionnaire. *Journal of Social and Clinical Psychology*, 14:134–146.

Thompson, J. K. 1990. *Body-Image Disturbance: Assessment and Treatment.* Elmsford, NY: Pergamon Press.

Thompson, J. K. (ed.) 1996. *Body Image, Eating Disorders, and Obesity: An Integrative Guide for Assessment and Treatment.* Washington, D.C.: American Psychological Association.

Tiggemann, M., and E. D. Rothblum. 1988. Gender differences in social consequences of perceived overweight in the United States and Australia. *Sex Roles*, 18:75–86.

Wadden, T. A., A. J. Stunkard, and J. Liebschutz. 1988. Three-year follow-up of the treatment of obesity by very low calorie diet, behavior therapy, and their combination. *Journal of Consulting and Clinical Psychology*, 56:925–928.

Wiseman, C. V., F. M. Gunning, and J. J. Gray. 1993. Increasing pressure to be thin: 19 years of diet products in television commercials. *Eating Disorders: The Journal of Treatment and Prevention*, 1:52–61.

Wolf, N. 1991. *The Beauty Myth: How Images of Beauty Are Used against Women.* New York: Morrow.

Wooley, W., and S. Wooley. 1984. Feeling fat in a thin society. *Glamour*, 198–201.

WordStar International Incorporated. 1991. *Correct Quotes*, version 1.0. Novato, CA: WordStar International Incorporated.

Yates, A. 1991. *Compulsive Exercise and the Eating Disorders: Toward an Integrated Theory of Activity.* New York: Brunner/Mazel.

Young, J. E. 1990. *Cognitive Therapy for Personality Disorders: A Schema-Focused Approach.* Sarasota, FL: Professional Resource Exchange, Inc.

Other New Harbinger Self-Help Titles

The Daily Relaxer, $12.95
Living with Angina, $12.95
The Power of Two, $12.95
Living with ADD, $17.95
The Body Image Workbook, $17.95
Taking the Anxiety Out of Taking Tests, $12.95
The Taking Charge of Menopause Workbook, $17.95
It's Not OK Anymore, $13.95
PMS: Women Tell Women How to Control Premenstrual Syndrome, $13.95
Five Weeks to Healing Stress: The Wellness Option, $17.95
Choosing to Live: How to Defeat Suicide Through Cognitive Therapy, $12.95
Why Children Misbehave and What to Do About It, $14.95
Illuminating the Heart, $13.95
When Anger Hurts Your Kids, $12.95
The Addiction Workbook, $17.95
The Mother's Survival Guide to Recovery, $12.95
The Chronic Pain Control Workbook, Second Edition, $17.95
Fibromyalgia & Chronic Myofascial Pain Syndrome, $19.95
Diagnosis and Treatment of Sociopaths, $44.95
Flying Without Fear, $12.95
Kid Cooperation: How to Stop Yelling, Nagging & Pleading and Get Kids to Cooperate, $12.95
The Stop Smoking Workbook: Your Guide to Healthy Quitting, $17.95
Conquering Carpal Tunnel Syndrome and Other Repetitive Strain Injuries, $17.95
The Tao of Conversation, $12.95
Wellness at Work: Building Resilience for Job Stress, $17.95
What Your Doctor Can't Tell You About Cosmetic Surgery, $13.95
An End to Panic: Breakthrough Techniques for Overcoming Panic Disorder, $17.95
On the Clients Path: A Manual for the Practice of Solution-Focused Therapy, $39.95
Living Without Procrastination: How to Stop Postponing Your Life, $12.95
Goodbye Mother, Hello Woman: Reweaving the Daughter Mother Relationship, $14.95
Letting Go of Anger: The 10 Most Common Anger Styles and What to Do About Them, $12.95
Messages: The Communication Skills Workbook, Second Edition, $13.95
Coping With Chronic Fatigue Syndrome: Nine Things You Can Do, $12.95
The Anxiety & Phobia Workbook, Second Edition, $17.95
Thueson's Guide to Over-the-Counter Drugs, $13.95
Natural Women's Health: A Guide to Healthy Living for Women of Any Age, $13.95
I'd Rather Be Married: Finding Your Future Spouse, $13.95
The Relaxation & Stress Reduction Workbook, Fourth Edition, $17.95
Living Without Depression & Manic Depression: A Workbook for Maintaining Mood Stability, $17.95
Belonging: A Guide to Overcoming Loneliness, $13.95
Coping With Schizophrenia: A Guide For Families, $13.95
Visualization for Change, Second Edition, $13.95
Postpartum Survival Guide, $13.95
Angry All the Time: An Emergency Guide to Anger Control, $12.95
Couple Skills: Making Your Relationship Work, $13.95
Handbook of Clinical Psychopharmacology for Therapists, $39.95
Weight Loss Through Persistence, $13.95
Post-Traumatic Stress Disorder: A Complete Treatment Guide, $39.95
Stepfamily Realities: How to Overcome Difficulties and Have a Happy Family, $13.95
The Chemotherapy Survival Guide, $11.95
Your Family/Your Self: How to Analyze Your Family System, $12.95
Being a Man: A Guide to the New Masculinity, $12.95
The Deadly Diet, Second Edition: Recovering from Anorexia & Bulimia, $13.95
Last Touch: Preparing for a Parent's Death, $11.95
Self-Esteem, Second Edition, $13.95
I Can't Get Over It, A Handbook for Trauma Survivors, Second Edition, $13.95
Concerned Intervention, When Your Loved One Won't Quit Alcohol or Drugs, $12.95
Dying of Embarrassment: Help for Social Anxiety and Social Phobia, $12.95
The Depression Workbook: Living With Depression and Manic Depression, $17.95
Focal Group Psychotherapy: For Mental Health Professionals, $44.95
Prisoners of Belief: Exposing & Changing Beliefs that Control Your Life, $12.95
Men & Grief: A Guide for Men Surviving the Death of a Loved One, $13.95
When the Bough Breaks: A Helping Guide for Parents of Sexually Abused Children, $11.95
When Once Is Not Enough: Help for Obsessive Compulsives, $13.95
The Three Minute Meditator, Third Edition, $12.95
Beyond Grief: A Guide for Recovering from the Death of a Loved One, $13.95
Leader's Guide to the Relaxation & Stress Reduction Workbook, Fourth Edition, $19.95
The Divorce Book, $13.95
Hypnosis for Change: A Manual of Proven Techniques, Third Edition, $13.95
When Anger Hurts, $13.95
Lifetime Weight Control, $12.95

Call **toll free, 1-800-748-6273,** to order. Have your Visa or Mastercard number ready. Or send a check for the titles you want to New Harbinger Publications, Inc., 5674 Shattuck Ave., Oakland, CA 94609. Include $3.80 for the first book and 75¢ for each additional book, to cover shipping and handling. (California residents please include appropriate sales tax.) Allow four to six weeks for delivery.

Prices subject to change without notice.